READ WELL
AND
REMEMBER

A guide to more rapid,
more efficient reading

by

OWEN WEBSTER

SIMON AND SCHUSTER
NEW YORK

To M
who caused it
and to all my other students
who taught me

Acknowledgments

I am most grateful to authors and publishers who have generously given me permission to quote in this book from works written and published by them. The books quoted in the text and used as reading extracts are listed in Appendix II.

O.W.

Knowledge is basic. It is knowledge which enables us to understand the world and ourselves, and to exercise some control or guidance. It sets us in a fruitful and significant relation with the enduring processes of the universe. And, by revealing the possibilities of fulfillment that are still open, it provides an overriding incentive.

We, mankind, contain the possibilities of the earth's immense future, and can realize more and more of them on condition that we increase our knowledge and our love.

Sir Julian Huxley
Introducing *The Phenomenon of Man*
by Pierre Teilhard de Chardin

CONTENTS

9

CONTENTS

PART I

THE PROBLEM

Why We Read Badly

THERE IS A GREAT DEAL too much of the printed word about now-adays, and no one who lives intelligently in the modern world needs telling so. Universal literacy has brought us much of value, but this is part of the price. Unrestricted paper supplies and new methods of printing and copying have not only added to the bulk of books, magazines, and newspapers, they have also made possible a flood of trade and society journals, house magazines, reports, minutes, and memoranda, about every conceivable topic under the sun and beyond it.

Yet, at the same time, little or no concern is shown for the poor reader, who is presumed to be able to read and assimilate all that comes his way. Publishers and booksellers may joyfully announce from their sales figures that more people are reading more, but in fact they refer to high hopes rather than capable reading. There are no figures on the books unopened or half understood, the magazines idly dipped into, the publications that gather dust and good intentions, or go straight into the wastepaper basket.

With no satisfactory system for tackling it all—and consequently no time for devising one—the hapless reader responds in his own way. Reading may lose its pleasure and become a bore or a chore. It may be given up altogether, save for the commuter's newspaper, and another expensive education may be lost to the golf course or the riverbank. The printed page may be used merely as a safeguard against interruption during the pursuit of private thoughts or worries. For such an audience, an author might as well be lost to the golf course or the riverbank.

Many people, victims of the bad reading habits of half a lifetime, tackle the printed page so inefficiently that most of it goes out of their minds the moment they have read it; and many more read so slowly that the Sunday paper takes half the week and a whole book demands an effort of sustained tenacity that is hardly possible more than once a year.

Taking the population as a whole, it is a safe bet that the majority read only newspapers and magazines. For a considerable proportion of the rest, reading anything but newspapers is synonymous with work, which is synonymous with unpleasantness. In consequence, their reading is confined to three categories:

1. Technical material relating to their own specialty.
2. Technical material about subjects ancillary to their own specialty.
3. Administrative reports, memoranda, and White Papers.

This is just the kind of reading matter that can and ought to be dispensed with quickly and effortlessly, leaving time and energy for the pleasure and leisure of good books.

The truth of these statements should be confirmed by a few pointed inquiries about reading habits in any ordinary circle of acquaintances. It will be found that three generations' investment in compulsory education has not resulted in a very praiseworthy profit. What has gone wrong?

The fault has been where every human failing lies: in ignorance. In this case it has been ignorance firstly of how we read and then of what can be done to improve reading ability. Silent reading is one of the rapidest of all human processes, involving the coordination of a complex of different skills and functions. A good deal about the process is still unknown, which is hardly surprising, since psychologists and other investigators began experimenting in the study of reading behavior less than fifty years ago. On the other hand, a great deal of knowledge is available nowadays about how bad reading habits may be cured. In America, where much of the basic research has been carried out, the knowledge is used—and misused—extensively. In Britain still too few people know how much can be done to improve the average efficiency of adult reading, a fact which has not been helped by the inaccurate publicity the subject has received and the exaggerated claims that are often made for it.

When most children leave grade school, it is presumed that they can read and that no further instruction in that particular one of the three Rs is necessary. Yet by the time these same children start work or enter college, only a tiny minority of them can cope with their normal reading requirements. The rest carry into adulthood, perhaps for the whole of their lives, habits which become more and more fixed and serve them less and less well. They are the habits of the infant classroom, where, whatever the method by which they were taught to read, progress was demonstrated by reading aloud and perfection went no further than registering one word at a time.

Hence, many intelligent adults holding responsible jobs still spell out all but the commonest words letter by letter, or move their lips while they are reading. Others make throat movements akin to reading aloud, and many more read each word separately. My own experience of teaching adults to read more skillfully has shown me conclusively that neither intelligence nor success, wealth nor fame, professional qualifications nor academic degrees, are any index of capability in reading. Top people, in fact, are quite likely to be bottom readers, and are no less prone than anyone else to read like schoolchildren and to misunderstand what they read more disastrously than schoolchildren. Anyone who can misunderstand through inefficient reading a simple, unequivocal newspaper report, is no less likely to misinterpret a written instruction, or to miss the point of a clearly reasoned argument. Men may well have been sent to their deaths through faulty reading. Yet anyone who can read at all has the capacity to read much better—and even uses this capacity sometimes. A letter from a loved one is usually read with meticulous care. If everything worth reading were to be read—and written—as efficiently as almost any love letter, the administrative and executive wheels of our world might run more smoothly, albeit perhaps a little more slowly.

As far as I know, the first comprehensive investigations into how adults read were undertaken at the University of Chicago during the twenties and thirties under the leadership of Guy Buswell, their professor of educational psychology. Some earlier work on the physiology of the eyes in reading lay behind it, and there were some other concurrent studies, such as the work on problems of visual perception for the British Medical Research Council by Professor M. D. Vernon.

One of Buswell's biggest experiments took place between 1935 and 1936, when nearly a thousand adults from all walks of life, with no qualification in common but that of having left school ten years or more previously, were each asked to read some short passages of about a hundred words ranging from a simple tale to rather difficult technical matter. As they read, their eye movements were plotted on film and then translated back to the passage they had been reading.

It was already known that the eyes do not move smoothly along a line of print: nothing whatever can be seen when the eyes are in motion. All our seeing is done by means of short pauses of fixation linked by quick and sightless movements of the eyes within their sacs, hence properly called *saccadic* movements.

On the opposite page are three examples of different reading habits similar to those revealed by Buswell's investigation. Each vertical line represents the center of a fixation pause made by the reader's eyes. The upper line of figures represents the serial order in which the pauses were made, and the lower figures are the time of each pause in thirtieths of a second. The marginal figures are the total times for each line.

The first reader is so unpracticed as to be almost illiterate. The second is more like an average reader who would turn to a book such as this one in the hope of improving. His speed over a long passage would be something less than 250 words a minute. The third is a highly capable reader with a speed of between 500 and 600 words a minute. A complete book of average complexity could be taken at a rhythm varying little from this. Note that each fixation pause is of a shorter and more uniform duration than those of the other readers, that regression is reduced to a minimum, and that the fewer pauses to each line involve register-

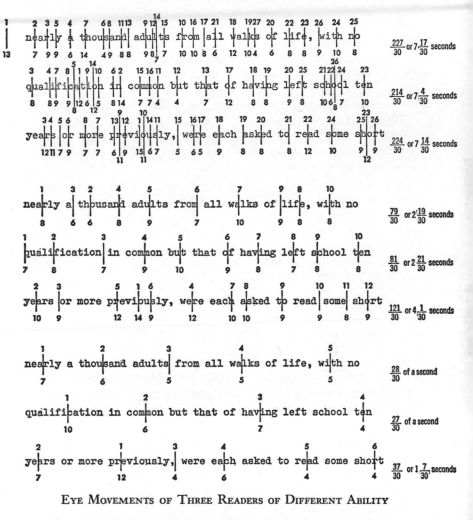

EYE MOVEMENTS OF THREE READERS OF DIFFERENT ABILITY

Each vertical line represents the center of a fixation pause.
The upper line of figures gives the serial order of the pauses.
The lower line gives the duration of each in thirtieths of a second.
The marginal figures are the total times for reading each line.

ing more characters of type at a glance. It will be obvious that the last reader could read a book in less than half the time of the second one. The first could not tackle an entire adult book.

One of the significant conclusions of Buswell's experiment led him to say this:

> No more serious handicap retards the adult education movement than the low reading ability of many adults. The independence of thinking that comes from wide reading, and is necessary even in a non-academic environment, is beyond the power of large sections of the adult population.

In the autumn of 1936 he organized three groups of adults into the first classes of students of efficient reading, teaching them principles and methods derived from his discoveries. He wrote:

> The most mature process of silent reading consists in the fusion of groups of words into units of meaning, which in turn flow into and become part of a larger stream of thought constituting the total substance of the material being read. This process of mature silent reading is characterized, psychologically, by a complete absence of attention to words as such and by an absorption in the meaning unfolded.

If you have read this far, you are probably interested enough in your own reading processes to want to try to improve them. And however powerful a reader you may be, there is always some room for improvement. Properly used, and provided that you suffer from no visual defects to prevent you from reading normally, this book will help you toward reading maturity. It is intended for readers with a little more than average interest in the printed word, because the subject of developmental reading is already well covered at the most elementary levels (some manuals are suggested in Appendix IIA). A good teacher can never be completely replaced by a book, but if you can understand printed instructions and can discipline yourself to follow them intelligently and sympathetically, the gulf between self-tuition and personal tutoring can be considerably narrowed.

First of all, then, how well are you understanding what you

read? Every chapter of this book has a comprehension test at the end of it. The one that follows this chapter is a multiple-choice recognition test in which you have to select the best of four alternative answers. Remember: there is only one "best." And beware: the alternatives do not always contradict one another. If three of the four were blatant nonsense, it would be possible to answer most of the questions without having read the passage to which they relate. Choose that one of the four alternatives which, from the chapter you have just read, gives the best answer to the question. Do not answer from your own experience or, if you can help it, from something else on the subject that you may remember reading.

Before you begin the test, ask yourself this: What, in essence, has the author been saying? Try to remember, before tackling any of the comprehension tests in this book, to ask this question about the central idea of every chapter and reading extract. Jot down the answer in a notebook, briefly, in your own words, and without referring back to the text. Keep the same notebook at your elbow whenever you are reading this book. It will be of great use to you.

EXERCISE 1

Choose the best answer to each question without referring back to the text.

1. According to the author, the figures of book sales are:
   a. false;
   b. misleading;
   c. evidence of too much printed matter;
   d. no indication of how much is actually read.
2. People who have to read reports and White Papers, the author says, ought to deal with them:
   a. meticulously;
   b. quickly and effortlessly;
   c. with unerring accuracy;
   d. with as much pleasure as a good book.
3. Bad reading habits, according to the author, are a result of:
   a. idleness;
   b. willful ignorance;

    c. ignorance of how we read;

    d. a poor educational system.

4. The meticulous care with which love letters are usually read is evidence that:

    a. we can all read accurately when we are really interested;

    b. we can all read fast when we try;

    c. people write love letters better than they write more prosaic things;

    d. the receipt of a love letter is an important event.

5. The author asserts from his own teaching experience that:

    a. top people are usually bottom readers;

    b. the worst readers are those with poor educational backgrounds;

    c. poor readers can be found in all walks of life;

    d. most people misunderstand what they read.

6. The Chicago experiment described in the chapter was carried out:

    a. in the middle 1930s;

    b. during the war;

    c. in the late 1940s;

    d. forty years ago.

7. The eyes of the skillful reader:

    a. move smoothly and quickly along the printed line;

    b. make short, sharp saccadic movements;

    c. take in several words with each fixation;

    d. make no regressive movements.

8. Mature silent reading, according to Buswell, means:

    a. reading fast and accurately;

    b. becoming absorbed in the meaning without paying attention to the actual words;

    c. making fewer pauses to the line;

    d. understanding and remembering effortlessly.

9. When the author asserts that an instructional book can never be a complete substitute for a good teacher, he means that:

    a. such books are not very helpful;

    b. the intelligent and disciplined use of such a book is the next best thing to a good teacher;

    c. teachers are necessary to answer questions that a book cannot answer;

    d. teachers are indispensable.

10. The main idea of this chapter is:

    a. It's never too late to learn.

b. Too many people idle away their time when they could be improving themselves.

c. Inefficient reading is jeopardizing the workings of democracy.

d. Understanding how we read is the first step toward taking control of the process and improving it.

Now check your answers against the correct ones in the table in Appendix I (page 301). If you have less than six correct, read the chapter once more and answer the questions again. If there is anything you have not understood, make a note of it. You may encounter the explanation as you read on. If you scored six or seven, ask yourself whether it was because of the unfamiliarity of the test, or because you have been reading carelessly. For example, in Question 5, did you honestly think I could have said that top people are usually bottom readers? If you refer back to page 15 you will see that I said, in connection with the statement that position is no indication of reading ability, that top people are quite likely to be bottom readers. The difference is important, isn't it? Note the kind of errors you make: your comprehension needs some extra work. Scores of eight or more at a single, unprepared reading are good.

Now try a passage in a different style, still reading in your usual way, but this time in the knowledge that a similar test awaits you at the end.

READING EXERCISE

How to Read a Page

BY I. A. RICHARDS

We all enjoy the illusion that we read better than we do; not least, no doubt, those who set out to write about *How to read.* But most of us—or those, at least, who are likely to open a book with this title—are satisfied that other people read badly, that they can miss any point and will put their own wild interpretations on even the most obvious remark. In recent years books, papers, and articles which labor this point and accuse the general reader of incompetence with language have been coming out in plenty. Some of them hint despondingly that things are getting worse and threaten us even with universal intellectual collapse unless something is done about it. Authorities tell vast conferences of English teachers every few weeks that they are failing to teach reading. Texts simplified and written down to tenth-grade level are adopted in university courses because the undergraduates cannot, it is alleged, read anything harder. Publicists lament, in popular volumes, the plain man's helpless acceptance of verbal nonsense. Specialists complain that their contributions are wasted because the other specialists do nothing but misread them. And prophets foretell the downfall of democracy through a decline in the citizen's ability to follow any discussion worth a hearing.

Behind all this there is enough solid evidence to make anyone who studies it very uncomfortable. If most people's reading is really as inefficient as it seems when carefully enough examined, the main staff of education is hardly worth leaning on. What is the advantage of toiling on through thousands of pages, if a chief outcome is an accumulation of misunderstandings? Surely it should be possible to go directly to the root of the trouble, to study verbal misunderstanding, its nature and causes, deeply enough to find and apply a cure?

Accordingly, a considerable literature is coming into being which discusses the theory of language: classification, abstraction, naming, metaphor, and the rest. Unfortunately, it cannot be said to offer us much hope of immediate remedies. And this is not surprising. The questions which our theory of language has to discuss are hardest of all to write clearly about. They are the meeting points of tremendous pressures coming from rival philosophic systems used consciously or unconsciously by those who discuss them. We should expect not only great divergences of view but persistent drastic misinterpretations among their students. Everyone who writes on such matters sighs to think how often he seems to be misread. The layman who looks into this literature extensively enough will be shocked to discover how much seemingly fundamental disagreement it contains. If he does not go into it far enough to see this, he should be warned not to suppose there is anything at present there corresponding to the agreed doctrines the sciences can offer him. There is no agreed theory of language—as elementary mechanics, for example, is an agreed theory. Moreover, to get any adequate view of what the rival professors are maintaining, the inquiring layman would have to become as adept at a peculiarly difficult sort of reading in which one is specially apt to suppose he has understood when in fact he has not. It is not likely, therefore, that perusal of those confusing pages will make many people better readers. There is evidence, on the contrary, that misunderstandings acquired from them have made intelligent people more foolish and imperceptive as readers than they would otherwise have been.

The belief that knowledge of linguistic theory will make a man a better reader comes itself from such a misunderstanding. Theory and practice are not so simply connected. It is true that bad theory does lead to bad reading. But good theory will not necessarily produce good reading. Between the principles in the theory and the actual words to be read comes the task of seeing which principles apply to which cases, the problem of recognizing what the actual situation is. Theory can give us no *direct* help in this, more's the pity! We have to rely on whatever sagacity we have developed. Nothing, alas, is easier than to fit our distinctions to the wrong instances. And in most reading there are strong motives at work which tempt us to do this.

We are all of us learning to read all the time. All our thinking is a part of the process as affecting the way we will on some occasion take some sentence. Whenever we use words in forming some judgment or decision, we are, in what may be a painfully sharp sense, "learning to read." The lover scanning his mistress's scribble or her scowling brows is learning to read.

There is an ambiguity here which is brought out by asking, Learning to read what?—the written word? or by means of that word the face, or the heart, of Nature?

The answer, of course, is, "Both." We cannot separate them.

We always read for some purpose—unless some sad, bad, mad schoolteacher has got hold of us. There is no such thing as merely reading words; always through the words we are trafficking or trying to traffic with things—things gone by, present, to come, or eternal. So a person who sets up to teach reading should recognize that he may be more ambitious than he seems. He may pretend he is only concerned to help people not to mistake one word for another, or one construction for another. *That*, so far, doesn't look like an attempt to finger the steering wheel of the universe. But "Which word is it?" turns into "Which use?"; and the question "Which construction?" into "What implications?" Before long the would-be authority on interpretation has become indistinguishable from an authority on "What's what?"—a question which belongs to a more divine science than he may wittingly aspire to.

Nonetheless, by being more aware of this he will be better able to pursue his main task—the cultivation of general verbal sagacity.

From: *How to Read a Page*
(1,200 words)

EXERCISE 2

Choose the best answer to each question without referring back.

1. Richards' attitude toward complaints and warnings about the effects of incompetent reading is one of:
   a. disagreement;
   b. unqualified agreement;
   c. disquiet;
   d. anger.
2. The root of the trouble, he suggests, is:
   a. verbal misunderstanding;
   b. ignorance;
   c. poor reading habits;
   d. oversimplified university courses.
3. The theory of language discusses questions which are difficult to be clear about because:

a. they are basically nonsensical;
b. they are unscientific;
c. linguistic philosophers disagree among themselves;
d. abstractions are confusing.

4. Misunderstandings acquired from books on the theory of language have made some people:
   a. more foolish than they were before;
   b. more foolish and imperceptive readers;
   c. more able to enjoy ordinary books;
   d. more aware of the complexities of linguistic philosophy.

5. Theory alone cannot help us to become better readers. We also need a certain amount of:
   a. practice;
   b. sagacity;
   c. education;
   d. personal tuition.

6. We learn a little more to read whenever we:
   a. look at the face of a loved one;
   b. open a book;
   c. think about the use of language;
   d. use words to make a judgment or a decision.

7. By "learning to read," the author means reading:
   a. people's faces;
   b. Nature;
   c. the printed word;
   d. the word and the world.

8. The teacher of reading, according to Richards, has to be:
   a. ambitious;
   b. aware that his subject has unsuspected ramifications;
   c. experienced in helping people to distinguish the meanings of words;
   d. aware that he may be steering the universe.

9. The main idea of this passage is:
   a. Democracy will fail unless the population becomes better educated through the use of better reading methods.
   b. Linguistic theory is so difficult to understand that most people would be better advised to avoid any but the simplest books on it.
   c. With an intelligent application of linguistic theory, common sense, and experience, we should cure many of our ten-

dencies to misunderstand words, and hence read to better
advantage.
d. The disagreements of linguistic philosophers are more confusing than illuminating.
10. Authors of books about *How to read*, according to Richards:
a. are probably expert readers;
b. are no more expert than anyone else;
c. probably think they read better than they do;
d. believe that most people read badly.

*Check your answers against those on page 301. This passage was
a little more difficult than the previous one, but if you scored
lower than you did before, read it again and answer the questions
again, noting where you went wrong. An added difficulty this
time was that the subject was not very dissimilar from that of
the preceding passage. You ought not to have confused the two,
especially as a different voice was addressing you, but if you did,
remember that this may be a general tendency of yours, and
make a note to work at it later on. If you scored nine or ten on
both tests, there is no cause yet for undue confidence: more
difficult passages and tests are to follow.*

*Now close this book and return to reading whatever it is you
normally read. But this time, try to notice what you are doing
as you read. Resume this book with Chapter Two tomorrow.*

Reading Speeds and Needs

IF YOU HAVE STARTED to read this chapter immediately after finishing Chapter One, you have ignored the instruction in its last
paragraph. You may not think this very important; but what is
important, surely, is that you are aware of ignoring it. You have
chosen to read an instructional book, and although you are free
to ignore its instructions if you choose, be sure it is through
choice and not faulty reading. Every day, probably, you have
to read some instruction or other, and you can imagine the consequences of faultily reading road signs, public notices, contracts,
medicine labels, directions on containers, operating instructions
for household gadgets, and so on. You may rightly think that
many such instructions are unnecessary or inapplicable to you,
but reflect upon the kind of intelligence that gives rise to many
of them, and you may imagine how little of what we "read"
(in I. A. Richards' omnibus sense of the word) is applied or retained, and understand why we are beleaguered by so much print
in consequence. In my kitchen is a gas stove with an enameled lid
to close over the burners. Under the lid a metal inscription forever declares: *Do not close lid while burners are in operation.*
If ever I become too optimistic about the ability of my fellow
men to learn by practical or verbal experience, I think of the
intelligence that devised that instruction and the intelligence that
made it necessary. It is my conviction that more conscious and
efficient reading habits can help to increase our awareness to
a point where all our experience is accurately evaluated and
sensibly applied.

The instruction at the end of the last chapter, then, was given with a deliberate purpose. You are going to be learning a skill and, as with any kind of skill, practice is imperative. Indeed, the skill of efficient reading may be more difficult to learn than many other skills if it has been practiced inefficiently and unconsciously for most of your life. So the practice gained from reading this book alone is not enough. You must give yourself time to become aware of the complexities of your reading behavior, even if at first you become self-conscious and your comprehension is impaired. Then you need time to gain enough control of your reading habits to change them. Thus, in addition to the time taken reading this book and heeding its instructions, you should spend as much time as possible with other kinds of reading: an hour a day or seven hours a week at least, and the longer you spend at any single sitting the better.

You will encounter difficulties enough as you read, from this point onward and perhaps for several weeks to come, so try to avoid adding to them by discomfort or distractions. Avoid, for example, important reading while traveling, unless your powers of concentration are already prodigious. Avoid reading anything important in bed before falling asleep. This is a time of reading for relaxation and, if you are fond of reading in bed, your relaxation reading probably achieves its purpose and so is efficient enough. From now on, however, you are going to learn to work at reading, too; and the ideal and most worthwhile conditions for this are in an easy chair with the page evenly illuminated by shaded daylight or a sixty-watt bulb in a reading lamp directed over the shoulder. Compare the strain of reading in bright sunlight or in the dappled shadow of a tree.

Make yourself comfortable, but not so comfortable that you fall asleep over your book. See that the room temperature is temperate, that the light is neither too dim nor too bright, that the dog is not barking and the children not demanding attention, that the television, radio, record player, tape recorder, vacuum cleaner, spin drier, are all switched off and, if you can arrange it, that there are no aircraft screaming overhead, no nearby road drills or pile drivers to pulverize your nerves, and no local youths displaying potency by motorcycle. Noise, whether we notice it or not, is helping to make us all a little more stupid every year. For noise restricts the freedom of the conscious imagination, and everything we do is done as well as we can imagine it beforehand.

It is therefore desirable at the outset to have a clear imaginary picture of what we want to achieve with our reading; of what can and what cannot be achieved with knowledge and practice. Since Buswell's pioneer work in Chicago, the subject of "rapid reading" has been thoroughly exploited in America and much of the rest of the English-speaking world; it has produced small fortunes and large claims.

The following Reuter report, for example, appeared as a paragraph in the *Guardian* of September 21, 1962:

GONE WITH THE WIND?

Brisbane, September 20

An Australian soldier who took a 13-day course in "quick reading" can comfortably read *Gone with the Wind* before breakfast or Shakespeare's complete works in about two days—at 80 words a second—an army spokesman said here.

Perhaps you have read long articles reporting similar claims.

Now, whether or not you think that Margaret Mitchell's saga of the American Civil War is worth no more than a late breakfast, or even that two sleepless days spent with Shakespeare are two wasted days, you would do well to wonder at the point of reading anything as quickly as that. Either a book is worth reading or not; if not, why spend as much time finding out as the Australian soldier did?

I shall discuss later the amount of truth likely in that newspaper paragraph; meanwhile, let me simply assert that no one who takes a whole book at eighty words a second, 4,800 words a minute, the half-million words of *Gone with the Wind* in an hour and three-quarters flat, is really reading, whatever else he may be doing. If you should be reading this book in the hope of learning a technique for reading *War and Peace* while the children are brushing their teeth, then either you are reading the wrong book, or you should persist with this one until you are persuaded of the futility of your ambition.

Let us suppose that you are an average reader; a little above average, perhaps, since at this moment you are actually doing something to improve your reading ability. You have had no formal instruction about how to read since before you left grade school, but you like reading books enough to have joined the local lending library, and perhaps you buy a book occasionally to add to a small library of your own. You may even think that the cost of a book is money better spent than on cigarettes, the movies, or a round of drinks at the corner bar. I am describing the average *reader*, remember, not the average citizen.

You probably spend more time than you need in reading the daily paper and too much of Sunday—and perhaps the three following days—with a couple of Sunday papers and some kind of weekly review. Your normal reading speed, as you may confirm in a few minutes, is likely to be between 225 and 275 words a minute and, on a single reading of something that interests you, useful comprehension of 70 or 80 per cent.

Now 275 words a minute is a perfectly adequate rate for reading certain types of material such as poetry and serious literature. The only fault with it is that you probably read everything in much the same way, at a more or less uniform speed, and with comprehension varying according to the difficulty of the material and the amount of interest you have in it. You may find many subjects and styles too difficult to read at all, and much that you do read will be disappointing. With all but the most absorbing books, your concentration may not be all you would like, and you may even wish that you could discuss books more knowledgeably and with keener appreciation. If your work entails much routine reading, you probably find it encroaching on your leisure and spoiling your appetite for what you want to read.

Perhaps you are worried about the time you take to read a book, or have other reasons for thinking that your reading ability is below average. Then you may find that your speed is around 200 words a minute or even as low as 180. Your comprehension, except over fairly short passages, may well be as low as 50 per cent or less. If your reading speed and comprehension were to be much less than that, you would be unlikely to call yourself a reader of books at all and you would be reading this only if you happened to be one of those rare beings with a greater thirst for knowledge than your reading experience allows you to quench.

A reading speed, in your own language, of about 250 words a minute is minimal; and I can think of no instance when it is not better to read something twice at 300 words a minute than once at 150. Even poetry, which it is sometimes fruitful to read more slowly than anything else, should not be taken too slowly. In his series of stimulating lectures, published as *Key to Modern Poetry*, Lawrence Durrell has said:

> You should let the whole poem flow through you as a cinema film flows across your vision. You should be receptive in the way that you are when you see an exciting film. You do not think too consciously about it, you let the successive scenes flash upon you, surprising you. In a moment they are gone, yet your attention is busy with the new image on the screen. Only when the film or the poem has ended should you begin to think about it and call up your powers of judgment. But while you are experiencing it you should be receptive—nothing more. Do not blunt its impact by too much headwork.

The time for reading at length at 250 to 300 words a minute is when your feelings are involved, when you want to surrender yourself to whatever mood the author is evoking, letting him lead you through an experience which, like life, you want to take at its own organic pace. Some parts of all great literature deserve to be so treated; and in any novel that you find worth serious reading there ought to be moments that move you to surrender. Whenever an author uses words with meanings additional to their simple face values, with studied intricacies of style, with overtones of euphony and cadence, and undertones of allusion and symbolism, then also, if you do not want the depths to evade you, is a time for slower reading.

But when the language is direct and unequivocal, when the author is pursuing an argument or dispensing information and nothing more, as I am most of the time in this book, then you may lose comprehension by reading too slowly. You will allow time for your attention to wander, for your own ideas and arguments to intrude between you and the full attention you want to give the author, for the body of the author's argument to disappear amid its constituent parts: for the wood, in other words, to be lost among the trees. Speeds of 350 to 450 words a minute are therefore more appropriate, varying with the complexity or unfamiliarity of the subject matter.

The more familiar the subject, of course, the more quickly it can be read without loss of comprehension. You ought to be able to take books and articles on your own specialty, when you already know most of the information they contain, at speeds of between 500 and 800 words a minute. But it demands considerable confidence and an attitude of attack and hard work that you may never have thought of applying to the printed word. Later, I hope to show you that the same mode of attack can be used to read a great deal of material that at present you might call unfamiliar; not only because much of all we read is simple and not worth reading carefully, but also because you are already familiar with many more subjects than you are probably aware.

I shall presume that your "slow" speed of less than 300 words a minute is adequate for your slow reading purposes. If not, it should become more efficient indirectly, as your techniques for other purposes improve. You will therefore be studying in detail only two of these three "gears" of reading, together with a fourth device, skimming, which is neither reading nor a substitute for it, but an adaptable aid to all types of reading. To describe a skimming speed in terms of words a minute would be meaningless. It would be like saying that if you take half a minute to look up a number in the Central London telephone directory, you have skimmed the directory at seventeen million words a minute.

All I need to do for the present is to establish the principle underlying this ideal. The most capable reader is one who can read anything at whatever speed is appropriate to it, comprehending as much of it as is appropriate to his needs.

EXERCISE 3

Choose the best answer to each question without referring back.

1. The author's view of written instructions is that:
   a. there are too many of them;
   b. they must be read carefully;
   c. they should be obeyed;
   d. they should be obeyed or ignored only when understood.
2. Reading is most efficiently done in:
   a. silence;
   b. comfort;
   c. the light of a reading lamp;
   d. one long session a day.
3. The function of the imagination, in the context of this chapter, is to:
   a. understand an action before performing it;
   b. decide whether an instruction should be obeyed or not;
   c. understand what an author is driving at;
   d. develop one's powers of concentration.
4. The Australian soldier's reading rate was said to have been:
   a. 80 pages a minute;
   b. 80 words a second;
   c. 8 seconds a page;
   d. 1,800 words a minute.
5. The hope of reading *Gone with the Wind* before breakfast is, in the opinion of the author:
   a. attainable with different tuition;
   b. all right for people who breakfast late;
   c. unrealistic and not worth pursuing;
   d. provoked by sensational newspaper reports.
6. According to the author, the average reader:
   a. reads at 250 to 300 words a minute;
   b. belongs to his local lending library;
   c. can learn to read much better than he does;
   d. wants to discuss books knowledgeably.
7. According to Durrell, poetry should be read:
   a. slowly;
   b. not too slowly;
   c. aloud;
   d. without too much headwork.

33

8. The author thinks that when your feelings are involved in your reading of literature you should:
    a. allow the book to lead you;
    b. take it slowly;
    c. ignore the feelings aroused;
    d. avoid too much headwork.
9. The quickest reading can be done:
    a. when the subject is familiar;
    b. when the material is factual;
    c. by skimming;
    d. by taking in a page at a glance.
10. The main idea of this chapter is:
    a. Many quick-reading experts make ridiculous claims.
    b. Most people read badly.
    c. One's reading speed should vary according to requirements.
    d. Noise is helping to make us all a little more stupid every year.

Check your answers against those on page 301. If you have scored four or less, read the chapter again, then do the test again, checking each of your answers against the relevant part of the chapter. If you scored between five and seven, read the chapter again quickly and see where you went wrong. If you scored eight or nine, it may be because on one or two points you disagreed with the emphasis of my answers. Note why you disagreed and try to understand why I gave the answer I did. For example, in Question 2, I know I emphasized the need for quietness, but this was only one of several aspects of comfort, in which condition everything is done more efficiently. But disagreement with my answers is not important at this stage. I shall discuss the problem later, together with more general questions of comprehension and the value of these tests.

Now perhaps it is time to assess your reading speed. Make sure that you are not going to be interrupted for the next five or ten minutes and prepare to read the following article at your normal speed, timing yourself as you do so. A stop watch is not obligatory, but if you can provide yourself with one to accompany your notebook, you will have plenty of use for it, and it will allow you to time yourself with a minimum of distraction. Before you start timing, take half a minute for glancing at the length of the passage, considering its title, author, and source, and picking up any indications you can of what the passage is about. Later, you will learn to do this methodically and to considerable purpose. Then return to the beginning to read the article, and start timing as you begin. Make a note of your time when you have finished, and then answer the questions at your own pace.

Pot

BY WAYLAND YOUNG

Pot, Indian hemp, Cannabis Indica, reefers, kif, marijuana, mahjnoun—what do the names make us feel? Probably something dark and desperate, an evil habit, brought here by dissolute black men from somewhere we'd sooner not know about, the kind of thing our children are bound to take to if we don't have them inside and locked up by ten o'clock. If they do they will surely become degraded, unrecognizable, tragic wrecks, sexually depraved, thin, with burning eyes, exploited by gangsters and criminal entrepreneurs, paying more and more for their necessary doses, etc., etc. Our laws reflect all this; cannabis is covered by the dangerous drugs legislation, those who deal in it are imprisoned amid toots of obloquy, and the stuff fetches magnificently high prices.

The whole thing is one of the most mysterious bits of our mores. Pot is not a habit-forming drug at all; the last interdepartmental committee set up to inquire into drug addiction, reporting in a White Paper in 1961, stated quite flatly that "cannabis is not in our opinion a drug of addiction." It did not waste further words on it, but continued its discussion of the large number of drugs in common use as tranquilizers and pain-killers which are. It also committed itself to the view that addiction to alcohol was a serious problem in Britain, and seemed to regret it was outside its terms of reference.

It would indeed be difficult to devise a study which would yield valid figures about this, but I guess that if you introduce a hundred adolescents to liquor (who would not otherwise ever have met it) you make one alcoholic; if you introduce them to pot you make one pot-addict; if you introduce them to tobacco —cigarettes, you make five lung-cancer deaths; if you introduce them to heroin you make eighty junkies.

Pot is not habit-forming, it is not even a *drug*, in the sense that cocaine and heroin and morphine and the barbiturates are. It is, as the White Paper said, an intoxicant, like alcohol. Its effects are very like those of alcohol. It increases both happiness and depression, according to which was present when it was taken. A tremendous lot gives rise to rather pleasant disturbances (though hardly hallucinations) in the visual sense; things look brighter, like Van Gogh, more sharp-edged, like Botticelli, more important. It is something to be taken at parties as drinks are. There is no joy in taking it alone, and nobody does. All in all, it feels like a variant of alcohol. It is not aphrodisiac; it doesn't seem to deaden the inhibition mechanisms in the way alcohol does. Nor does it make for vomiting or "stupor." You have to smoke lots of reefers in quick succession to feel anything much: to compare it with alcohol, one reefer is perhaps rather less than half a pint of beer. It can produce a hangover, though, just as alcohol can.

In some parts of the world, notably North Africa, it is socially equivalent to our use of alcohol. People smoke it, or eat it in spoonfuls of jam, after meals, and above all at parties. They feel about mahjnoun, as they call it (marijuana is the Spanish form of this Arabic word) as we feel about alcohol, and they feel about alcohol as we feel about marijuana. They fear and despise alcohol; it is prohibited to Moslems by the Koran.

Naturally, after the French occupation, and during the strenuous puritanism of their own nationalist revolutions, mahjnoun is getting a bad name, but that is an infection from European attitudes and does nothing to prove they are justified.

Now we surely have enough things in life to make us miserable without inventing more. I don't know how we first came to fear cannabis; it seems as though some mistake was made.

Perhaps it arose during the times when we feared everything about people who were darker-skinned than us. We feared their religion, their politics, their geography, their art forms (steel bands were actually *prohibited* in Trinidad until after the Second World War, when at last an unsquare governor went out and danced in the street) and so why not their intoxicants, too? The fear of cannabis goes with the feeling that brown and black people are dirty sexy beasts, and that sitting on the floor and eating with one's fingers is disgusting, instead of just different. The tragicomedy is that our simple little mistake led us to bracket pot with the really dangerous drugs, heroin, cocaine, etc., against which all possible sanctions are justified. It may prove hard to disentangle it, but the attempt ought to be made quite soon.

If it is not, the trouble will not so much be that we deprive ourselves of an innocent pleasure; we have alcohol, which is just as good. The trouble is that many people are deeply distressed if they hear of the spreading of this habit, and their distress is unnecessary. For one thing, it introduces a needless strain between the races and between the generations. A reform of the law would do something to remove this strain. A possible way to go about it would be to permit the growth, processing, importation, and sale of hemp and reefers on the same footing as alcohol; taxed and regulated alike.

It is not deadly, like tobacco, and might be a good alternative source of revenue.

From: *Guardian*
October 23, 1963
(900 words)

Note in seconds the time you have taken to read the preceding 900-word passage. From now on, every chapter and passage for timed reading will have its length in words noted at the end of it. To find your reading rate, see the instructions and tables on pages 313–316. When you have found your reading rate in words a minute, make a note of it. Then answer the following questions.

EXERCISE 4

Choose the best answer to each question without referring back.

1. The subject of the article is:
   a. a few harmless drugs;
   b. a single harmless intoxicant;
   c. habit-forming drugs;
   d. an alcohol substitute.
2. The departmental committee's inquiry into drug addiction discussed commonly used tranquilizers and pain-killers as:
   a. harmless drugs;
   b. drugs of addiction;
   c. no worse than marijuana;
   d. substitutes for alcohol.
3. The writer implies that reefers are:
   a. less harmful than cigarettes;
   b. more harmful than cigarettes;
   c. as bad as cigarettes;
   d. as satisfying as cigarettes.
4. The usual effects of taking pot are:
   a. mildly intoxicating;
   b. hallucinatory;
   c. aphrodisiac;
   d. stupefying.
5. Pot is taken:
   a. at parties;
   b. alone;
   c. in reefers;
   d. with a hypodermic needle.
6. The differences between Moslems and ourselves, for the purposes of this article, may be said to be that:
   a. they are dirty sexy beasts;
   b. they are forbidden alcohol and marijuana, but get contraband supplies of the latter;

38

    c. they take marijuana and fear alcohol;

    d. they drink smuggled alcohol as Europeans take smuggled marijuana.

7. The writer suggests that our fear of Indian hemp arose with:
    a. the thought that it might turn us into dirty sexy beasts;
    b. the fact that it has been bracketed with really dangerous drugs;
    c. the mistaken belief that it is habit-forming;
    d. our erstwhile fear of everything connected with people darker-skinned than us.

8. The writer's tone in this article is that of:
    a. a libertarian;
    b. a libertine;
    c. a satirist;
    d. a social reformer.

9. "Pot, Indian hemp, Cannabis Indica, reefers, kif, marijuana, mahjnoun . . ." the article begins. Why?
    a. They are all harmless intoxicants.
    b. They are words that shock us.
    c. They are alternative names for the same substance.
    d. It is an arresting way to begin.

10. The main idea of the article is:
    a. There is no reason to be distressed upon hearing about the spread of the use of marijuana.
    b. The dangerous drugs acts are depriving us of an innocent pleasure.
    c. Because Negroes and others prefer reefers to alcohol, we encourage racial discrimination by forbidding them.
    d. A number of social problems would be solved and a good source of revenue gained if hemp and reefers were permitted, controlled, and sold on the same footing as alcohol.

The answers are on page 301. If you have scored less than five, follow the former procedure of rereading the passage and doing the questions again, with the passage before you if necessary. Remember to do the same throughout this book whenever your comprehension score is less than half. If you have scored seven or less and your reading speed is more than 400, slow down a little for the next few chapters until your comprehension scores are regularly nine or ten. If you scored seven or less with a speed of between 300 and 400, your comprehension needs more attention and for the time being I suggest a second quick reading of everything. If you scored seven or less with a speed of much below 300, you may be reading too slowly for good comprehension. See what happens as your speed increases. If you scored nine or ten at less than 300 words a minute, you can afford to speed up a little, even at the risk, to begin with, of a point or two in comprehension. If you scored nine or ten with a speed of more than 400, have patience. You will meet more demanding material later on. With any score less than the maximum, check back, now and after each subsequent test, to see why your answers disagreed with mine.

Now put aside this book until tomorrow and return to whatever else you happen to be reading. It should be a book, preferably, not a newspaper or magazine, and for the present something not too demanding.

·3·

Beginning to Improve

ONE OF THE COMMONEST FAULTS of all but the most capable readers is that of frequent and compulsive regression. To go back a few paragraphs deliberately, to compare or to check something you may have misunderstood, is not a fault. Failure to do so, indeed, may be a sign of inattention. If you have forgotten, for example, to start timing yourself at the beginning of this chapter, you may need to go back and start again. Most of the time, however, regression is no more than a kind of nervous tic, a symptom of poor concentration or an anxious compulsion to hang upon the author's every word. You will remember the diagram in Chapter One illustrating characteristic eye movements of different readers. You may recall that one of the habits of the two less efficient readers was meaningless regression on each line. (If you have forgotten, take it on trust for the moment and refer back at the end of the chapter.) The diagram did not show the regression over several lines or even a page or two that most readers heedlessly indulge. We shall be studying the habit in detail later; meanwhile, practice correcting it as much as you can by reading the rest of this chapter without going back for anything. If you miss something important, you can always pick it up afterward. You should find an increase in speed and perhaps even an increase in comprehension. Gradually, by such means, you will come to understand various components of the complex process that is your silent reading behavior. Eventually you will gain control of them.

It is an important part of my thesis in this book that anything can be learned from books, given the determination, and provided that they are well written and properly read. Mechanical aids to learning may contribute to the amusement of any course of training or study, but they detract from the sense of personal achievement. And in the long run it is questionable whether they do much to speed up the learning process, unless their alternative is bad books, poor teachers, or unlettered students.

There are a variety of mechanical aids to quicker reading, all of them expensive, many of them aggressively sold, and none of them, in my opinion, indispensable. There are three main types: the film, the reading-rate controller, and the tachistoscope. The main function of them all is to control the reading rate by progressive increases in the speed at which the printed word is revealed to the eye. There is even today a teaching machine providing a self-administered reading course.

The different series of films project a page of print onto a screen and reveal it gradually from top left to bottom right in a rough simulation of a good reader's eye movements. Their chief disadvantage is that their pace cannot be varied and they make no allowance for the needs of the individual reader.

A more individual device, the reading-rate controller, is often sold for an extra few dollars with correspondence courses and books of the "Rapid Reading in Two Weeks" variety. It is popular with commercial quick-reading establishments where they charge high enough fees to afford one for every student. Essentially it is a frame for a printed sheet with a control knob to vary the speed at which a bar moves down the page, forcing the eyes to move with it. Its disadvantage is that only one page at a time can be fitted into it; a page of a particular size and format containing a measured number of words.

The tachistoscope (Greek: *tachys*, swift; *skopein*, to see) is simply a slide projector with a camera shutter attached to its lens. Words and phrases of varying lengths are projected onto a screen at different speeds: one-fifth, one-tenth, one twenty-fifth, one-fiftieth of a second, and so on. If you happen to be looking at the right part of the screen and do not blink at the time, it is possible to read the words "Gone with the Wind" if they are shown to you for one-twentieth of a second. You can thus be said to have read four words in one-twentieth of a second: a reading rate, one might say, of eighty words a second. You will readily see, therefore, how simple arithmetic can be used to prove that you could read *Gone with the Wind* before breakfast or Shakespeare's complete works in a couple of days.

In fact, much of the literature on quicker reading will tell you that you can do a lot better than the voracious Australian soldier. The authors of the Harvard University Reading Course[1] quote from two scientific investigations into the physics of sight and reading[2] and place the facts in proportion.

> The *normal*, average reader can "see" (without special training) four related words totaling approximately twenty-four characters of type in a single tachistoscopic flash of .01 sec. But this same reader will not use a fiftieth of this visual capacity in reading. In fact his average glance will be twenty-five times as long and involve less than ten characters. In the face of this astounding discrepancy it seems, to us, frankly absurd to train a normal reader tachistoscopically to "see" more words in less time in the belief that it will directly improve his reading. It may improve his confidence, but on grounds we are disposed to question: He can already see more in less time than his mind is ever likely to be able to handle on the job itself.

In other words, you can "see" *at a rate of* 24,000 words a minute; and a fiftieth of this capacity still gives you 480 words a minute. In fact, a glance twenty-five times as long, or a quarter of a second, with an eyespan involving, say, eight characters, or the same twenty-four characters of type in three-quarters of a second, gives sixteen words in three seconds, or a good average reading speed of 320 words a minute.

The chief disadvantage of the tachistoscope, in my opinion, is that even the irrelevant evidence and nugatory confidence it is alleged to produce are open to question. I may be mistaken, but it was my distinct impression, when I saw a tachistoscope in use,

[1] William G. Perry, Jr. and Charles P. Whitlock (1949).
[2] M. Luckiesh and F. K. Moss: *The Science of Seeing* (1937) and *Reading as a Visual Task* (1942).

that the sudden flash of light in the dark room left behind a negative image on my retina which I proceeded to read at my own speed.

But perhaps the evidence of subliminal advertising does suggest some validity for the tachistoscope. If the words BUY ICE CREAM are flashed onto a cinema screen for a fraction of a second during the showing of a film, no one in the audience, allegedly, is aware of having read the message, but in the interval the sales of ice cream increase. If training by tachistoscope could make one aware of being thus advertised at, there might be some chance of averting the panic of superstition that arises whenever subliminal advertising is discussed, as if it were somehow more perverse than any other form of advertising.

For my own reading-efficiency courses of ten or twelve weekly sessions, mostly with heterogeneous groups of adults with various levels of reading ability, I find a fruitful source of discussion and entertainment and a valuable aid to group cohesion in the films of the Harvard Course. Neither I nor my students would care to manage without them; but I frankly cannot decide whether or not they contribute directly to increasing the speed of comprehension, and no amount of "controlled" experimenting would help me to do so. Indeed, as long as my students continue to improve, I have ceased to care. As with all the other mechanical aids, I suspect that their principal function is their amusement value.

What, then, apart from mechanical aids, is the difference between taking a course in efficient reading and learning the subject from a book? Quite simply, the classroom has two elements that a book has not: other students and direct contact with a teacher. The former provide stimulus and encouragement by creating standards of comparison, asking questions, articulating individual problems, and reporting progress; the latter, if he is really a teacher and not merely a lecturer, can sense the needs of his students and adapt his instruction to meet them. The point of articulate need is the time when everything is learned best. One possible disadvantage of the classroom is that the rate of progress has to be pitched at a mean between the slowest and the brightest student, so that the slowest will not be discouraged and the brightest not bored. One hopes to stimulate the slow students and invite a creative contribution from the bright ones. The main drawback of a classroom course is that the exercises have to be done in artificial reading conditions with the distractions of timing, other students turning over pages, and symptoms of quite unnecessary but often ineradicable examination nerves. Self-tuition from a book, especially with a subject like this one, has all the advantages of reading and studying in normal conditions and plenty of opportunity for contemplation and creative introspection.

No course of efficient reading, whether **in a classroom** or a book, can do more than found a new set of **reading** habits and reveal weaknesses that must lead to further work. What I can state with confidence is that the techniques you do acquire, properly and continually applied, should last you a lifetime. The rest is up to you.

(1,450 words)

Now stop timing and turn to page 314 for your reading rate. Remember to follow the drill of jotting down in your own words the essence of what the author has been saying. When you have answered the questions you can consider any problems of regression or other difficulties that the chapter may have presented.

EXERCISE 5

Choose the best answer to each question without referring back.

1. Regression must be:
   a. avoided at all costs;
   b. practiced whenever the reader thinks he has missed something;
   c. practiced deliberately and only with good reason;
   d. avoided when trying to speed up one's reading.
2. Anything can be learned from books, according to the author, provided that:

    a. the books are not trying to sell anything other than them-
       selves;
    b. they are also entertaining;
    c. the student is determined enough;
    d. determined authors write them well and determined stu-
       dents read them well.

3. Mechanical aids to learning, in the author's opinion, are:
    a. indispensable;
    b. amusing;
    c. of limited usefulness;
    d. better dispensed with altogether.

4. The common factor in all mechanical aids to quicker reading is:
    a. their high cost;
    b. their gimmick value;
    c. their forcing of the reading rate by progressive increases in
       speed;
    d. they all have disadvantages.

5. Training by tachistoscope, in the author's opinion:
    a. helps to increase confidence;
    b. proves nothing;
    c. adds to the cost of teaching;
    d. is a useful gimmick on a rapid-reading course.

6. One may infer that the author's attitude to advertising is one of:
    a. cautious approval;
    b. amusement;
    c. extreme caution;
    d. cynicism.

7. The author finds the Harvard films:
    a. a fruitful source of discussion;
    b. no help in increasing speed of comprehension;
    c. indispensable;
    d. expensive.

8. The chief advantage of learning efficient reading from a book
  is that:
    a. one studies in conditions more like ordinary reading;
    b. there is a more individual contact with the teacher;
    c. one is free from the distraction of other students;
    d. one can determine one's own rate of progress.

9. One may reasonably suppose that the author has chosen to write
  this book in a direct, personal style because:

    a. he likes talking better than writing;

    b. he is trying as far as possible in a book to establish a sound teacher-pupil relationship with his reader;

    c. he wants to make a dull subject as entertaining as possible;

    d. he writes more easily that way.

10. The main idea of this chapter is:

    a. There is not much to choose between a well-written book on efficient reading and a classroom course with all its mechanical aids.

    b. Although self-tuition from a book is different in many important respects from a classroom course, the former has certain advantages which can be turned to good account by a conscientious student of reading.

    c. Statistics of reading speeds and comprehension scores are not much of a guide to what a reader can really do when he is alone with a book.

    d. Anything can be learned from books.

The answers are on page 301. Keep a bookmark between that page and the page of conversion tables, so that after every test and without further reminders, you can turn there for your results.

It is very important to remember throughout this book that instructions will seldom be repeated and reading techniques, once applied to one passage, should continue to be applied throughout the book unless you are instructed otherwise.

So far, then, you have received the following instructions about using this book. There will be additions to them as you progress.

1. *Read the book in the order in which it has been arranged. (This is not necessarily the best way to read every book, as you will discover later.)*

2. *Follow its instructions as closely as you can.*

3. *Keep a notebook at your elbow when working on it.*

4. *Do not try to read more than one chapter and one extract a day.*

5. *Practice with other kinds of reading for at least an hour a day and think about your reading habits.*
6. *Glance at the length of each chapter and passage before reading it. Read its title, note anything else that catches your attention, and prepare your mind as well as you can for the subject matter it seems likely to contain. (Later you will learn to do this more efficiently.)*
7. *Start timing as you start reading properly.*
8. *Keep all regression to a minimum.*
9. *Aim at good comprehension before trying to increase your speed.*
10. *Stop timing when you finish the chapter or extract and look up your reading rate in the conversion table on pages 314–316.*
11. *Note briefly, in your own words, the essence of what the author has been saying.*
12. *Answer the questions without referring back to the text, taking as long as you need, and check your answers against those on page 301.*
13. *Check back or reread the passage until your comprehension score is at maximum. If you disagree with the answer given, make a note of the difference of opinion.*
14. *Try to understand and, if possible, make a note of your faults and weaknesses, but do not try to correct them too hurriedly or drastically.*
15. *Be aware of as many of your reading processes as possible, and of your points of disagreement with the author.*

Make a special note of any of these instructions you think you may be likely to omit. If, for example, you found that you were delayed while reading this chapter by the footnotes connected with the Harvard Course, perhaps it was because you omitted to carry out Instruction No. 6. (Do not check back to see what it was; read on.) If you had noted, during your first glance through the chapter, that the footnotes contained nothing of immediate importance, you could have ignored them as you read. I shall discuss the problem of footnotes in more detail later. (Do you now, after deduction and recall, still need to check back on Instruction No. 6? If so, do so. If not, remember that by reading on you can often recall something you may have thought forgotten, or deduce something you may have missed.)

READING EXERCISE

Predigested Thinking

BY ROBERT H. THOULESS

In the days when a central issue at elections was the question of whether a duty should be paid on imported goods the difficult and complicated problem of the effect of such duties on prices and employment was summed up in such phrases as "Food taxes mean dear food" on the one side, and "Tariff reform means work for all" on the other. A similar process of simplification may transmute and distort a scientific theory. Professor Freud's theory of psychoanalysis was a body of doctrine complicated enough to give exercise to the most highly developed brain. Many of those who talk about his work, however (and these are not all persons deficient in education), are quite content to sum it up simply as "Everything is sex."

Let us call this tendency "predigested thinking." We find it is a widespread reaction to the complications of actual fact. Darwin's complicated and beautiful theory of the course of evolution was popularly reduced to the simple formula: "Men are descended from monkeys." More recently the difficult mathematical physics of Einstein's theory of relativity were supposed to be adequately summed up in the phrase: "Everything is relative." What science has discovered about the values of different kinds of food is similarly summed up in predigested form as: "Milk is nourishing," "Jam contains calories," and "Lettuce is rich in vitamins." In all these cases the extreme proposition is the less complicated

49

one, and therefore the one that we are prone to accept by our tendency to predigested thinking.

A man, for example, begins to argue against the teachings of Freud. He will almost certainly begin to attack the view that "everything is sex." His opponent may be better informed on the matter and try to explain which activities Freud thinks are related to sex and which he does not. This, however, is of no interest to the first speaker, and he escapes by protesting that his opponent is too "learned" or too "subtle" for him. He protests that he is a plain man and that nothing will convince him that art, romantic love, and religion are just sex, which is generally agreed by everybody to be the teaching of Freud. Thus he entrenches himself in his predigested thinking, and if the dispute takes place before an audience he can generally be sure of having their sympathy, for his opponent will seem to be a person trying to make himself out to be too clever and who makes serious argument impossible by throwing doubt on what everyone knows to be true.

The popular controversialist has indeed a serious complaint against those who do not accept the predigested thought formulas ordinarily current, because these are the agreed postulates for popular discussion. "The Scots are a healthy race because they are bred on a diet of oatmeal," "The Germans were responsible for both World Wars," "The higher critics tried to prove that the Bible was not true, but their conclusions are now out of date," "The welfare of the nation is based on the sanctity of its home life," "The Socialists wish to reduce all men to a dull uniformity" —these are samples of the predigested postulates of newspaper controversy. Without them such controversy could not be carried on. Yet there is not one of them that can reasonably either be denied or affirmed: they are simple statements on a number of matters about which the truth could hardly begin to be told in less than several pages.

A statement expressed in predigested form has the great practical advantage that it can be easily remembered and easily passed from one person to another. It is, therefore, easy for belief in it to be increased by the force of "suggestion." No kind of suggestion is stronger than the conviction that "Everybody says so-and-so." I was living in a village during an epidemic of influenza when word was passed from one back garden to another: "Bananas are so nourishing." Neither proof nor authority was demanded. Whoever heard these words went off to buy bananas for those who were in bed. Apparently lettuce, bread crumbs, or mushrooms could have been fitted into the formula with equal effect. This tendency to accept any predigested statement is being exploited by the advertiser who prints: "Snooks's mixture cures your cold."

A predigested thought formula expressed in a form of words which is handed from one person to another may be called a "slogan." A successful slogan may possess great power in influencing the behavior of a large number of people in one direction. No complicated statement of the doctrines of Rousseau could have been as effective in directing the French Revolution as the slogan "Liberty, fraternity, equality." Now, this slogan is obviously predigested. It is a very simple statement which would need a complicated expansion to mean anything exactly. Such an expansion of "liberty" would need to explain what the people were and what they were not to be free to do; of "fraternity," to explain with whom they were to be fraternal (not aristocrats or enemies of their country); of "equality," in what respects they were to be equal. Yet such an expanded account would not serve any of the purposes of the slogan: that it should be readily accepted in its entirety, easily remembered, and able to stimulate a large number of people to similar action.

The use of slogans as a method of influencing people is by no means unreasonable. A skillful leader of men, however complicated were his own thought processes, would need to express his doctrines in predigested form for them to be widely accepted, and, for the purposes of mass action, this could most conveniently be done by inventing slogans. Thus the second Russian revolution was directed not by a preaching of the subtleties of Marx to the people, but by the slogan, "All power to the Soviets." This was a legitimate use of a slogan; slogans can reasonably and properly be used to stir people to action but not to induce belief.

Probably there is no single explanation of the tendency to accept and respond to predigested thinking. There is the difficulty of grasping a complex proposition. The most finely developed brain reaches at some point the limit of the complexity it can grasp. With the majority of men this limit is rather early. Long before it is reached, however, mental idleness steps in, making us tend to accept mental food well below the limits of our digestion.

From: *Straight and Crooked Thinking*
(1,000 words)

EXERCISE 6

Answer the following questions briefly without referring back to the text. Be sure you read them accurately.

1. What is "predigested thinking"?
2. What conviction does the author quote as having the strongest force of suggestion?
3. The author names two great thinkers whose ideas have been unjustly subjected to predigestion. Who were they?
4. The author names two great thinkers whose ideas he considers became legitimately predigested. Who were they?
5. How does the author account for the fact that everyone can sometimes fall victim to predigested thinking?

Mark your answers by checking them against the passage. Allow two marks for each question you have answered rightly in your own words, or reduce the score by a mark for each error or omission.

Now put this book aside for a week and enjoy your practice reading. Try to read at least two complete books in the following week, but do not try anything too formidable at first. Choose light, factual material with a strong line of continuity and try, if you can, to find an uninterrupted stretch of three or four hours for reading one short book at a sitting. If you are not already a member of your local public library, go and join it. You help to pay for it. Here are some suggestions if you need them for suitable practice reading.

SUGGESTED PRACTICE READING (PART I)

Thomas E. Gaddis	*Birdman of Alcatraz*
Thor Heyerdahl	*Kon-Tiki*
Gavin Maxwell	*Ring of Bright Water*
Alan Moorehead	*Cooper's Creek*
Slavomir Rawicz	*The Long Walk*
A. J. A. Symons	*The Quest for Corvo*

PART II

QUICKER READING

·4·

Word Recognition

SINCE YOU SHOULD HAVE SEEN and read on your first glance through this chapter the curious arrangement of words in the middle of this page, it is best to begin by explaining them. If, for some mistaken reason, you did not notice them on your initial skimming of the chapter, you will surely have done so by now. Perhaps it is worth observing that because the words are so familiar and their arrangement so unfamiliar, they may already have caught your eye several times since you first acquired this book. No matter: you have probably read the same thing each time.

The cat
sat on the
the mat

Make a quick mental note now of what it was you read. You may think the task is rather childish. *The cat sat on the mat.* But if that *was* what you read, then go back and read the words again, taking care this time to read each word separately.

Have you discovered your mistake? The reason you made it was not because you were careless, nor because the words were arranged that way capriciously, to deceive you. The much more likely reason is that you read the whole of that familiar sentence in a single fixation, making use of the vertical as well as the horizontal part of your vision. This essentially is what the mature reader does most of the time. He would have read that sentence, as well as a good deal of other material, in much the same way as you were intended to, and quite rightly so. There is nothing wrong with failing to notice a printer's error unless you are a proofreader, in which case you would use a different reading technique altogether, because your purpose would be a specifically limited one, having nothing to do with comprehension. The mature reader is so absorbed in the meaning of the words that the only errors he would notice in a normally well-printed book would be those of the author, such as contradictions and ambiguities, flaws in his arguments or misstatements of fact.

So, if you failed to make the "mistake" in reading the sentence about the cat—if, to put it pedantically, you observed three definite articles in a sentence with only two nouns—then you may take it as fairly conclusive evidence that, although you might make a good corrector of the press, your reading habits could do with some cultivation. On the other hand, if, only once, you read "the cat sat on the mat," you may take this as evidence that you can read maturely sometimes. You may be doing so more often than you think.

But before analyzing mature reading habits in more detail, let us consider how immature habits are acquired. Perhaps "acquired" is the wrong word to use. Immature behavior of any kind was appropriate and mature enough when it was first adopted. It is its persistence into realms in which superior behavior is appropriate and possible that qualifies it as immature. A child of four who puzzles simple words out of the letters of the alphabet is using a mature reading technique. If he is still doing so at the age of ten, his reading is immature. And if he continues to do so as an adult, he is illiterate.

When you first learned to read, you did so by one of two methods or, if you were lucky, by both of them. If you are over, say, thirty, the chances are that first you learned your alphabet, then you learned the phonetic values of the letters, and then you began to combine the letters phonetically: c-a-t, cat. If you are under thirty, there is more chance that you were taught by the "look-and-say" method, in which the pupil learns with the aid of pictures to recognize a word as a whole, like a sign or a Chinese ideogram, by its outline instead of its separate letters.

An example of the look-and-say method struggling to establish itself in a child who had also been subjected to the old method was once told to me by a nursery school teacher. Studying the caption under the picture in his primer, the little boy read: "Sam had some (*pause*) h-a-m." He looked at the picture and said, with a proud air of achievement: "Corned beef!"[1] I have also heard it authoritatively recommended to earnest parents of preschool children that if familiar objects about the house are labeled in big, clear letters—chair, table, window, baby buggy, washing machine, cat, and so on—the child will learn to associate the word with the object and read, not only without tears, but also without thinking about it. I would rather send mine to a nursery school, corned beef or not.

It is my suspicion, incidentally, that whatever help look-and-say might be in establishing more efficient reading habits in later life, it may well be largely to blame for the extremely inefficient spelling habits of the postwar generation. Jacques Barzun discusses the two methods in a similar way in *Teacher in America* (1945); in fact, part of his chapter on "How to Read and Be Right" has been used as the text of one of the Harvard Reading Course films, at 305 words a minute. "The older way," says Barzun, "did not prevent the acquiring of the one-glance reading habits, and it did help to learn spelling and pronunciation. So that my choice, if I had any, would be for starting the old way and making sure that the child does not bog down at the letter or the syllable stage." It remains to be seen what kind of adult readers and spellers develop from the children now being taught by the new Initial Teaching Alphabet with its additional symbols and simplified spelling, and for which such promising claims are made. But the whole subject of the connection between childhood reading methods and adult reading habits must be commended to the researches of an educational psychologist or a thesis hunter. I must remain with my chosen task of encourag-

[1] The story may be apocryphal, but it serves as an illustration of the difference between the two methods. Indeed, every time I tell it, the more unlikely it seems, and the more difficulty I have in visualizing how the h-a-m could have been illustrated. But perhaps I have repeated it too often.

ing adults to transcend the traumas of whatever teaching they received.

If you have been able to read with interest this far, it is unlikely that you need to spell out words to yourself letter by letter, except probably for long and completely unfamiliar words. Even the best reader has to enucleate a pronunciation, if not a meaning, from a word he has never encountered before, and at best this is done syllable by syllable. Nobody, not even the most sesquipedalian writer, has a working vocabulary as big as an average-sized dictionary. And anyone learning a foreign language must begin with the muttering habits of childhood.

Any reader who is troubled by the vocabulary of his own language should compile word recognition exercises for himself. With the aid of a dictionary, make a list of, say, 500 difficult words of at least seven or eight letters each. Set them down one under another in a notebook in a left-hand column about an inch and a half wide. On the remaining part of each line, make lists of five or six words of equal length and similar appearance to those in the left-hand column and include among them the same word as the one that stands alone. The very act of compiling this formidable list should do something to improve your vocabulary. Have the list typed if you can, and the words on the right of the page jumbled, by someone else. Divide the list into equal sections of, say, fifty lines each. Then, timing yourself, go through one section at a time as quickly as possible, avoiding saying the words to yourself, and underlining on the right of the page the word corresponding to the one on the left. Try to do each section more rapidly than the one before.

That description should be enough to tell you what to do. If it is not, you ought to put in some more homework on the comprehension of written instructions by taking up a practical hobby that interests you and learning it from the bottom up with the aid of all the instructional manuals you can lay your hands on.

Henceforward I must assume that your vocabulary is adequate for reading this book and following its instructions. Remember that there is nothing like wide and determined reading for extending your vocabulary, and nothing like an extensive vocabulary for wider and more confident reading.

The extent of a vocabulary, for the purposes of this context, may be defined as the number of words that require only a single glance to comprehend them. And one comprehensible word at a glance is probably a fair definition of your ability when you last had a reading lesson at school. It probably also explains one of the habits you are still indulging today—if you have been reading this book at less than about 300 words a minute. But if you find a word of fourteen letters comprehensible at a glance, what is to prevent you from reading, say, three words of four letters, or any other arrangement of fourteen characters of type, in a single pause without uttering them one after the other in the mind's ear? When you read the sentence in the middle of the page about the cat, you read at least twenty characters at a glance because, as I said, you were able to employ your vertical vision. If the sentence had been normally printed, it would have contained twenty-six characters including the spaces, requiring a couple of fixations, during which you would have spotted the mistake. *The cat sat on the the mat.*

If you will recall again the diagram in Chapter One illustrating characteristic eye movements of different readers, you may remember that in the case of the superior reader, not only regression was reduced to a minimum. He also made fewer and shorter pauses in each line because on an average he registered as many as twelve characters of type with every glance, not counting the overlap at the periphery of each visual fixation. He was aided by the regularity both of the span and the duration of each fixation.

There are thus three principal components responsible for the pace and rhythm of the efficient reader's eye movements: a minimal number of fixation pauses; minimal duration of each; minimal regression. A fourth component is produced by the other three: a fast and accurate return sweep from the end of a line to the beginning of the next.

How far it is possible to train an individual to make the correct eye movements has been a subject of dispute among teachers of adult reading ever since the days of Buswell. You may recall from the previous chapter that in 1949 the authors of the Harvard University Reading Course were arguing that "it seems absurd to train a normal reader to 'see' more words in less time. . . . He can already see more in less time than his mind could ever handle on the job itself." The question is, does one read better by learning to make the correct eye movements, or does one make the correct eye movements by reading better—that is, by having a more confident and sophisticated attitude toward what one reads? It is fashionable nowadays to deny the former and affirm the latter, but both parts of the question have been affirmed after "scientific" investigation.

For me, observing empirically, the problem is still not resolved, and until it is I shall continue to assert that the protagonists of both sides are partly right and that, as with so many other contradictions, including scientific ones, there need be no conflict. And if my students and readers should not improve by training their eye movements, but in some other way, I shall persist in explaining to them what happens to their eyes when they read, however old-fashioned I may be thought. For I believe that any skill is, in the long run, more efficiently performed if we know all that there is to be known about the way we perform it. So at the end of this chapter, before you put this book aside until tomorrow, I shall suggest some ways in which you might study and practice eye movements.

(2,100 words)

EXERCISE 7

Answer the following questions briefly.

1. What was the purpose of the sentence about the cat, set in the middle of the page? (2 marks)
2. In the author's opinion, the look-and-say method of teaching children to read has one main advantage and one main disadvantage for laying the foundations of full adult literacy. What are they? (1 mark for each)
3. The author cites two occasions on which even the most capable reader has to make use of the practices of the childhood learner.

What are they? (1 mark for each)
4. What are the four components of pace and rhythm in the efficient reader's eye movements? (½ mark for each)
5. What was the main idea in this chapter? (2 marks)

Check back through the chapter for the answers.

It is possible that your speed and comprehension scores were lower than before. There are several likely reasons for this, none of which needs give cause for discouragement.

1. *You have picked up this book for the first time in a week. During the week you have probably become more self-conscious about your reading habits than ever before, and you may be spending more time reading than you are accustomed to do. All this can be inhibiting at first.*
2. *The chapter was rather technical and much of its content probably unfamiliar. You may have found it difficult to read about your reading processes without reflecting about them, experimenting with them, or visualizing them, all of which would tend to slow you down.*
3. *The awareness that you were reading more slowly may have caused you to worry about why you were doing so, which involved you in paying more attention to your reading processes than to what you were reading, with commensurate results on the comprehension test. Remember that you are learning to do skillfully something you have been doing only passably well for years. What would happen to, say, your game of tennis or your typing ability if, having practiced it untutored for years, you decide to take professional coaching?*
4. *Your comprehension score may also have been lower because some of the questions did not cover the points you think you remembered. Question 4 may have been troublesome, for example. The reason is not that you have a poor memory, for it is not your memory you are testing, but your comprehension. And if, as may have been the case, you*

failed to register the right emphasis of the chapter, you therefore failed to understand it properly. As you improve your techniques you will learn to take more notice of the important points and rather less of the unimportant ones. If you do not agree that the questions in Exercise 7 cover the important points in the chapter, check back again and list what you think was important. The exercise will come in useful later.

5. *Lastly, the footnote may have distracted you, because it was a different kind of footnote from the one about the Harvard Course in the previous chapter. I included it deliberately as an example of what may be called a parenthetical footnote, because it takes the place of an observation that could have gone into the main text between brackets, but would have arrested the development of the argument if it had done so. If you had read it during your initial skimming, you may not have understood the point of it, but you could have decided safely to ignore it. The best time to have read it would have been after finishing the chapter, or during a second quick reading of it. If you delayed yourself by reading it when you came to it, there was nothing inherently inefficient in doing so, provided that it was deliberate. I hope you resumed reading the text where you left it and not at the top of the page following the footnote. You may have been further delayed by uncertainty about how to treat the footnote. Never mind; you have begun to think about one of the many elements of reading a book, which is all to the good. There were also some other elements to interrupt the normal flow of discourse that you may have come to expect from the main text of this book. There was the reference back to the diagram in Chapter One, for instance, when you may have been uncertain about whether to refer to it or not. I also used at least two unfamiliar words—quite deliberately, as you can see from their context; and one word,* comprehensible, *in a dual sense, both for its everyday meaning and to employ an example of a word*

*of fourteen letters. There was also the cat on the mat, whom
we can now leave there, once and for all.*

*Now forget all about eye movements, footnotes, and self-analysis
for a few minutes to see if there is some improvement when you
time yourself reading straight through—with enjoyment—the
following passage. Remember to skim through it first, for a
measured forty-five seconds.*

Learning by Ear and Eye

BY H. J. CHAYTOR

Children can learn languages more easily than adults, because
they can concentrate wholly upon audition and are not hampered
by habits of visualization; just for that reason, they forget almost
as rapidly as they learn, unless they are in continual contact with
the language concerned. For the adult to return to the infantile
stage of simple auditory perception is a task of extraordinary
difficulty for those who are obliged to face it, as, for instance, the
missionary who proposes to reduce an unwritten language to
writing. He must first learn it as a spoken tongue until he is so
fully master of it as to be able to decompose the words he has
heard into their component sounds and find a symbol to represent
each sound, in fact, to form an alphabet. But in this task he will be
continually hampered by the fact that he has been accustomed to
regard language as visualized in the garb of a written ortho-
graphy.

But when the ordinary well-educated man is learning a new
language and hears an unfamiliar word, supposing him to have
reached the stage of ability to separate the words of a new
language, his instinctive inquiry is: how is it spelled? what does it
look like in writing? from what is it derived or with what known

words is it cognate? Given this help, he can associate the new acquisition with his previous experience and has a chance of making a permanent addition to his vocabulary. But if he has to depend upon audition alone, he will certainly forget the new word, unless circumstances oblige him to make use of it forthwith and frequently. Such is the consequence of association with print; in printer's ink auditory memory has been drowned and visual memory has been encouraged and strengthened.

Thought, in the full sense of the term, is hardly possible without words. When ideas rise above the threshold of consciousness, they are formulated by the mind in words; accustomed as we are to impart and receive information by means of language, we inevitably follow the same method when we are occupied by mental consideration; we discuss a matter with ourselves as we might discuss it with an interlocutor, and such discussion cannot be conducted without the use of words. Hence, until ideas can be formulated in words, they can hardly be regarded as fully conceived. Here, an objection is raised: unless the thinker possesses words, he cannot think; but, unless he has thought, he cannot possess words; how then was the process begun? Did ideas precede language, or is capacity for speech innate and waiting only the stimulus of ideas provoked by external accident, in order to break into action? In other words, did the hen or the egg come first? This question has interested those concerned with the origins of language, but it does not affect the reality of inner speech as the method of inner thought. This reality has been admitted from the days of Homer to our own time. Odysseus, alone upon his raft and confronted by the rising storm, "in trouble spake to his own great soul" for some twenty hexameter lines; and a barroom orator, describing his domestic troubles, will say "then I says to myself, this has got to stop," and will conclude his catastrophic narrative, "so I says to myself, I gotta have a shot, so I come down here." If the thinker is illiterate, the images that arise in his mind will be auditory; if he is literate, they will be visual; in either case, immediate vocal expression can be given to them, if necessary.

This vocal expression is necessary to children who are learning to read or to inexperienced adults; they cannot understand the written or printed symbols without transforming them into audible sounds. Silent reading comes with practice, and when practice has made perfect, we do not realize the extent to which the human eye has adapted itself to meet our requirements. If we take a line of printed matter, cut it lengthwise in half, so that the upper half of the lettering is exactly divided from the lower half and then hand the slips to two friends, we shall probably find that the man with the upper half will read the line more easily than the man with the lower half. The eye of the practiced reader does not take in the whole of the lettering, but merely so much as will suggest the remainder to his experienced intelligence. Similarly, if we listen to a speaker with a difficult delivery, we instinctively supply syllables and even words which we have failed to hear. Nor does the eye halt at each separate word. When we read our own language, we halt at a point in the line, notice a few letters on either side of it, and proceed to another halting point; the eye has not seen the whole formation of every word, but has seen enough to infer the meaning of the passage. Hence the difficulty of proofreading; our usual method of reading allows us to pass over misprints, because we see enough of any one word to take its correctness for granted. The number of these halting places will vary with the nature of the matter to be read; in a foreign language they will be more numerous than when we are concerned with our own familiar tongue, and if we are reading a manuscript in a crabbed hand with many contractions, we shall be forced to proceed letter by letter.

Very different was the case of the medieval reader. Of the few who could read, few were habitual readers; in any case, the ordinary man of our own times probably sees more printed and written matter in a week than the medieval scholar saw in a year. Nothing is more alien to medievalism than the modern reader, skimming the headlines of a newspaper and glancing down its columns to glean any point of interest, racing through the pages of some dissertation to discover whether it is worth his more careful consideration, and pausing to gather the argument of a page in a few swift glances. Nor is anything more alien to modernity than the capacious medieval memory which, untrammeled by the associations of print, could learn a strange language with ease and by the methods of a child, and could retain in memory and reproduce lengthy epic and elaborate lyric poems. Two points, therefore, must be emphasized. . . . The medieval reader, with few exceptions, did not read as we do; he was in the stage of our muttering childhood learner; each word was for him a separate entity and at times a problem, which he whispered to himself when he had found the solution; this fact is a matter of interest to those who edit the writings which he produced. Further, as readers were few and hearers numerous, literature in its early days was produced very largely for public recitation; hence, it was rhetorical rather than literary in character, and rules of rhetoric governed its composition.

> From: *From Script to Print:*
> *An Introduction to Medieval Literature*
> (1,200 words)

EXERCISE 8

Choose the best answer to each question.

1. Children learn languages easily, the author says, because the images they use are predominantly:
   a. symbols;
   b. word shapes;
   c. visual;
   d. auditory.
2. The educated adult's difficulties in language learning, according to the passage, are likely to be aggravated by his:
   a. forgetfulness;
   b. desire to visualize it in print;
   c. poor auditory perception;
   d. demand to know its grammar and structure.
3. Most thought, the author says, is wholly dependent upon:
   a. the ability to read;
   b. words;
   c. a good visual memory;
   d. an inner dialogue.

4. The difference between the mental images of the literate and illiterate thinker is that:
    a. the former depends on words and the latter does not;
    b. the former's are visual and the latter's are auditory;
    c. the former's are auditory and the latter's are visual;
    d. the former has his knowledge of print to help him.
5. When reading, children and inexperienced adults:
    a. cannot understand the symbols without transforming them into sounds;
    b. have to practice silent reading;
    c. can read the upper half of the line more easily than the lower half;
    d. cannot supply the words and syllables they miss.
6. The main difficulty with proofreading is that of:
    a. knowing the correct spelling of every word;
    b. reading too quickly;
    c. most people's inefficient reading habits;
    d. the normal habit of seeing enough of every word to take its correctness for granted.
7. The main difference between the medieval reader and the efficient reader of today is that the former:
    a. read so little;
    b. could memorize much of what he read;
    c. muttered every word;
    d. had to read in manuscript.
8. Medieval literature was written:
    a. in manuscript, often beautifully illuminated;
    b. for inexperienced readers;
    c. in epic and lyric poems;
    d. to be spoken.
9. We may infer that Chaytor's purpose in writing this passage was to:
    a. emphasize the differences between modern and medieval reading habits;
    b. deduce the everyday conditions in which medieval literature was produced and read;
    c. argue the superiority of auditory over visual perception;
    d. encourage students of medieval literature to read it slowly and meticulously.

10. The main idea of the passage is:
  a. Anyone who is only just literate, whether a child of today or a scholar of the Middle Ages, would read slowly but memorize easily because they read by ear, a fact which should be borne in mind by students of medieval literature.
  b. The modern reader differs from the medieval reader in the amount of written or printed matter that the former consumes and consequently in having a poorer memory.
  c. The modern reader could improve his memory by reading more carefully and cultivating a respect for words.
  d. The medieval reader had a capacious memory because he treated every word he read as a problem, so that once he had found the solution he could hardly forget it.

PRACTICE EXERCISES
FOR TRAINING EYE MOVEMENTS

The following techniques should be applied only to unimportant material, such as newspapers and magazines, and not to anything requiring adequate comprehension until they have become second nature and in need of no further conscious thought. They are not an obligatory part of developmental reading and need not be practiced by anyone who finds them irritating or unduly distracting. But for anyone who enjoys performing mechanical drills they may be found a useful aid to increased speed.

They are designed to increase the pace and regulate the rhythm of the fixation pauses by reducing to a minimum the three main components of number, duration, and regression. They should be practiced at first at a comfortable rate, and continued with gradual daily increases in speed, but never so fast that comprehension disappears entirely. Regression should be eliminated altogether during the practice of these exercises.

1. In any popular newspaper with narrow columns, try to read by making one fixation pause to every line, thus encouraging your span of perception to cover as much of each line as possible. Repeat the exercise daily at an increased rate.

2. In any printed matter with wider columns—thirty characters to a line or more—rule a vertical line down the center of every column and use it as a guide to make one fixation pause each side of the line, trying to keep the pauses as regular and metronomic as possible.

3. Divide the pages of an unimportant, easily read book vertically into three equal parts with the use of two straight pieces of wire or two rubber bands, and practice reading at three rhythmic pauses to each line.

4. Anyone with difficulty in controlling regression should use a white straight-edged card to cover each line as it is read. The card can be used to simulate the reading-rate controller by increasing the pace at which it is moved down the page.

5. As an aid to regulating the rhythm of fixation pauses, beat with an index finger line by line down the margin of an unimportant book, keeping pace with the finger. Beating down the left-hand margin should encourage a swift return sweep; beating down the right-hand margin should increase the pace across each line.

Remember that all these mechanical crutches—including fingers —are in the long run slower than the eye of the efficient reader. Sooner or later they must be dispensed with, and there is much to be said for learning without them from the start.

·5·

Anticipation

THE MEDIEVAL READER had another attitude to words which Dr. H. J. Chaytor did not describe. He believed that they were sacred. This was hardly surprising, since so many of the words he read belonged to sacred writings. And if his laborious method of reading them is thought to account for his prodigious memory, it should not be forgotten that their sanctity, their scarcity, and their limited subject matter were also significant aids to memory.

Words for us today have neither limited subject matter nor scarcity. But once anything is invested with magical properties, the magic tends to adhere long after all its magical uses have been forgotten, so that superstitions still attach to such things as sweeps, Sunday, knives, Negroes, kings and Christmas, as well as words, as if they had the same meaning for modern life as they had in the world of five or six centuries ago. The most prevalent and dangerous superstition (I was about to say) is the one that gives words some special sanctity; but I wonder if some of the other superstitions of the modern world are not even more pernicious. I shall let the statement stand because, if education is the only antidote to superstition, and words are the primary vehicle of education, it is vital for us to set our relations with words to rights to begin with.

Words are tools, marks on bits of paper, symbols, ciphers, hieroglyphs, a set of conventions, what you will; but their only meaning is the meaning we invest them with ourselves. An amusing and conclusive example of the irrational power of words can be demonstrated by uttering some obscenities in a language you do not know to someone whose language it is. Their effect on you compared with their effect on him will reveal both aspects of the problem at once.

As for the printed word, it is still invested with magical properties in many ways. Any day in any court of law you can see the magic of a printed book being invoked in the ceremony of oath taking. Four-letter words in everyday conversational use were believed until quite recently by responsible people in the United States to develop special corrupting powers if allowed to appear in print. Natural functions which healthy people everywhere perform and discuss nearly every day of their lives, if described in print, are still thought in some towns and villages of Britain to have an evil influence upon the young and to summon incubi if permitted across the thresholds of maiden ladies. Printers, who are an interesting race anthropologically speaking, have been known to refuse to set up a manuscript because certain words and statements it contained might have invoked the wrath of their patron saint and brought misfortune upon them and their machines.

It is a commonly held belief to this day that the appearance of any statement in print invests it with a quota of absolute truth. "It must be true because I read it" is dying almost as hard as its offspring: "It must be important because I saw it on television." It is amusing to speculate upon what would become of the popular newspaper industry if one morning the whole population awoke with the courage of a healthy rationalism toward the tyranny of the printed word; almost as amusing, in fact, as it would be if just as suddenly the utterances of all politicians were treated with the same rationalism, like a party political broadcast on television with the sound turned off.

A rational attitude to words, spoken or printed, together with the urbanity it engenders, are in my opinion an essential part of the efficient reader's equipment. And one of the commonest ways in which conscious or unconscious semantic superstition contributes to inefficient reading is through a compulsion to read every word.

If in all your reading lately you have been seriously resisting the temptation to go back whenever you think you have missed something, you may not yet have succeeded in doing so without its concomitant guilt or discomfort. In fact, the guilt may have been so uncomfortable at times that your comprehension was impaired until you succumbed to its pressure and, by then, had to go back several pages. It is a consequence of a compulsion to read every word, first instilled, perhaps, by some primary school teacher. It may also be a sign of superstition about words.

So examine it. And then recall some occasions when you have gone back to read something you thought you had missed. How often have you been able to add anything to your comprehension of what you have read? Very seldom, I suggest. There are several possible reasons for this. You may have read it the first time and forgotten it because it was unimportant. You may have omitted only one or two insignificant words and felt so guilty that it seemed like one or two sentences. You may have skipped over it because it was of no consequence or because you anticipated it. You may actually have read it very quickly but without hearing the sequence of words in your mind's ear. Or you may really have missed it, but deduced what it was from what followed, as you do if your attention wanders when listening to somebody speaking.

For a good deal of literature, all poetry, and any detailed instructions, it is certainly desirable to read every word; but the great majority of all we read is merely communicating information to us, if not actually in clichés, at best in language very similar to the kind we use in conversation. And to demand that every word of such material should be heard and registered, even when you know what the author is going to say, is as boring a procedure as to insist on completing every sentence in a conversation when you know your listener has taken your point. Listen to the phrasing of any conversation between two people who know each other and note how often a sentence remains uncompleted because the speaker knows he is understood or his listener chips in with a reply. The closer and more familiar two people are, indeed, the more situations there are in which words can be reduced to a bare minimum.

There is no reason why a similar relationship, albeit more one-sided, should not be established by a reader with an author.

Anticipation

Unfortunately, it is not possible for an author to write in such a way that he   . An author is bound by the conventions of the written word because he cannot know whom he is addressing and because any breach of convention would be likely to confuse the printers so that they   . But there is no reason for a reader to be bound by the same conventions. If a word or a phrase, a whole antithetical statement or even a complete stage in an argument can be anticipated, it is quite in order to omit it and resume reading at the beginning of the next sentence.

And if it is possible to anticipate what is to come, it is equally possible to deduce what has gone before if you read past it.

The point I am making is a relatively small one which perhaps will be conclusively demonstrated by the time you have done the three exercises at the end of this chapter.

(1,200 words)

EXERCISE 9

Choose the best answer to each question.

1. The medieval scholar's prodigious memory for what he read was probably assisted by the fact that he:
    a. puzzled out each word as a separate problem;
    b. believed that words were sacred;
    c. read relatively little;
    d. read the same things on the same subject again and again.
2. The author's argument about the superstitions attaching to words is intended to:
    a. amuse;
    b. shock any Mrs. Grundys who may read it;
    c. startle the reader into examining his preconceptions;
    d. satirize the law courts and the press.
3. One can infer that in the author's opinion superstition in general is:
    a. a sign of ignorance wherever it is found;
    b. quaint when kept in its place;
    c. a suitable study for anthropologists;
    d. handy to invoke when bad luck threatens but irrelevant when applied to words.

75

4. One can infer that the author's attitude to censorship would be one of:
   a. amusement;
   b. urbanity;
   c. hostility;
   d. support in certain circumstances.

5. A good guess at the author's political affiliations would be that they are:
   a. conservative;
   b. radical;
   c. revolutionary;
   d. nonexistent.

6. The statement: "It must be true because I read it" is:
   a. a symptom of superstition;
   b. an expression of a commonly held belief;
   c. dying hard;
   d. false.

7. A compulsion to read every word is:
   a. useful when applied to poetry;
   b. a possible sign of superstition about words;
   c. the cause of guilt feelings when you omit to read something;
   d. part of the efficient reader's equipment.

8. For a complete understanding of this chapter, an appreciation of the author's opinion of printers is:
   a. irrelevant;
   b. imperative;
   c. advisable;
   d. illuminating.

9. The main idea of this chapter is:
   a. Medieval scholars once thought words were sacred but that is no reason for us doing so today.
   b. Freedom from the tyranny of words will help to free us from many other tyrannies.
   c. An appreciation of why we feel compelled to read every word will help to release us from the compulsion and make us better readers.
   d. It is not necessary to read every word.

10. The questions in this exercise have been mainly concerned with testing comprehension of:

a. much the same things as the previous tests;
b. the facts;
c. the direction and importance of the chapter as a whole;
d. the author's argument.

It is quite likely that your reading speed on this chapter was a little higher than before. If so, the reason may be that the chapter was shorter than some of the others and more loosely written, containing fewer facts, and hence easier to read. If any of it angered or offended you, however, your speed may have been slower than usual. I shall have more to say eventually about the effect on our reading ability of material that offends us.

Whatever may have happened to your reading speed, there is even more likelihood that your comprehension score decreased. This was an important test because it was concerned with your appreciation of other levels in your reading than that of what is obviously being said. The ability to read in depth is an invaluable part of the learning process. So if you had any wrong answers, be sure to check back with special care and compare your answers with mine. Do not be content merely to agree or disagree, but try to understand how your thinking fell short or why I chose one answer as better than another. It was a difficult test also because, with a few exceptions like Question 7 (d), any of the alternative answers could have fitted the question. Take Question 4, for example, the one about my attitude to censorship. Certainly, I hope I was both amusing and urbane in my references to it. But to imply, as I did, that it was nothing but a consequence of superstition demanded an attitude far stronger than amusement or urbanity. You might have hoped to find an alternative suggesting prejudice, but none was given. You might then have hoped I would support censorship in certain circumstances, but there was nothing in the text to suggest such a reservation. It was an answer implying a more specific and reasoned attitude than the context warranted. But if you still

77

hesitated to infer that I was hostile, consider the images I used. ". . . still thought in some towns and villages of Britain to have an evil influence upon the young and to summon incubi . . ." Is it not the language of an anthropologist recording with a foreign detachment the folklore and magical practices of a primitive culture? Since I am not an anthropologist and, however hard I try, I could not be that objective about the culture that produced me, surely it can be presumed that I am feigning detachment in order to dissociate myself from a practice to which I am hostile. Although there is nothing like articulate analysis to wreck a joke or blunt the point of a conceit, let me risk analyzing one more question and then leave it to you to apply similar reasoning to any other questions that you answered wrongly. In Question 6, all the given alternatives can be applied to a statement like "It must be true because I read it," but one is better than the rest. You can take that on trust. To say merely that it is false, when you are supplied with more specific alternatives, is clearly mistaken. I said that the idea was dying hard, but that says little more about it. That it is a commonly held belief says something, but if it were not it would not have been worth discussing. The fact that it was a symptom of superstition was both the reason it was mentioned and the only possible alternative to choose.

There remains for this chapter only the task of explaining how to use the three tests which demonstrate some ways in which words and phrases can be anticipated. In three different passages, words and phrases have been omitted and your task is to replace them. Each example is concerned with a different dimension of anticipation, because if all three were superimposed upon the same passage there would be too few words left to make it comprehensible.

The first example, an ordinary newspaper report, has omitted mostly words that are repeated several times: "specialized" words that belong with the subject of the article. It should be possible to read it through quickly, ignoring the blanks, and still to compre'   nd it adequately.

The second example leaves gaps of several words for you to complete in any way that makes it comprehensible. The task will take a little longer than ordinary reading because you may want to pause over the best choice of words or to read on before the sense is revealed. But do not spend too long puzzling, or you will destroy the point of the exercise. Remember that it represents a device to be applied to normal reading when, if you cannot easily anticipate the author's words, they are always there to be read. The purpose is to show you that when the author's diction is such as to convey nothing more than information, you may use different words; but as long as the meaning is the same, they are as good as the author's—you anticipated accurately. Read the passage through once quickly, letting as much register as possible. Then go through it more slowly, jotting down whatever you think the gaps should contain. If you cannot articulate the idea for the gap, note whether you know it or not, and the answer in Appendix I may produce the necessary recognition of your partly formed thought. The length of the gap is no indication of the number of words omitted, although in the first and third examples each x represents a letter, thus superficially giving the passages the look of a printed page.

Read the third passage through twice or three times, until you have understood as much as you can. In this case, I have omitted what might reasonably be complete fixation pauses, giving you, for instance, only the beginning of one word and the end of the next. I have also tried to introduce some elements of the other two examples, as far as possible without depriving the extract of its text. You should be surprised at how much of it you can read. The original versions are on pages 301–304.

EXERCISE 10A

Migration Gave Australia 58 Per Cent
of Postwar Population Increase

Australia's xxxxxxxxxx reached 11 xxxxxxx last Saturday, on official estimates prepared by the Commonwealth Statistician. Speaking in Adelaide, the Minister of Immigration, Mr. Downer, said that about 58 xxx xxxx of the net postwar xxxxxxxxxx increase could be attributed to xxxxxxxxxxx.

Although it took 80 xxxxx for xxxxxxxxx'x xxxxxxxxxx to rise to one million, it is only four years and eight months since the 10 xxxxxxx mark was passed. said Mr. xxxxxx. The number of people in xxxxxxxxx has been increasing steadily since 1949 at about 213,000 a year.

Mr. xxxxxx said that since xxxxx War II, and allowing for departures, 1,460,000 xxxxxx from Britain and Europe had settled in xxxxxxxxx. This was 39 per cent of the xxxxxxx net gain of xxxxxxxxxx.

To this must be added 720,000 children born in xxxxxxxxx to families where one or both the xxxxxxx were migrants. These comprised 19 xxx xxxx of the 3.7 xxxxxxx births reported in xxxxxxxxx since 1945.

Immigration had thus contributed about 58 xxx xxxx of xxxxxxxxx'x total postwar xxxxxxxxxx xxxxxxxx. Without xxxxxxxxxxx, xxxxxxxxx'x xxxxxxxxxx would not have reached 11 xxxxxxx until 1975.

The xxxxxxxx was speaking at a special church xxxxxxx held on the banks of Port Adelaide River to mark the 125th xxxxxxxxxx of the first xxxxxxx in xxxxxxxxx of members of the Lutheran xxxxxx. The xxxxxxx was at the spot where, in 1838, about 200 Lutherans went ashore after a sea xxxxxx of 19 weeks from Hamburg, xxxxxxx.

Mr. xxxxxx said that of nearly 1.5 xxxxxxx xxxxxx from Europe and Britain who had xxxxxxx in xxxxxxxxx since xxxxx xxx II, about 95,000 were Germans, many of them Lutherans.

Australian News
November 21, 1963

Odd Ways at Westminster

The oddest thing about the House of Commons is the meeting-place
in which   more than 100 years. This unique chamber
was gutted   ,
but was restored in its original rectangular shape. Legislative halls
            so planned that   can have a seat and can sit
                                      . But in the
there have never been benches for more than two-thirds   .
And those who occupy them do not face the Speaker   ;
                        . New members sometimes
no individual seats are assigned and there are current stories of
freshman commoners making   to the clerk in the hope
of   . A first glance around   gave the impression of a
chapel or huge choir stall. The subdued light which fell from overhead threw a mellowness   .   dignity,
leisure, and comfort intermingled with venerableness—all
                    the bustling auditorium in which the American House
of Representatives semicircles around its Speaker.
    It is not astonishing that time had rendered the old
                        too small   . It is under-
standable, too, that its peculiar plan of antiphonal banks of seats
derived from the historical accident of its
in a choir-chapel. Some there were who wanted a new and
                    . But the characteristically
                        just as it was in its two essentials: the
banks of benches for
                    facing each other, and seats for about two-thirds
            . Winston   eloquently in favor of retaining
            . The oblong shape, he said, favors the two-party
rather than   . To slip a bit to left
or right is easy; to "cross the floor" is a decisive act "which requires
serious consideration." A small   the easy, conversational
style of speaking, traditional   , rather than "harangues from
a rostrum." It also prevents the feeling of being lost in a vast hall
when the business is not such   . Further-

81

more, "there should be on great occasions a sense of crowd and
urgency," with

From: *The Governments of Europe*
by William Bennett Munro
and Morley Ayearst (1954)

EXERCISE 10c

What Do We Mean by "Thinking"?

Aristotle selected rationality, the capacity to think, as the defining
attribute of Man. Descartes sought xx xxxxxxguish mind from xxxxxx
by characterizing xxx xxxmer as "that which thinks." It is not sur-
xxxxxxx xxxx these xxx xxxxxxxxxxxx should seize xxxx one of the
xxxx distinctive human xxxxxxxxxx in their definitions. It is true xxxx
many xx xxx activities involved in human thinking are present lower
xxxx xxx evolutionary xxxxx, xxxxxxxlarly among vertebrate xxxxxxx;
but the human xxxxxx has developed these xxxxxxxxxx to such an
xxxxxx that xxxxx xx x huge gap xxxxxxx man and xxx xxxx most
intelligent livxxx xxxxxxxx. Thought is not necxxxxxxxx the most
signixxxxxx psyxxxxxxxxxx function, but no xxxxxxxanding xx xxxxx
behxxxxx can be comxxxxx xxxxxxx xxxx study xx xxx fact xxxx
human xxxxxx have the capaxxxx xx xxxxx in ways which no xxxxx
xxxxxx is xxxx xx achieve. No psychology xxx xx xxxplete xxxxxxx
xxxx attempt xx xxxxxxxx and explain what a man xxxx when he is
descxxxxx xx "thinking"—xxxxxxx much certain psychxxxxxxxx emphasize the irratxxxxx xxx xxxxxscious factors xx xxxxx make-up.

But what xx xxxxxxxx? This might xxxx x pointless xxxxxxxx,
xxxxx everyone xxxxx by acquaintance xxxx xxxxxxxx is from his
own first-hand xxxxxxxxxx xx xxxxx xx. We all xxxxx from time xx
xxxx. Even xx xx are not philxxxxxxx or scixxxxxxx we xxxx xx
least follxxxx xx xxxxxxxx put to us by a schoolxxxxxx or preaxxxx.
We have sometimes been bright xxxxxx xx spot a flaw in such xx
xxxxxxxx and have manxxxx xx xxxxulate a cogent objxxxxxx xxxxxxx
xx. We have xxxx xxxeated by chess or bridge xxxxxxxx or have
battled xxxx xxxx teasers xxxxx we have succxxxxx xx reaxxxxx a
xxxxxxxx. We know very xxxx how some xxxxxxxx sticks xx xxx
xxxxx and moves steadxxx xxxxxx xxx xxxxxusion while xxxxx thinking runs xxxxxx xx xxxxxxx or drifts xxx xxxx blind xxxxxx or gets
xxxxxx xxxx! Some ansxxxx xx xxxxlems come xx xx in a xxxxx,

whxxx xx xxxxx times we xxx xxxfused and befxxxxxx xx spite xx xxxx efforts. In xxxxx, xx know xxxxx a lot about xxxxxxxx xxxx xxx own practical xxxxxxxxxx xx xxxxxxxx.

From: *The Psychology of Thinking*
by Robert Thomson (1959)

·6·

Vocalizing

THERE HAVE BEEN SEVERAL REFERENCES in previous chapters to the practice of reading each word separately and hearing the author's voice in your mind's ear. You may have become aware already of your need of this inner voice to assure you that you are comprehending what you read. Perhaps you have also realized that your speed of comprehension is closely related to that voice. If not, I am afraid that now I have mentioned it, you will do so hereinafter until you have either cured the habit or ceased to care any more.

In the jargon of the reading experts it is called sub-vocalizing. There are cruder forms of it, such as muttering or lip moving. But I am assuming that you have already discovered for yourself the undesirability of these habits and abandoned them, preferably while you were still at school. If you are in any doubt about whether you move your lips, or make some kind of movement in your throat akin to speaking, ask someone to observe you while you read. Diagnosis and practice are the best cure. Such habits restrict your reading speed to your speaking speed, with all the attendant dangers to comprehension and limitations to learning. Those of us who have grown out of the habit probably did so by accident rather than education. It is a very early stage of development from reading aloud in the classroom to mature silent reading.

Sub-vocalizing is a subtler process, because it has no apparent physical concomitant, save that of turning over the pages too slowly. The only observer who can evaluate it is the reader himself, and the chances are that anyone who interrupts his comprehension enough to think about it will find himself doing it. In its commonest form, it restricts silent reading to a speed very little quicker than speaking. A fluent speaking speed is around 200 words a minute, give or take twenty. I once heard the sports commentator Raymond Glendenning say in a radio interview that when his speaking rate was measured over the length of a greyhound race, in which he described all the runners from start to finish, it was found to be 325 words a minute. This suggests that sub-vocalizing still occurs at that reading speed. I have heard a teacher of rapid reading insist that sub-vocalizing persists at speeds of up to 600 words a minute or more, and in the face of such an assertion it is not difficult to understand why the elimination of sub-vocalizing is one of the foremost problems of rapid-reading schools and their students. Out come the tachisto-scopes and the pacers; tricks like counting over and over to one-self while reading—onetwothreefourfive, onetwothreefourfive— are suggested as therapy; and, I even suspect, reading passages and comprehension tests of ever more beguiling simplicity are given in the hope of supplying the student with the confidence of the illusion that he can comprehend with his eyes alone and his money has not been wasted.

For the sake of urbanity, let me expose myself to the con-tumely of all who breakfast on Bacon and Proust by confessing here and now that, as far as I can apprehend, I still sub-vocalize, whether I am savoring at 300 words a minute, devouring at 600, or picking the meat out of a book at even higher average rates. But whatever it is I do when I sub-vocalize, it is obviously some-thing different at 600 than it is at 300. The only difference I can describe is that at the lower speed I appear to sub-vocalize nearly every word, whereas at 600 I sub-vocalize only the key words while my eyes register independently of my ears the connecting words on either side. Allowing for the fact that the moment I try to ascertain what I do, I stop reading, the process would seem to be partly illustrated by Exercise 10C, and partly, perhaps, by assuming that I sub-vocalize only the words underlined in a sentence such as this one. That unsatisfactory description may not concur with your experience, still less with your articulation of your experience, so it should not be taken too literally. Trying to describe what you do while reading is, as you will discover, rather like counting the number of trains of thought clattering over the junctions of your mind at any one moment.

Though I have seldom met one and never trained or tested one, I am prepared to concede that there are prodigious individuals scattered about who can read accurately in depth at high speeds entirely without sub-vocalizing. I would be surprised if any of them were men and women of letters, for a writer must use all his senses when dealing with the raw materials of his craft, and it would therefore be next to impossible to subtract his auditory sense from his reading. I have heard tales, as we probably all have, of feats like reading and remembering a page at a glance. But for me they remain mere legends of potency that cling like incense around the images of great men. I would like the chance of testing such claims.

My contact, of course, is chiefly with readers in need of remedial training, and among them I have seen so many resigned to irremediable ignorance, or worried to the point of reading with neither pleasure nor comprehension, by exhortations to stop sub-vocalizing, that I long ago decided to concentrate on those aspects of reading which were amenable to training and suggestion, and let the sub-vocalizing take care of itself. I have so far found no reason to change.

Why, then, do I mention it at all, albeit at a later stage than usual in the analysis of reading? Firstly, because the relation between the auditory and the visual is an important part of the reading process, and I have already explained that everything is done more efficiently if we understand it; secondly, because a great deal of harmful nonsense is talked and written about it, both by rapid-reading merchants and in the press, and some corrective is desirable; and, thirdly, because it provides me with a stopper for the jar in which I hope to pickle the notion that efficient reading can be acquired by short cut, gimmick, or inoculation.

Various patent remedies for sub-vocalizing are peddled by

those whom I can no longer resist calling quack reading experts which give rise to divers popular notions of how to be cured of slow reading. "Yes, I've heard about it: you learn to read down the middle part of the page." Or: "Don't you have to read just the top half of every line, or something?" And the answer has to be: "No, it's more complicated than that. But also simpler, in a way. You only have to read, in fact. And, most important, you have to really want to. After that, it's mostly a matter of practice and confidence."

There are aids, of course, which an attentive reader can employ for reducing sub-vocalizing, word by word reading, and so on, as well as enhancing the ease and pleasure of reading, but they are nothing more extraordinary than the typographical design and arrangement of books, magazines, and newspapers. I have already suggested a way of attacking the narrow columns and short sentences of popular newspapers, by reading straight down the column at roughly one fixation to a line. At the other extreme, the reader can enrich all aspects of his reading and living with an awareness of the sheer aesthetic pleasure there is to be found in handling and reading a well-designed book.

The past decade or so has seen a dramatic growth of design consciousness in all sorts of fields, and it is my impression that developments in typographical design have made a bigger contribution than is usually recognized. The de-rationing of paper and new printing techniques made it possible, the pressures of rising costs and competition from television and paperbacks made it necessary, and a slowly awakening demand for education made it desirable. New type faces were designed, some a little eccentric and obtrusive, but many extremely pleasing. Magazines appeared so thoroughly remodeled that only their titles connected them with their former selves. Newspapers entered for design competitions. In London *The Times* changed its masthead. Turn out and compare some old magazines sometime, or change the newspapers under the linoleum. You will soon see what I mean and realize which is preferable.

Unfortunately, although the average reader's needs were probably considered when many of these innovations were undertaken, the efficient reader's needs were not, partly, no doubt, because too little research had been done on the relation between efficiency of reading and typographical layout and design. One of the most dangerous examples of willfully ignoring this problem can be seen wherever important road signs giving instructions or directions are still designed and composed entirely of capital letters. They are more difficult and confusing to read than they need be, not only because of frequent careless siting and ill-considered coloring but also, and mainly, because they are of the capital letters. Words in capital and lower-case letters, as in the text of this book, are more easily recognized from their overall shape and therefore much more easily read.

The most comprehensive investigation into the relation between typographical design and efficient reading that I know was conducted by Sir Cyril Burt and published in 1959 as *A Psychological Study of Typography*. Ordinary adults were given simple passages in a variety of type faces and sizes, their times and comprehension scores on reading each were compared and their opinions about legibility were asked. Nearly all of them were inclined to confuse legibility with their private aesthetic preferences and tended to read more easily the types that they preferred. "Preference depends largely on custom," the author concluded; "and throughout it seemed evident that almost everyone reads most easily matter set up in the style and size to which he has become habituated." Furthermore:

> The legibility of a page of print is the resultant of many different facts—the size, the form, the thickness or "boldness" of the letters, the width of the line, the spacing between successive words, the distance between successive lines, the texture of the paper, the ink, the presswork, the lighting, and, what is too often overlooked, the intrinsic interest of the subject matter itself.

In the course of reaching these conclusions, Burt discovered and confirmed some other important facts. Too long a line of print, for instance, gives difficulty in making a quick and accurate return sweep to the beginning of successive lines. Too short a measure, on the other hand, which necessarily gives widely varying spaces between words and many broken words at the ends of lines, demands a narrower span of perception and more and longer fixations to every line, impediments which increase as the type becomes larger. By that token, the narrow columns of newspapers are less legible than books, whatever they may do for newspaper economics; and the "brighter" the make-up of the paper the longer, word for word, it takes to read. That is why other techniques are necessary for tackling newspapers. I have suggested one already; I shall devote a chapter to others.

What the efficient reader needs from typographical layout is a line measure that permits a comfortable return sweep, with margin width and line spacing wide enough in relation to page and type size to encourage a reader with a reasonably broad span of perception to return quickly and accurately to the beginning of each successive line. Close print can cause lines to be read twice or a line or two to be missed. Narrow margins may encourage the eye to pause at a prominent word in the middle of the succeeding line instead of alighting directly at the beginning of it. Of course, the broader the horizontal span of the reader's perception, the more flexibility there is for a single fixation to take in the first words of every line. The line width, or measure, should allow for word spacing to be even, and moderately close, not only to avoid "rivers" of white running down the page, but also to encourage phrase recognition and quicker comprehension. Spacing should not be too tight either, and an ample space after each full stop is desirable, to assist the reader's attention to make a brief pause.

Thus it would seem that paperbacks are likely to be less easy to read than their original hardcover editions, unless the format is the same. Some paperbacks are so well designed within their own limitations that the difference in legibility should be negligible. Others, especially some American series and most pulp publications, are so poor as to require extra careful reading techniques.

The correct spacing between both words and lines is more important than size or design of type. Burt found that with adults of normal vision, wide variations in design, size, or measure seemed possible without greatly affecting reading efficiency. Where there were marked differences in optimum type size, they were mostly connected with differences in sharpness of vision, although older subjects generally tended to find decreases in size less legible.

The value of this knowledge to you as a reader is that when you have to read any poorly designed publication, you can be prepared for a possible reduction in efficency and adjust your reading methods accordingly.

One last minor factor in the mechanics of quicker reading should be noted before we turn from mechanical techniques to the livelier business of analyzing the psychology of reading. Another of Buswell's discoveries in the Chicago experiment was that the good silent reader was also better than the poor one at reading aloud, because the good reader's eyes were always a line or two ahead of his voice, arranging the phrasing and emphasis of the spoken sentences, whereas the poor reader spoke each word as he read it, flatly and without fluency. The value of this in the present context, apart from simply knowing it, is that improved reading techniques should also improve your ability to read aloud; and that practice at reading aloud, if you feel inclined to do it, should help to improve some aspects of your silent-reading ability.

(2,250 words)

EXERCISE 11

Without referring back to the text, write a brief summary of the foregoing chapter. A summary, in this case, is not the same as a précis: you need not include a paraphrase of every paragraph. Only the main points are required, arranged in such a way as to indicate that you have not misunderstood anything. When you have finished, check back to see which of what you consider to have been important points you have missed, and reduce your maximum mark of ten accordingly. If you can, get someone else to read the chapter and check your summary against it. Make a note of the result against your reading speed and then, but not before, resume reading this book.

Perhaps some explanation of that surprise test is called for. I do not expect you to have done well; if you have, perhaps you have less need of this book than you think. Indeed, the more faults there are, the more use you can make of the exercise when, in succeeding chapters, you can study how this sort of thing can best be done, and when you learn more about learning. You are not supposed, by the way, to have learned this chapter as you read it. No one could have done so, not by rote, at a single reading. Learning requires a different set of ancillary skills. But if your summary had been a perfect one, prepared with the original text before you, it would have provided a basis for learning or for discussing with someone else. The test was to help you discover how well you can pick out essentials as you read. It would have been a mistake, for example, to pause and memorize the title and date of Burt's book, or even the author's name, if it was unknown to you. Keep your version of the exercise for reference, take note of your mistakes, and see how many of them you can eliminate for yourself when you know before beginning something your purpose for reading it. Try to keep up your speed over the following passage with the knowledge that you are to write a similar summary when you have finished. Remember to look through the passage—say, for a minute—before you start timing.

READING EXERCISE

A Look Around the Modern World (1937)

BY STUART CHASE

If original sin is an assumption without meaning; if people as one meets them—Mr. Brown and Mrs. Smith—are, in overwhelming proportions, kindly and peaceful folk, and so I find them; and if the human brain is an instrument of remarkable power and capacity—as the physiologists assure us—there must be some reason, some untoward crossing of wires, at the bottom of our inability to order our lives more happily and to adapt ourselves and our actions to our environment.

91

Nobody in his senses wants airplanes dropping bombs and poison gases upon his head; nobody in his senses wants slums, *Tobacco Roads,* and undernourished, ragged schoolchildren in a land of potential economic plenty. But bombs are killing babies in China and Spain today, and more than one-third of the people in America are underfed, badly housed, shoddily clothed. Nobody wants men and women to be unemployed, but in Western civilization from twenty to thirty million are, or have recently been, without work, and many of those who have recovered their jobs are making munitions of war. In brief, with a dreadful irony, we are acting to produce precisely the kinds of things and situations which we do not want. It is as though a hungry farmer, with rich soil, and good wheat seed in his barn, could raise nothing but thistles. The tendency of organisms is strongly toward survival, not against it. Something has perverted human-survival behavior. I assume that it is a temporary perversion. I assume that it is bound up to some extent with an unconscious misuse of man's most human attributes—thinking and its tool, language.

Failure of mental communication is painfully in evidence nearly everywhere we choose to look. Pick up any magazine or newspaper and you will find many of the articles devoted to sound and fury from politicians, editors, leaders of industry, and diplomats. You will find the text of the advertising sections devoted almost solidly to a skillful attempt to make words mean something different to the reader from what the facts warrant. Most of us are aware of the chronic inability of schoolchildren to understand what is taught them; their examination papers are familiar exhibits in communication failure. Let me put a question to my fellow authors in the fields of economics, politics, and sociology: How many book reviewers show by their reviews that they know what you are talking about? One in ten? That is about my ratio. Yet most of them assert that I am relatively lucid, if ignorant. How many arguments arrive anywhere? "A controversy," says Richards, "is normally an exploitation of a set of misunderstandings for warlike purposes." Have you ever listened to a debate in the Senate? A case being argued before the Supreme Court? . . . This is not frail humanity strapped upon an eternal rack. This is a reparable defect in the mechanism. When the physicists began to clear up their language, especially after Einstein, one mighty citadel after another was taken in the quest for knowledge. Is slum clearance a more difficult study than counting electrons? Strictly speaking, this may be a meaningless question, but I think you get my point.

It is too late to eliminate the factor of sheer verbalism in the already blazing war between "fascism" and "communism." That war may end Europe as a viable continent for decades. To say that it is a battle of words alone is contrary to the facts, for there are important differences between the so-called fascist and communist states. But the words themselves, and the dialectic which accompanies them, have kindled emotional fires which far transcend the differences in fact. Abstract terms are personified to become burning, fighting realities. Yet if the knowledge of semantics were general, and men were on guard for communication failure, the conflagration could hardly start. There would be honest differences of opinion, there might be a sharp political struggle, but not this windy clash of rival metaphysical notions.

If one is attacked and cornered, one fights; the reaction is shared with other animals and is a sound survival mechanism. In modern times, however, this natural action comes *after* the conflict has been set in motion by propaganda. Bad language is now the mightiest weapon in the arsenal of despots and demagogues. Witness Dr. Goebbels. Indeed, it is doubtful if a people learned in semantics would tolerate any sort of supreme political dictator. Ukases would be met with a flat *"No comprendo"* or with roars of laughter. A typical speech by an aspiring Hitler would be translated into its intrinsic meaning, if any. Abstract words and phrases without discoverable referents would register a semantic blank, noises without meaning. For instance:

> The Aryan Fatherland, which has nursed the souls of heroes, calls upon you for the supreme sacrifice which you, in whom flows heroic blood, will not fail, and which will echo forever down the corridors of history.

This would be translated:

> The blab blab, which has nursed the blabs of blabs, calls upon
> you for the blab blab which you, in whom flows blab blood, will
> not fail, and which will echo blab down the blabs of blab.

The "blab" is not an attempt to be funny; it is a semantic blank.
Nothing comes through. The hearer, versed in reducing high-
order abstractions to either nil or a series of roughly similar events
in the real world of experience, and protected from emotive
associations with such words, simply hears nothing comprehensible. The demagogue might as well have used Sanskrit.

If, however, a political leader says:

> Every adult in the geographical area called Germany will receive
> not more than two loaves of bread per week for the next six
> months,

there is little possibility of communication failure. There is not
a blab in a carload of such talk. If popular action is taken, it will
be on the facts.

Endless political and economic difficulties in America have
arisen and thrived on bad language. The Supreme Court crisis
of 1937 was due chiefly to the creation by judges and lawyers of
verbal monsters in the interpretation of the Constitution. They
gave objective, rigid values to vague phrases like "due process"
and "interstate commerce." Once these monsters get into the zoo,
no one knows how to get them out again, and they proceed to
eat us out of house and home.

Judges and lawyers furthermore have granted to a legal abstraction the rights, privileges, and protection vouchsafed to a
living, breathing human being. It is thus that corporations, as well
as you or I, are entitled to life, liberty, and the pursuit of happiness. It would surely be a rollicking sight to see the Standard Oil
Company of New Jersey in pursuit of happiness at a dance hall.
It would be a sight to see United States Smelting and Refining
being brought back to consciousness by a squad of coastguard-

men armed with a respirator, to see the Atlas Corporation enjoying its constitutional freedom at a nudist camp. This gross animism has permitted a relatively small number of individuals to throw the economic mechanism seriously out of gear. By economic mechanism, I mean the operation of factories, stores, machines, whereby men, women, and children are fed, sheltered, and clothed. If people were armed with semantic understanding, such fabulous concepts could not arise. Corporations would not be interpreted as tender persons.

Corporations fill but one cage in a large menagerie. Let us glance at some of the other queer creatures created by personifying abstractions in America. Here in the center is a vast figure called the Nation—majestic and wrapped in the Flag. When it sternly raises its arm, we are ready to die for it. Close behind rears a sinister shape, the Government. Following it is one even more sinister, Bureaucracy. Both are festooned with the writhing serpents of Red Tape. High in the heavens is the Constitution, a kind of chalice like the Holy Grail, suffused with ethereal light. It must never be joggled. Below floats the Supreme Court, a black-robed priesthood tending the eternal fire. The Supreme Court must be addressed with respect or it will neglect the fire and the Constitution will go out. This is synonymous with the end of the world. Somewhere above the Rocky Mountains are lodged the vast stone tablets of the Law. We are governed not by men but by these tablets. Near them, in satin breeches and silver buckles, pose the stern figures of our Forefathers, contemplating glumly the Nation they brought to birth. The onion-shaped demon cowering behind the Constitution is Private Property. Higher than Court, Flag, or the Law, close to the sun itself and almost as bright, is Progress, the ultimate God of America.

Looming along the coasts are two horrid monsters, with scaly paws outstretched: Fascism and Communism. Confronting them, shield in hand and a little cross-eyed from trying to watch both at once, is the colossal figure of Democracy. Will he fend them off? We wring our hands in supplication, while admonishing the young that governments, especially democratic governments, are incapable of sensible action. From Atlantic to Pacific a huge, corpulent shape entitled Business pursues a slim, elusive Confidence, with a singular lack of success. The little trembling ghost down in the corner of Massachusetts, enclosed in a barrel, is the Taxpayer. Liberty, in diaphanous draperies, leaps from cloud to cloud, lovely and unapproachable.

Here are the Masses, thick, black, and squirming. This demon must be firmly sat upon; if it gets up, terrible things will happen; the Constitution may be joggled—anything. In the summer of 1937, Mr. John L. Lewis was held to be stirring up the Masses; and the fear and horror of our best people knew no bounds. Capital, her skirts above her knees, is preparing to leave the country at the drop of a hairpin, but never departs. Skulking from city to city goes Crime, a red loathsome beast, upon which the Law is forever trying to drop a monolith, but its aim is poor. Crime continues rhythmically to Rear Its Ugly Head. Here is the dual shape of Labor—for some a vast, dirty, clutching hand, for others a Galahad in armor. Pacing to and fro with remorseless tread are the Trusts and the Utilities, bloated, unclean monsters with enormous biceps. Here is Wall Street, a crouching dragon ready to spring upon assets not already nailed down in any other section of the country. The Consumer, a pathetic figure in a gray shawl, goes wearily to market. Capital and Labor each give her a kick as she passes, while Commercial Advertising, a playful sprite, squirts perfume into her eyes.

From the rear, Sex is a foul creature, but when she turns, she becomes wildly alluring. Here is the Home, a bright fireplace in the stratosphere. The Economic Man strolls up and down, completely without vertebrae. He is followed by a shambling demon called the Law of Supply and Demand. Production, a giant with lightning in his fist, parades reluctantly with Distribution, a thin, gaunt girl, given to fainting spells. Above the oceans the golden scales of a Favorable Balance of Trade occasionally glitter in the sun. When the people see the glitter, they throw their hats into the air. That column of smoke, ten miles high, looping like a hoop snake, is the Business Cycle. That clanking goblin, all gears and switchboards, is Technological Unemployment. The Rich, in full evening regalia, sit at a loaded banquet table, which they

may never leave, gorging themselves forever amid the crystal
and silver. . . .

Such, gentlemen, is the sort of world which our use of language
fashions.

The United States has no monopoly of menageries of this
nature. Kingsley Martin, editor of the *New Statesman,* devoted
a book to the Crown, the greatest spook in the demonology of
the British Empire.[1] It is a careful study in contemporary fetish-
ism, tracing the growth and pointing out the dangers of that
totem-and-taboo culture which has been substituted in the British
Isles for the rites of the Druids and painting the body blue. Mr.
Martin questions whether the labors of the shamans and witch
doctors in creating the perfect "father image" have not been a
little overdone. It will be hard now to build the new King into a
god after the decidedly human behavior of Edward VIII.

From: *The Tyranny of Words*
(2,100 words)

EXERCISE 12

*Without referring back to the text, write a brief summary of the fore-
going passage. Check back afterwards for the important points you
have missed, and reduce your maximum of ten marks accordingly.
Keep your version of the exercise for reference.*

*Now put this book aside for a week and return to your practice
reading. During the week, try to read at least one average-sized
book at a single sitting of up to four hours. A single sitting should
not exclude short breaks for refreshment or some other change
of activity. If you are satisfied with your progress and feel you
could enlarge the scope of your reading to include slightly more
difficult material, choose some books of ideas—popular philosophy
or psychology—discussing personal or everyday matters that you
can easily relate to your own experience. Here are some examples
of the kind of thing I have in mind.*

[1] *The Magic of Monarchy.* Nelson, 1937.

SUGGESTED PRACTICE READING (PART II)

Eustace Chesser	*Love without Fear*
Erich Fromm	*The Art of Loving*
John MacMurray	*Reason and Emotion*
Anthony Storr	*The Integrity of the Personality*
Henry David Thoreau	*Walden*
Lin Yutang	*The Importance of Living*

PART III

SKIMMING

·7·

Looking for Something

SKIMMING, IT IS IMPERATIVE TO REPEAT, is not a substitute for reading. It is a technique of selection, and as such is as valuable a part of the efficient reader's equipment as a good vocabulary or membership in a library. Since there is no possibility whatever of reading everything that is printed, or even everything we feel we ought to read, some process of selection is unavoidable. And for too many of us it is an entirely random one. What we really want is to be able to choose accurately, for ourselves, so that the maximum of our reading time is spent with purpose or pleasure, and, if possible, both.

For every kind of selection, in whatever sphere, we must have a *purpose*. The purpose is fulfilled more easily to the extent that there is *arrangement*. This applies whether we want to buy olive oil in a supermarket, find lubricating oil in a toolshed, or discover our name in a list of sweepstake winners. When our purpose is to look up a number in a telephone directory, we depend upon an alphabetical arrangement and, as with anything else that is arranged alphabetically, a single item can be found in a few seconds with *forethought* and *concentration*. As with a telephone directory so, of course, with any other form of index, dictionary, reference book, or encyclopedia. And as with alphabetical so with numerical arrangements, from libraries to lotteries. So, too, with every other kind of properly written book, document, or text. For everything that is properly written has some form of arrangement; and if we know the arrangement and have a clearly defined purpose, we can skim. The more limited the purpose, the more rapid the skimming; the more thorough the forethought and concentration, the more accurate the skimming.

AIDS TO SKIMMING

If you have referred back, at the end of any chapter in which I quoted them, to the examples of different readers' eye movements, you will remember that because you knew exactly where to find Chapter One, you had only to flip quickly over a few pages to discover the illustration. But suppose you wanted to note the exact date of the Chicago experiment. Perhaps you remember from the first questionnaire in this book that all you needed to note as you read was that it took place in the middle 1930s. You may have forgotten that too by now, unless you made a point of remembering it at the time or it had special significance for you. This is not a sign of an inferior memory, by the way; the most formidable scholar could have done no better. What you probably do remember is that the Chicago experiment was associated in some way with the illustrations of eye movements. Hence you have only to turn back there and glance down the adjacent pages to see the date standing out prominently, as numerals always do in a page of letters, and letters would, of course, in a page of figures. A further moment's forethought would have reminded you that you were looking only for a date—19-something—so you were able to find it by *recognition*, like a familiar face in a crowd. (Do not look back now. You can time yourself doing so when you have finished this chapter. The exercise should not take more than ten seconds.)

Similarly, you will note that the italicized word "recognition" is prominent in this page of roman type, as were the four other components of efficient skimming discussed above: purpose, arrangement, forethought, and concentration. And of course there are many other devices which give prominence to words, phrases, or short passages, such as larger, smaller, or bolder type, capital letters small and large, variations in spacing, and so on. Headings, subheadings, and paragraph signs help to clarify an arrangement, or separate one topic from another. Textbooks are often full of them, American textbooks especially. I am using some of them here as examples, but since this book is littered already with distractions enough, both with its exercises and its demands on the reader for self-analysis, I am avoiding them wherever possible. It is my concern to write a book which can be read with pleasure as well as purpose, and it seems to me that both qualities are discouraged by the clutter of typographical emphases to be found in many textbooks.

Perhaps they are popular with the incurious student whose way through his studies needs signposting because his horizons are obscured by the fog of an exam. They tend to be employed by the pedant who believes that work should be set apart from pleasure and addresses his reader accordingly ("I am your teacher, or *pedagogue,* with knowledge of the Word, or *Logos*"); by the author who wants to sell something, or persuade with a threadbare argument ("With the right DETERMINATION it is EASY to read a PAGE at a GLANCE"); and as a last bid for order and lucidity by the expert who knows his subject but is unwilling to learn how to write about it (§ *Three final points*).

Such devices, incidentally, are commonly associated with the kind of style that Barzun[1] has called the Impersonal Voice, when

> absence of tone passes for scholarliness, for impartiality and "objectivity," but it is usually a shirking of responsibility. . . .

The human being addressing the reader (if he is human) is never revealed.

> The Truth drones on, with the muffled sound of one who is indeed speaking from a well.

But there are plenty of good reasons for reading inferior books, and still more for reading selected parts of them, having first made the selection by a proper use of skimming. This is not to say, by the way, that headings, subheadings, italics, and so on, are always superfluous and only to be found in inferior books. Some authors make masterly use of them, and the efficient reader can do so too, wherever they are encountered.

In books and respectable journals generally, a subheading is at

[1] Op. cit.

least a reliable guide to what follows it, and an italicized passage more important than what surrounds it, which is more than can be said of their use in popular newspapers, where they are merely intended to look pretty or persuade you to read on.

It is complete independence of typographical pointers, however, which should be the aim of the efficient skimmer, so that he may use them, but not be directed by them unwittingly. With a contents list and chapter headings at most, plus confidence and a clear picture of what one is looking for, it should be possible with any book or printed document to fulfill a purpose in skimming as quickly and accurately as if the words sought were actually printed in bold type.

TECHNIQUES OF SKIMMING

By now it should be apparent that skimming is successful to the extent of our knowledge of where to find what we are looking for. It is seldom possible, of course, to find something in a printed text with the speed and precision of looking up an entry in an alphabetical list, so a certain amount of *scanning* is usually necessary. The physical process of scanning is an individual one; for instance, it may be more comfortable to glance down either margin than to run down the middle of the page or column. Remember, though, that the eyes see nothing while they are in motion, so the swiftest scanning is but a series of jumps from one brief fixation to the next. It is worth repeating here, too, that the aid of a pencil or index finger is not to be recommended for, as with every other reading technique, the slowness of the hand can deceive the eye.

Scanning should be reduced to a minimum by first accurately estimating the most likely position in a chapter or article for what we are seeking. If headings and subheadings are too sparse or imprecise, then it may be necessary to glance through the opening paragraph for an idea of the contents of what follows; and perhaps also through the final paragraph for a conclusion, a summary of the contents, or some other indication of what ground has been covered since the introduction.

For still further precision, we must recall from our school days the simple rules of paragraphing. When a new topic is begun, another voice or idea introduced, a further step taken in the development of an argument, then is the time to start a fresh paragraph. And it follows that the end of a paragraph marks the end of the topic or idea with which the paragraph began. Hence, when skimming anything which has been properly put together, is it not reasonable to suppose that the first and last lines of each paragraph, or perhaps the first and last sentences, are enough to give the reader a pretty reliable idea of what the rest of the paragraph contains?

Finally, if confirmation of a paragraph's contents is needed, it is usually possible to register in passing a word or phrase, often a repeated one, if not a complete topic sentence, which is a key to the subject matter and upon which the rest of the paragraph pivots. The topic sentence of the next paragraph is: *It would be better to read laboriously through the whole of something and select what we want from it than to select the wrong thing by inaccurate skimming.* Often the topic sentence is the first sentence of a paragraph.

APPLICATIONS OF SKIMMING

Unless our skimming techniques are accurate, they are nothing. Just as there is no point in reading at twice the speed if by doing so we understand half as much, so it is useless to skim unless our purpose for doing so is fulfilled. It would be better to read laboriously through the whole of something and select what we want from it than to select the wrong thing by inaccurate skimming. But with practice, confidence, and intelligent application of the principle, it should be possible to skim rapidly and accurately, thus saving hours that were once spent undermining our confidence and destroying our pleasure by plowing through material for which we had no immediate need.

Plenty of practice is imperative. Indeed, if you have never made conscious use of skimming before, it is unlikely that a mere abstract description of its principles will be enough to show you all its uses; and not until you have begun to apply them as a matter of course will you fully understand the method. At the end of this chapter are some skimming exercises that make use of this book, and some suggestions of how you might devise further exercises for yourself. The more practice you give yourself, the more accurate your techniques should become, and the more applications of them you will discover.

The applications of the kind of skimming described in this chapter fall into two main groups. The obvious one is that of finding information quickly which is known to be there, as in all kinds of indexes, directories, dictionaries, encyclopedias, and many other reference books. The other, less obvious but equally important, is that of finding information quickly which may or may not be there, and doing so without the tedium of reading irrelevant material. It is this use of the technique that I find to be of most value to my students, especially those such as business executives and certain professional people who, at the end of nearly every crowded working day, have to fill their briefcases with a residue of reports and trade journals, and annihilate many leisure hours reading without pleasure and with no other purpose than that of looking out for anything that may be of importance.

Suppose your work is in one of the many branches of the radio and electronics industry. You are doubtless bombarded daily with a bewildering assortment of literature—trade journals, reports, learned papers, catalogues, handouts, memoranda—all of which *might* contain something vital to you which, if missed, puts you behind in your knowledge of latest developments. But suppose the only branch of the vast industry to concern you is that of transistors. You know the jargon of your specialty, its technical vocabulary, the contexts in which it is used. Then if, with forethought and concentration, you can keep a clear general picture in the front of your mind of what any reference to transistors is going to look like, the skimming techniques I have described should enable you to leaf confidently through each day's literature in a few minutes and mark, for reading and noting later, anything you *recognize*. It is as if you were a detective watching a crowd pass through a row of turnstiles to pick out for questioning every bald man with rimless glasses wearing a blue raincoat and suede shoes.

Among others who can use skimming techniques profitably are lawyers confronted with law journals and weekly law reports, doctors needing to keep pace with new drugs and medical discoveries, administrators and civil servants with analytical reports and minutes of meetings, and journalists with a few lively paragraphs to write quickly on the essence of some important public document. The ramifications seem inexhaustible.

But perhaps the nature of your work is such that it is impossible to formulate a simple picture of what to look for when skimming. You are not quite sure what you seek, but you know when you see it. A student once described it as *sifting*. The only practical difference is that your purpose is more generalized. You are asking: "What is there here for me?" rather than: "What does it say about so-and-so?" The process will be slower because it is more detailed, but the same rules apply: typographical pointers, first and last paragraphs, first and last lines of paragraphs, key words, topic sentences.

One last warning word. The immediate attraction of skimming will be to reduce the amount of chore in your daily work. But if you try to do this too soon, before you are completely confident of the accuracy of your techniques, you will certainly find yourself without chore, but you may also find yourself without work. When skimming all important work material, therefore, please double check for several weeks until your accuracy is certain.

In this chapter we have been examining techniques for rapidly *discarding irrelevant material* so that our time is spent reading only what we need to read. But skimming can also be fruitfully used *in association with* all our thorough reading and studying, to increase speed, comprehension, and appreciation. The techniques are basically the same; only the purposes are different. We shall study these purposes in the next chapter.

(2,250 words)

EXERCISE 13

Answer the following questions briefly.

1. The author distinguishes "skimming" from "scanning," although many people use both words synonymously. To ensure avoiding subsquent confusion, describe in your own words the distinction the author makes between them.   (2 marks)
2. The applications of skimming described in this chapter fall into two main groups. What are they?   (1 mark for each)
3. What are the four prerequisites of efficient skimming?
                                        (½ mark for each)
4. List four of the aids in every printed text which should be read when skimming.   (1 mark for each)

Skim back through the chapter to check your answers, taking special care with the answer to Question 4. Write out the answers to all these questions again, with the chapter at your elbow, and keep them as a summary of the chapter for reference. I could have summarized the same points for you, but, as you will discover when we come to discuss the theory of learning, you will find them more meaningful, and therefore memorable, if you prepare the summary for yourself.

Your reading speed on this rather difficult chapter is not significant. If you have never thought about these matters before, it will probably have been slower than usual, unless you noticed as you read that it was repetitive and loosely written and decided to speed up from impatience and unsuspected resources of efficiency. To anyone who knows something about skimming, it should have presented no difficulty and resulted in an increase of speed. I hope that the footnote did not delay you. Again, it was something to register during your initial skimming of the chapter so that, whether you understood it or not, you could ignore it as you read. You will find the words "op. cit." as a repeated footnote in many books, and if you have not yet de-

duced its meaning, or troubled to look it up in the back of a dictionary if you needed to, it ought to be explained that it is an abbreviation of the Latin opere citato, *which means "in the work cited." Sometimes you will also see the footnotes "loc. cit."* or loco citato, *in the passage, or place, cited; and "ib." or "ibid."* which means ibidem, *in the same place.*

PRACTICE EXERCISES IN SKIMMING

Using this book, try to do the following skimming exercises in the time indicated. It is now, when working quickly in very short periods, that you will find a stop watch most useful. If you cannot answer the questions in the time given, persist with the search until you can. Think about where you should look before you start timing, and stop timing before you jot down the answer. The first ten questions relate to material you have already read.

1. What was the date of the Chicago experiment? (10 secs.)
2. What was the title of the "op. cit."? (30 secs.)
3. What is a minimum efficient reading speed for unfamiliar, factual material? (20 secs.)
4. What are the two Greek words from which "tachistoscope" is derived? (15 secs.)
5. When was the report of the departmental committee on drug addiction published? (20 secs.)
6. How many words are there in the Central London telephone directory? (30 secs.)
7. What is the name of Australia's Minister of Immigration? (30 secs.)
8. In what book is one advised not to blunt a poem's impact by too much headwork? (30 secs.)
9. What word was passed around a village during an influenza epidemic? (40 secs.)
10. Who worked on problems of visual perception for the Medical Research Council? (40 secs.)

Now do the same thing with the rest of the book and find the answers to the following questions. Employ the contents page at the beginning of the book for the most likely chapter containing the answer. Start timing as you open the book at the contents page.

11. When did Dewey publish his decimal system of classifying books? (30 secs.)
12. Who was "Datas"? (20 secs.)
13. Where and when did he make his first stage appearance? (20 secs.)
14. How many books on religion were published in Ireland in 1961? (30 secs.)
15. Who wrote: "The sure mark of an unliterary man is that he considers 'I've read it already' to be a conclusive argument against reading a work"? (1 min.)
16. Who is quoted as saying, and on what occasion, "I could have done it a little quicker, sir, but I hope you will agree it was quite expeditious and efficient"? (1 min.)
17. What is the source of "A book is a machine to think with"? (1 min.)
18. What was the publication date of the Report of the Committee on Weights and Measures Legislation? (1 min.)
19. Who was Hermann Ebbinghaus? (90 secs.)
20. Imagine you are reviewing this book for a popular newspaper. Your literary editor has warned you that the author has some harsh things to say about the press. You decide to write a hostile notice "proving" that the author has a chip on his shoulder about newspapers and those who produce them. Find five quotations (not more than three from the same chapter) which can be taken out of context and used to this end. (5 mins.)
[Write the entire notice if you wish.]

Read the following passage with a view to writing a summary at the end of it. Try to increase your speed as you do so, but before you begin timing, give yourself a measured minute for skimming through it to get a sense of what it contains and how it is constructed.

Medicine and Defective Vision

BY ALDOUS HUXLEY

Medicus curat, natura sanat—the doctor treats, nature heals. The old aphorism sums up the whole scope and purpose of medicine, which is to provide sick organisms with the internal and external conditions most favorable to the exercise of their own self-regulative and restorative powers. If there were no *vis medicatrix naturae*, no natural healing powers, medicine would be helpless, and every small derangement would either kill outright or settle down into chronic disease.

When conditions are favorable, sick organisms tend to recover through their own inherent powers of self-healing. If they do not recover, it means either that the case is hopeless, or that the conditions are not favorable—in other words, that the medical treatment being applied is failing to achieve what an adequate treatment ought to achieve.

ORDINARY TREATMENT OF DEFECTIVE SIGHT

In the light of these general principles let us consider the current medical treatment of defects of vision. In the great majority of cases the only treatment consists in fitting the patient with artificial lenses, designed to correct the particular error of refraction which is held to be responsible for the defect. *Medicus curat;* and in most cases the patient is rewarded by an immediate improvement in vision. But in the meanwhile, what about Nature and her healing process? Do glasses eliminate the causes of defective vision? Do the organs of sight tend to revert to normal functioning as the result of the treatment with artificial lenses? The answer to these questions is, No. Artificial lenses neutralize the symptoms, but do not get rid of the causes of defective vision.

And so far from improving, eyes fitted with these devices tend to grow progressively weaker and to require progressively stronger lenses for the correction of their symptoms. In a word, *medicus curat, natura NON sanat.* From this we can draw one of two conclusions: either defects in the organs of seeing are incurable, and can only be palliated by mechanical neutralization of symptoms; or else something is radically wrong with the current methods of treatment.

Orthodox opinion accepts the first and more pessimistic alternative, and insists that the mechanical palliation of symptoms is the only kind of treatment to which defective organs of vision will respond. (I am leaving out of account all cases of more or less acute disease of the eyes, which are treated by surgery and medication, and confining myself to those much more commonplace visual defects now treated by means of lenses.)

CURE OR PALLIATION OF SYMPTOMS?

If orthodox opinion is right—if the organs of vision are incapable of curing themselves, and if their defects can only be palliated by mechanical devices—then the eyes must be totally different in kind from other parts of the body. Given favorable conditions, all other organs tend to free themselves from their defects. Not so the eyes. When they show symptoms of weakness, it is foolish, according to orthodox theory, to make any serious effort to get rid of the causes of those symptoms; it is a waste of time even to try to discover a treatment which will assist nature in accomplishing its normal task of healing. Defective eyes are, *ex hypothesi*, practically incurable; they lack the *vis medicatrix naturae*. The only thing that ophthalmological science can do for them is to provide them with the purely mechanical means for neutralizing their symptoms. The only qualifications to this strange theory come from those who have made it their business to look into external conditions of seeing. Here, for example, are some relevant remarks taken from the book *Seeing and Human Welfare* by Dr. Matthew Luckiesh, Director of the General Electric Company's Lighting Research Laboratory. Eyeglasses

(those "valuable crutches," as Dr. Luckiesh calls them) "counter-
act effects of heredity, age and *abuse;* they do not deal with
causes." "Suppose that crippled eyes could be transformed into
crippled legs. What a heart-rending parade we would witness
on a busy street! Nearly every other person would go limping
by. Many would be on crutches and some on wheel chairs. How
many of these defects of the eye are due to poor conditions for
seeing, that is, to indifference toward seeing? Statistics are not
available, but a knowledge of seeing and its requirements indicates
that most of them are preventable and most of the remainder can
be improved or arrested by adequate and proper conditions."
And again, "even the refractive defects and other abnormalities
of eyes induced by abuses are not necessarily permanent. When
we become ill, Nature does her part, if we do ours, toward
getting well. Eyes have various recuperative powers, at least to
some degree. Reducing their abuse by improving seeing conditions is always helpful, and there are many cases on record where
great improvement has followed on this procedure. Indeed, without correction of the abuse, the disorder generally becomes
progressively worse." These are encouraging words that leave us
with the hope that we are to be given a description of some new
and genuinely aetiological treatment of visual defects, to take
the place of the purely symptomatic treatment at present in vogue.
But this hope is only imperfectly fulfilled. "Poor lighting," Dr.
Luckiesh goes on, "is the most important and universal cause of
eyestrain, often leading to progressive defects and disorders."
His whole book is an elaboration of this theme. Let me hasten
to add that, within its limitations, it is an admirable book. To
those suffering from defects of vision the importance of good
lighting is very great indeed; and one can only be grateful to
Dr. Luckiesh for his scientific clarification of the meaning of
"good lighting" in terms of standard, measurable entities such as
foot-candles. One's only complaint is that foot-candles are not
enough. In treating other parts of the organism doctors are not
content to ameliorate merely the external conditions of functioning; they also seek to improve the internal conditions, to work
directly on the physiological environment of the sick organ as

well as on the physical environment outside the body. Thus when legs are crippled, doctors refuse to let their patients rely indefinitely on crutches. Nor do they consider that the laying down of rules for avoiding accidents constitutes sufficient treatment for the condition of being crippled. On the contrary, they regard the use of crutches as merely a palliative and temporary expedient, and while paying attention to external conditions, they also do their best to improve the internal conditions of the defective part, so that nature may be helped to do its work of healing. Some of these measures, such as rest, massage, applications of heat and light, make no appeal to the patient's mind, but are aimed directly at the affected organs, their purpose being to relax, to increase circulation and to preserve mobility. Other measures are educational and involve, on the patient's part, a coordination of mind and body. By means of this appeal to the psychological factor astonishing results are often obtained. A good teacher, using the right technique, can often educate a victim of accident or paralysis into gradual recovery of his lost functions, and through that recovery of function, into the re-establishment of the health and integrity of the defective organ. If such things can be done for crippled legs, why should it not be possible to do something analogous for defective eyes? To this question the orthodox theory provides no answer—merely takes it for granted that the defective eye is incurable and cannot, in spite of its peculiarly intimate relationship with the psyche, be re-educated toward normality by any process of mind-body coordination.

The orthodox theory is, on the face of it, so implausible, so intrinsically unlikely to be true, that one can only be astonished that it should be so generally and so unquestioningly accepted. Nevertheless, such is the force of habit and authority that we all do accept it. At the present time it is rejected only by those who have personal reasons for knowing it to be untrue. I myself happen to be one of these. By the greatest of good fortune I was given the opportunity to discover by personal experience that eyes do not lack the *vis medicatrix naturae*, that the palliation of symptoms is not the only treatment for defective vision, that the function of sight can be re-educated toward normality by appropriate body-mind coordination, and finally that the improvement in functioning is accompanied by an improvement in the condition of the damaged organ. This personal experience has been confirmed by my observation of many others who have gone through the same process of visual education. It is therefore no longer possible for me to accept the currently orthodox theory, with its hopelessly pessimistic practical corollaries.

From: *The Art of Seeing*
(1,400 words)

EXERCISE 14

Write a summary of the foregoing extract, without referring back.

When you have finished, go through the passage again using skimming techniques and copy out the key sentence of each of its six paragraphs. Compare these six sentences with the main points that should have been included in your summary, and award your marks out of ten for comprehension accordingly.

·8·

Sense and Structure

ANYONE WHO ATTEMPTS to express thoughts in writing always does so not only with some kind of sense but also with some kind of structure. The sense may sometimes be revealed only by the application of one form or another of expertise or insight, but the structure is always easily discerned. The writer can be the most woolly or semi-literate of letter writers, the most ponderous of public functionaries, the most pompously prolix of bureaucrats, but however tiny his mind or muddled his thoughts, he can do no more when he writes than proceed from statement to statement, from fact to fact, from platitude to platitude. And if the essence of all his statements were distilled from his verbiage and listed, a pattern would emerge, even though some rearrangement might be necessary to make it a coherent one.

Material written professionally, or written by amateurs and edited professionally—most printed matter, in fact—has a structure which can be discerned in a few seconds and analyzed and noted in a few minutes—a technique of which the efficient reader will make the maximum use, as an aid to accurate selection, quicker comprehension, and subsequent study.

The structure of a sentence is something I must assume you remember from your school days. Now you need only recall the subject-verb-predicate elements and the fact that the three can be arranged in any order and interspersed with various kinds of phrases and modifying clauses. Of course, you remember: you/know/the structure of a sentence. Subject, verb, predicate. So much is elementary, and the knowledge helps when skimming or reading at very high speeds to get merely the general sense of something.

Sentences are linked into paragraphs, and you have already begun to understand the present relevance of paragraph structure. A paragraph contains an introductory sentence, a topic sentence or main idea, and a concluding sentence. The topic sentence can stand alone, or be either the introductory or the concluding sentence. The four sentences of this paragraph provide a simple example of introduction, topic, extra information, conclusion.

Some paragraphs contain no topic sentence, either because the main idea is implied, or because the paragraph consists of a series of details developing the theme. Such is the case with this paragraph.

A rapid appreciation of paragraph structure is especially useful when quickly reading material on familiar subjects. It may often be sufficient to read the main idea alone, for whatever else supports it can be supplied by the reader from existing knowledge and experience. It is, moreover, an invaluable aid to all comprehension and learning because the fabric of each paragraph goes to build the structure of every article and chapter.

Consider the extract from *The Art of Seeing* that supplied your last timed reading passage. If you followed all the instructions associated with it, you should have read it only yesterday and you ought to remember quite a lot about it without referring back. Your work on comprehension of it should remind you that it contained a title, two subheadings, and six paragraphs, each with a topic sentence. The headings alone reveal quite a lot:

MEDICINE AND DEFECTIVE VISION

Ordinary Treatment of Defective Sight
Cure or Palliation of Symptoms?

Clearly, the passage is concerned with the age-old medical problem of whether disease can be cured or whether the sufferer must content himself with apparatus or medication. In this case, the question is applied to defective vision, so "ordinary treatment" must mean either the use of glasses (apparatus), or eye drops, lotions, and surgery (medication), or both. The six topic sentences disclose the answer and add nearly all one needs to know. Here they are, paragraph by paragraph, abbreviated where possible:

1. If there were no natural healing powers, medicine would be helpless.
2. Sick organisms tend to recover their own inherent powers of self-healing.
3. Artificial lenses neutralize the symptoms but do not get rid of the causes of defective vision.
4. Orthodox opinion insists that the mechanical palliation of symptoms is the only kind of treatment to which defective organs of vision will respond.
5. If . . . things can be done for crippled legs, why should it not be possible to do something analogous for defective eyes?
6. The function of sight can be re-educated toward normality by appropriate body-mind coordination.

The only difficulty might have been presented by the exceptionally long fifth paragraph, which can be subdivided and treated as a separate article. Its contents form a kind of subplot to the main theme, an argument within an argument. This is suggested by its opening words, "If orthodox opinion is right . . ." It is a familiar stage in any argument, as old as Socrates, when the case for the opposition is argued by the dissenter as favorably as he can put it. It follows, as "but" follows "therefore," that it will then be demolished or reduced to absurdity. Since orthodox opinion assumes that the eyes are incurable, they must, Huxley declares, be different in nature from every other organ of the body. He considers one concession—prevention—allowed by orthodox opinion, and quotes an authority on lighting in support of it. Then he describes the physiological and psychological means used successfully by orthodox medicine to cure other defective organs, such as crippled legs. The question asked in the topic sentence follows naturally.

From the six topic sentences, then, we can see the structure of the passage as that of a simple argument: thesis—antithesis—synthesis.

Thesis: Sick organisms have self-healing powers and without them medicine would be helpless (paragraphs 1, 2).

Antithesis: Glasses do not cure defective eyes and orthodox opinion insists, contrary to the evidence of principles applied to other organs, that eyes are incurable (paragraphs 3, 4, 5).

Synthesis: But the same principles can in fact be successfully applied to the eyes.

Q.E.D., one might say, but for the knowledge that poor Huxley, who indeed never went completely blind, lived and died as phenomenally nearsighted in his physical vision as he was clear-sighted in his metaphysical vision.

When a complicated passage like that first chapter of *The Art of Seeing* is so ruthlessly and simply reduced to something as commonplace as the basic form of any argument, it seems likely that any other text can be similarly stripped.

An article has a beginning, a middle, and an end—a truism of such bewildering banality that it must be immediately applied or deleted. The basic structure may occupy only the middle of an article, with the beginning and end fulfilling other functions. One of the commonest constructions to occupy an entire article is that used in all news reports and by journalists writing and editing in many other fields. This is the inverted pyramid. The beginning summarizes the contents of the middle, and the end occurs where it ends, or where the reader stops reading. I shall discuss the inverted pyramid in detail when we consider the reading of newspapers.

The summary introduction is a way of beginning articles with other constructions than the inverted pyramid, and there are several other beginnings, too. To take the analysis of Huxley's chapter a stage further as an example, his thesis was not properly stated until his second paragraph with: "Sick organisms tend to recover their own inherent powers of self-healing." The first can be regarded as an inductive introduction, by which the reader is led gently toward the main idea from familiar generalities: "The doctor treats, nature heals."

The inductive opening may lead in the opposite direction, that is, beginning with the particular and leading into the general.

The anecdotal opening is so similar to the introduction from the particular to the general that the difference can only be seen in the structure of the body of the article. The anecdotal opening is usually part of a simple chronological structure. Its most familiar form, of course, begins: "Once upon a time . . ."

Two other types of introduction, usually detached from the main structure of the article, are the mood and the shock. The former tries to heighten the reader's emotional interest in the subject and the latter is designed to startle him into reading on.

Pot, Indian hemp, Cannabis Indica, reefers, kif, marijuana, mah-jnoun—what do the names make us feel?

I interpret this example as a mood opening, but it may also be read as a shock. You will encounter a more conclusive example of the shock (though by now it ought not to shock you) in the reading extract preceding Exercise 26c in Chapter Thirteen:

When highly educated industrialists, businessmen, and senior Government officials, headed by the Lord Privy Seal, find it necessary to go back to school to learn to read effectively, one is justified in wondering how this situation arises.

A famous film director, whose name I do not know and dare not guess, once uttered a commandment which many people in the industry today would like to see engraved above the portals of their studios. It is far more honored in the industry than any Mosaic commandment, and you have only to switch on your television to see within a few minutes that it has been handed down another generation. The commandment is this: *Tell 'em you're gonna tell 'em. Tell 'em. Tell 'em you've told 'em.*

It could equally well exemplify a common way of constructing articles. It makes use of a third kind of ending. I have described two already: the rounding off, and just stopping because a summary introduction has covered the ground already. The third ending is merely a summary too, telling the reader what he has just been told.

We have now considered in passing three of the six basic

structures of articles: the film maker's commandment, the inverted pyramid, and the prototype argument. I have also touched upon a fourth: the chronological sequence. The simplest form of this begins in the past, narrates the story chronologically up to the present, and perhaps looks toward the future. "Once upon a time . . . and they lived happily ever after."

Past, present, and future, however, can be covered in any order. They can also be repeated several times in the same article if it has also a spatial structure, changing from place to place, or person to person. Once the order of chronology has been established, it is likely to be retained throughout any spatial changes. The middle of an article about a city's churches, for instance, might give a brief history of each church in turn.

A common form of spatial construction is the list, but it is usually contained in a larger overall structure, as with this chapter.

An uncommon chronological sequence is one that begins in the present and progresses backwards in time. It can be especially helpful to the learning process, because it begins with what is familiar and leads gradually into the more unfamiliar. There is much to be said for a wider use of it. I would like to see subjects such as history and literature being taught in this way in schools as well as in books.

A fifth type of structure is the cause and effect sequence. Consider again the ten paragraphs of Wayland Young's article "Pot," which preceded Exercise 4 in Chapter Two. Here are the main topics of each paragraph:

1. Cannabis is covered by dangerous drugs legislation.
2. —But it is not a drug of addiction.
3. Cigarettes and heroin are, in different degrees.
4. The effect of one reefer is rather less than half a pint of beer.
5. In some parts of the world it is socially equivalent to our use of alcohol—
6. —although the infection of European attitudes is getting it a bad name in some countries.

7. Some mistake has been made to cause us to fear it.
8. An attempt to disentangle it from dangerous drugs ought to be made soon.
9. This would prevent much unnecessary distress and strain between races and generations.
10. And it might be a good alternative source of revenue.

It is rather an unusual use of cause and effect, but that is what it is nevertheless. Cause: Fear of cannabis, which is irrational, ought to be allayed by new legislation (paragraphs 1 to 8). Effect: Prevention of distress, of strain between races and generations; and a source of revenue (paragraphs 9 and 10).

A sixth type of structure is a joker which may be kept in reserve for any new arrangement you discover, or used for any combination of the other five. Here is an example of a combined structure, often to be found in specialized forms of writing. It is a typical book review, analyzed topic by topic. One point may be spread over more than one paragraph.

1. Introduction: shock or inductive (general to particular) depending on the quality of the publication carrying the review.
2. Chronology: the subject matter of the book.
3. Spatial change to the author: narrative about him, possibly chronological.
4. Thesis: what the author was trying to do.
5. Antithesis: what others have done; what the reviewer thinks of what the author was trying to do.
6. Synthesis, or summary ending: judgment.

Structure analysis should be used as an aid to every kind of reading, including books. Books are divided into chapters, and a chapter is either a series of linked articles or an article in itself, such as Huxley's chapter. Hence any article or chapter may be skimmed rapidly before reading, and a suitable approximate rate is a minute for every 1,500 words. It should be possible, with the experience given by this book alone, to skim at about that rate without the measure of a watch and word count. An initial skimming can give no more than an impression of the structure and subject matter, but it should be enough to decide whether the material is worth further attention, and, if so, to use the framework as a foundation for detailed comprehension. Any advance impressions should be used to prepare one's mind for the subject matter by relating it to whatever one already knows about it. A sense of the author's tone may also be desirable so as to be prepared for possible antagonism or misunderstanding, as can all too easily occur if certain kinds of irony or satire, for example, are too casually read.

The rate of skimming after reading will depend on one's purposes. Note-taking of topic sentences for study or critical appraisal will obviously be slower than mentally noting points to be remembered, or checking back to ensure that there has been no misunderstanding. The rapidest skimming will be used to pick up some small point that was missed, or to note a name, a date, a technical term, or some other noteworthy detail.

With experience and confidence you ought to be able to skim, read, and skim again in less time than you previously needed for a single reading. The results should be greatly improved comprehension, a reduction in the chances of misunderstanding, and—a by-product that reaches beyond the range of this book—an improvement in the lucidity, order, and conciseness of anything you may write yourself.

(2,600 words)

EXERCISE 15

Write down the answers to the following questions without referring back to the text.

1. What is the main idea of Chapter One of Aldous Huxley's *The Art of Seeing?* (2 marks)
2. Describe, with your own quoted or invented examples, three of the typical openings to articles listed in the chapter. (3 marks)
3. Explain three of the basic constructions of articles described by the author. (3 marks)
4. Describe two practical applications of a knowledge of structure analysis. (2 marks)

Mark your exercise in relation to a formal plan of the chapter, drawn up by yourself. Skim back through it, noting the main idea of each paragraph to include brief descriptions of introductions, constructions, and endings. Reduce these twenty-nine topics to as few as are necessary to cover the essentials and then rearrange them in columns, so that when you finish you have a page in your notebook which is a diagrammatic abstract of the chapter.

EXERCISE 16

The extract that follows, "The Functions of a Prison," should not, properly, be read until after you have done this exercise. You are going to prepare a diagrammatic abstract of the passage by using only skimming techniques.

Firstly, note that it is 1,600 words long. This means that a minute should be sufficient for skimming through it to see what it is about, how the subject is covered, its source, and general structure. Now skim for a measured minute, and resume reading these instructions when you have done so.

Having done so, you should have found it is written in three main divisions, arranged in a certain order. You should also have an idea of why the writer chose this particular order, and which form of construction has been used for each part. If not, take another half minute and do so.

Next, divide a page of your notebook into three equal columns and put the writer's three headings at the tops of the columns. Set yourself five minutes for skimming the extract again, briefly noting the main topic of each paragraph in its appropriate column, together with any secondary facts that go to make up its substance. When you have finished, take a little extra time to rearrange anything that needs tidying up or simplifying, until your table is clear enough to be a diagram in the book from which the extract was taken.

You have now spent six minutes on a passage that once would have taken you at least that long to read, and with only a little extra time you have prepared detailed notes for reference or further study.

Now time yourself reading the passage as quickly as you can for comprehension adequate enough to confirm that your notes are accurate.

Lastly, can you answer this question without further reference to the passage? What is its underlying philosophy?

READING EXERCISE

The Functions of a Prison

BY SIR FRANK NEWSAM

A prison today serves three purposes, which may be described as custodial, coercive and correctional. Though the last of these, which concerns the use of imprisonment as a form of legal punishment, now takes the primary place, it is in historical perspective a comparatively new conception, not all the implications of which have yet been worked out. In its origins the prison served only the custodial function: it was a place in which an alleged offender could be kept in lawful custody until he could be tried and, if found guilty, punished. The judges went out to "deliver the jails"—to clear them, not to fill them. The punishments for treasons and felonies were banishment or death; for misdemeanors, public shame, physical punishments, or fines. It is less than a hundred years since the use of imprisonment as a primary punishment for crime began to receive serious consideration.

This first or custodial function of the prison has not lost its importance: in 1951 over 19 per cent of the total receptions into British prisons were of persons committed on remand or for trial who did not return again on conviction, that is to say they were either found not guilty or dealt with otherwise than by imprisonment. It is also applicable to aliens awaiting the execution of deportation orders, and to various categories of offenders awaiting removal to other types of institution to which they have been committed by the courts.

The coercive function means that imprisonment may be used to persuade a person to comply with an order made by a court of law, whether civil or criminal; if he complies, he is released. The first use of the prison in this way was against convicted offenders who had been ordered to forfeit property, or to pay fines, and had failed to do so. Prisons are still so used: in 1951 some 13 per cent of the total receptions of men on conviction, and some 22 per cent of women, were for non-payment of fines. All these persons could at any time obtain release by paying. The courts, civil or criminal, may also use imprisonment to persuade persons before them to comply with orders to do or refrain from doing certain things: persons deemed to be "in contempt of court" through failure to comply with such a direction of the court may be committed to prison until they "purge their contempt." Such persons are received from time to time. Here the function of the prison lies somewhat outside the field of crime, as does another use of its coercive function. Imprisonment has long been used in England to enforce the payment of moneys ordered by a court to be paid under civil process—not only the payment of rates and taxes due to public authorities, and of sums due under wife maintenance and affiliation orders, but of private debts recoverable in the county courts. In 1951 over 5,600 persons were received into prison in default of payments of this nature.

Finally, imprisonment takes its place as one of the punishments which a court may impose on those convicted of offenses against the criminal law. In dealing with persons over the age of seventeen convicted of indictable offenses, the courts in 1947 used fines for 39 per cent, probation for 11 per cent, and imprisonment for

29 per cent. Of all offenses indictable and non-indictable dealt with in that year, imprisonment was used for only 4.7 per cent. Thus it appears that the majority of persons convicted of crime are not nowadays sent to prison: nor is the correctional concern of the prison only with those who have committed the more serious offenses, since only 71 per cent of the men received on conviction in 1951, and only 58 per cent of the women, had been convicted of indictable offenses.

This statement of the functions of our prisons shows that their effort must be spent in various ways, all necessary for the support of the law, but by no means directed to their central function, which concerns those sent to prison as a punishment for crime.

IMPRISONMENT AS A LEGAL PUNISHMENT

Discussion of the principles of imprisonment as a form of legal punishment must start from the consideration that a sentence of imprisonment in itself is no more than an order that the offender be deprived of his liberty in a lawful prison. The problem of the correctional function of the prison is concerned with the question —how can the treatment of the convicted offender thus confined in prison best be made to serve the purpose of legal punishment, which is the prevention of crime. The view which in the early nineteenth century still prevailed in Parliament and on the Bench was that crime could be prevented only by the deterrent effect of uniform maximum severity, hitherto achieved by cutting the offender out of the community by banishment or death. There had been other views, notably those of John Howard and Elizabeth Fry, suggesting that in so far as the prison played a part in this purpose it would be better to use it to attempt to improve the offender, so that he would be less likely to revert to crime on release, rather than "by the greatest possible degree of misery, producing the greatest possible degree of wickedness . . . receiving [the prisoner] because he is too bad for society, you return him to the world impaired in health, debased in intellect, and corrupted in principles." These views did not however prevail in 1863, when a Committee of the House of Lords, set up to decide on the principles and practice of imprisonment and penal servitude, pronounced in favor of deterrence by severity as the object of imprisonment, with the reform of the prisoner as a subsidiary object which need not be sought and was scarcely to be expected.

This principle, to which statutory effect was given by the Prisons Act, 1865, held good to the end of the century. It was then assailed on both moral and practical grounds, and in 1895 a Departmental Committee under the Chairmanship of Lord Gladstone (then Mr. Herbert Gladstone) reconsidered the principles of 1865, and made a report on which the principles of the contemporary system still largely rest. They found that the system of 1865 had indeed, by creating "the greatest possible amount of misery," produced "the greatest possible degree of wickedness," and that in its primary purpose of preventing crime it had demonstrably failed. The prisoners had been "treated too much as a hopeless or worthless element of the community," and it would be better for the system to be designed "to turn them out of prison better men and women physically and morally than when they came in . . . prison treatment should have as its primary and concurrent objects deterrence and reformation." The Prisons Act, 1898, laid the statutory foundations of the new system.

During the next phase of development, up to the First World War, these more humane ideas spread throughout the penal system. Legislation was primarily concerned with the abatement of imprisonment by providing alternative forms of treatment, as in the Probation of Offenders Act, 1907, or in the Borstal system for young offenders provided by the Prevention of Crime Act, 1908; by ensuring the removal of the mentally defective from prison in the Mental Deficiency Act, 1913; and by reducing the numbers committed for non-payment of fines in the Criminal Justice Administration Act, 1914. The Act of 1908 further sought to remove habitual criminals, who were neither deterred nor reformed by prison sentences, out of the normal prison system into a form of prolonged internment known as preventive detention. Thus the courts were furnished with a variety of forms of punishment which enabled them to adapt the treatment of the offender to his character and needs as well as to the nature of his offense.

After the First World War, the prison system itself moved far in this direction of individualization of treatment, and also in a revaluation of its "primary and concurrent objects," deterrence and reform. Experience had shown that the difficult task of reconciling punitive deterrence and reform within one method of treatment would not succeed so long as the regime was based on a careful balance of "deterrent" and "reformative" elements. "Better men and women" could not be made by methods which sought at the same time to hurt and humiliate them. If this end was sincerely sought, the deterrent effect of prison must be deemed to lie in the *fact* of imprisonment, with all that this inevitably implies—complete loss of personal liberty; separation from home and friends; subjection to forced labor and disciplinary control; and deprivation of most of the amenities and intercourse of ordinary life. Further, it is not enough to seek the "reform" of the offender: that can only come from within, through the exercise of the right personal influences. The treatment should seek positively to fit him to lead a good and useful life after release: it is a grave danger of imprisonment, especially of prolonged imprisonment, that it may cause deterioration both of body and of mind, and the prevention of crime is not served if the offender returns to society unfitted rather than fitted to adapt himself to its life.

The system based on this reinterpretation of the Gladstone principles was evolved in administrative practice, not as the result of any further legislation or official inquiry. It is the system which led, in the Criminal Justice Act, 1948, to the provision that rules should be made for, *inter alia*, the "training" of prisoners, and to Rule 6 of the Prison Rules, 1949, which reads:

The purposes of training and treatment of convicted prisoners shall be to establish in them the will to lead a good and useful life on discharge, and to fit them to do so.

From: *The Home Office* (1954)

(1,600 words)

·9·

The Problem of Choice

THIS IS A DIFFICULT CHAPTER to write because I have never experienced the problem of not knowing what to read next. Once upon a time I was a slow and slavish reader, a worried and forgetful student, and perhaps for this reason I cannot remember a time when I have not had more books waiting to be read than I have ever had time to read. Even now that I am a better reader, there are still many unread books on my shelves, some of which have lived there unopened since my acquisitive adolescent years of inexpensive paperbacks and book club membership. From three libraries I still take out more books than I could ever hope to read before they were due back, which some may see as evidence of an uncorrected reading problem and others as evidence of something else, but I am not aware that it is a problem, and the fines can be claimed against tax. Back they go unread as often as not; my shelves slowly gather new ones, usually brought for future reference or rainy days; titles are entered into a notebook for an often unborn tomorrow; and meanwhile, between living what past reading has taught me, teaching others to read better, and adding to the amount that there is for others to read anyway, I manage to continue reading and assimilating what books I can: a modest fifty a year, if that. And it is enough. I never travel without at least one book, but I have not become a voracious reader, perhaps because books have taught me that reading is to living as skimming is to reading: an aid, not a substitute.

I claim no special virtue for any of these facts, and it does not surprise me to learn that most people seldom know what to read next, that many who would not call themselves illiterate read fewer books in a lifetime than I read in a year and others read in a couple of months, and that some are even frightened by books. An acquaintance of mine had a difficult time with his Notting Hill landlady, which is not by any means unusual, except that this was an affable fellow who usually formed successful functional relationships and was too well adjusted to society for anyone to dislike actively. It was his girl friend who discovered the reason for the landlady's hostility. When she had to clean her tenant's room she could not help seeing that he kept books. "My husband used to keep books too," she growled, confidential and sinister. "But slowly, one by one, so he didn't see, I burned 'em. He don't keep books no more."

My problem is to invent a sort of formula which anyone can apply to the question of what to read next so that in time it need arise no more. Let me straightway confess that I have not yet succeeded in doing so, nor have I discovered anyone else who has. The soundest suggestions I have found constitute the reading extract at the end of this chapter, and they are not unlike those I have made myself when students have persuaded me to think them out. Now, at the end of a discussion about techniques of selection, it seems worth considering some of the more formal aids that are available to selecting what to read.

The most obvious is the public library. It is perhaps not widely enough known that any public library member can borrow almost any nonfiction book. If it is not in the local library's collection, it may be obtained through an inter-library loan initiated by the local library.

But before employing this service it is necessary to ensure that the book you seek is not in your local library's collection. The librarian will do this in any case, but to search for it yourself will help you to become familiar with the library's catalogue or card index. More and more libraries nowadays are adopting the "dictionary" system of indexing, in which authors, titles, and subjects are all listed in a single alphabetical sequence. (Remember that for easy control of a card index, the cards should be fingered from the sides, not the tops.)

It is also useful to know something about your library's system of classifying books, especially when you seek a book by subject rather than title and author. The catalogue may sometimes be divided in two, with authors and titles in one index and subjects in another. The Dewey Decimal System of classification is now in use almost everywhere in Britain and the United States. Most libraries display notices listing their principal categories and leave reference booklets on shelves by the catalogues with a wide selection of subjects indexed with their class numbers. Every new book published is listed in bibliographical indexes with its decimal classification alongside its other descriptive particulars. This book, for example, will be classified under 028.8; and those figures alone would tell a skillful librarian quite a lot about it.

The first digit places it in one of ten classes into which all knowledge was divided by the inventor of the system, an American student called Melvil Dewey, who first published the idea in 1876 in a forty-two-page book. The system has been greatly enlarged and improved since, but Dewey's ten classes have remained unaltered. Hence an initial naught always represents general works, as distinct from: one—philosophy, two—religion, three—sociology, and so on to nine—history and biography.

The second digit of 028.8 gives its division. In this case it refers to works about library science and the use of books. Each class has ten divisions, and librarians have to learn them by rote, for they are arbitrary and do not follow a similar pattern from class to class. For example, class five is science and its respective divisions from naught to nine are pure science, mathematics, astronomy, physics, chemistry and allied sciences, earth sciences, paleontology, anthropology and biology, botanical sciences, and zoological sciences.

The third digit represents the section into which the type of book can be classified. Thus naught is again a general work on the subject, section one is a theoretical or philosophical exposition of it, section two is an outline or manual, section three a dictionary or encyclopedia of the subject and so on for ten sections. In 028.8, the eight before the point indicates a book miscellaneous in style or treatment. The same ten sections are applied as far as possible in each division.

The figures after the point, which sometimes go to four decimal places and in theory could go to any number, cover a multitude of subsections, and thus give the system its ingenuity, flexibility, and comprehensiveness. Dewey's original 1,000 sections now run into tens of thousands and are listed in a reference book of two volumes and, in the sixteenth edition, nearly 2,500 pages. Not every section has ten subsections, but the blanks are there to be filled one day, either by books on new subjects or by individual libraries giving a book a second classification. For example, 028.2 is a blank, but I have seen *Reading as a Visual Task* by Matthew Luckiesh and Frank K. Moss with this classification. It can be regarded as scientific research into the physics of either reading or lighting, and classified accordingly. In some circumstances, too, the present book might be treated as part of a special branch of education.

Class 028, in fact, is listed with only seven subsections: 028.1 is book reviewing, 028.3 reading courses, 028.5 children's books and 028.52 bibliographies and lists of children's books, 028.7 use of books and libraries as sources of information, 028.8 readers' guidance, 028.9 reading habits and tastes of the community.

Wherever possible, the same logic of the classification before the point is applied after it. Consider classes 027, general works about books and library science in relation to education, study and teaching, and 900, history and biography. Class 910 is reserved for geography and travel, 920 for biography, 930 for ancient history, and 940 to 990 for modern history in different parts of the world. Thus class 970 is for North American history, subdivided so that 973 means the history of the United States. The United States is therefore represented by 73 in this classification as well as in 027.473, public libraries in the United States.

A useful classification for the undirected reader is 016, the class for all sorts of bibliographies, among which may be found titles like *What Shall I Read Next?* They are admirable as a starting point for a few basic or standard books about a chosen subject, but their disadvantage is that they tend to get out of date fairly quickly and new editions are not published very often. A good general guide is the *Subject Guide to Books in Print*, which lists books by subject matter.

I have tried to include in this book some guidance for further reading which may soon become out of date. Anyone familiar with books ought to be able to date this one from its bibliography alone. No matter; I have made no special effort to be objective or topical, which may mean that some of the titles and most of the authors will endure, at least for the lifetime of this book. There are five different sources of bibliographical information, four of which are set out again in Appendix II. They are the timed reading extracts, the sources of quotations in the text, the practice reading suggestions at the end of each section, and the further reading in the subjects under discussion. The fifth source is in the text: titles mentioned in passing which, like all name-dropping, is less casual than it may seem.

Most of the extracts have been chosen and the titles mentioned both for their obvious role in the context of this book and as recommended reading. The recommendations should be regarded as nothing more than personal and the omissions should merely indicate that a line had to be drawn somewhere. I have tried to cover as wide a field as possible, avoiding specialist subjects, except for those connected with reading and literature. Any titles thought to be of less general interest may be stood upon the bridge between the two cultures, literary and scientific. I have for the most part avoided representing any author more than once, assuming that enjoyment of one book can lead to another work of the same author, or to further reading suggested by the author's own appended bibliography. Most of the authors will be known to readers familiar with books, but here and there I have popped in a curiosity.

A few of the titles are so well known that if perchance you have never read any of them, and you have read this far, I would not be surprised if you have been finding this book rather hard going. Never mind; it is no cause for shame. Either you are an inexperienced reader or such a specialist in your own field that you seldom read beyond it. Time, curiosity, and confidence in your reading techniques will cure both. Persevere for another three chapters, and if you continue to find it too advanced, turn first to a more elementary book of reading improvement in Class 028.8 and begin again with this book later.

All these aids are but beginnings of new explorations into the world of books. To continue, it is necessary to keep abreast of current books and the only practicable way I know for the ordinary reader to do so is by a weekly dose of book reviews.

The disadvantage of book reviews is not, as many people may think, that the reader's choice is likely to be governed by the state of the reviewer's digestion. A diligent reader of book reviews can soon learn to ignore anything as inconsiderable as a reviewer's opinion, making use instead of the way that reviewers often use a new book as a framework for the display of their own erudition which, among respectable journals' reviewing staffs, can be far from inconsiderable. A passing reference to an esoteric book, such as *The Universal Design of the Oedipus Complex,* or some little-known author, like Lawrence Hyde or Elias Canetti, could start a reader unexpectedly on a new adventure into books and thought before he ever reads the book under review. And there are many other ways that a reviewer's name-dropping may be a means of whetting a reading appetite. A case could be made, indeed, for reading book reviews for their own sake and disregarding the titles under review until the long-term repetition of them demands that they be read.

This approach at least eliminates the main disadvantage of book reviewing, the practitioners of which are as enslaved by fashion as the rest of us, so that 10 per cent of the authors get 90 per cent of the notices. That statement should not be taken too literally, for it may be an exaggeration if technical journals and specialist reviews are included, but it is safe to say that not more than 20 per cent of the books published are reviewed in newspapers, magazines, and weekly reviews of general interest.

Reviewing is a business, if not a racket, and, from the nature of the book world today, incapable of keeping up with everything published in the United States, let alone other English-speaking countries. The provincial reviewer or the specialist receives a batch of books from his literary editor and makes his own selection; he who can calls at the office and takes his pick from the huge weekly delivery of the publishing houses. The fact that, times out of number, the same half-dozen books constitute a major part of the reviews in any week's papers, probably without much deliberate intent on the part of literary editors and their staffs, is evidence either of literary fashion or a collective unconscious, which might after all be much the same thing.

What it all means for the author is that a reviewer's damnation is better than his inattention; and for the reader, that a book ignored may be better than one with rave notices. I am referring to book reviewing, incidentally, not scholarly criticism, which is a more considered and less ephemeral pursuit. Criticism has another value; reviews as an aid to selection provide guidance through the jungle of the publishers' lists and, taken with caution, are better than having no guide at all.

In addition to one daily and one Sunday book-reviewing newspaper, I take *The Times Literary Supplement* each week and I find it gives me an adequate coverage, albeit some weeks and even months in advance of the books reaching my public library. So I note the titles that attract me and wait. If, after several weeks, I am still reminded of a book and eager to read it, then I order from the library. I seldom buy a new book until I have first read a library copy.

If, however, you happen to be reading a library copy of this book, and have been following its instructions, you will soon have kept it out too long to be fair to the other readers, and I would suggest that you buy your own copy before passing on to Part IV next week. You may be surprised at how much more you will gain from this book once you have made the investment.

I also enjoy reading and noting any encounters I have with those annual features in which famous people describe the books they have enjoyed most during the past year. I do not seek the guidance of librarians and booksellers, although some readers, I believe, find it helpful to do so.

Perhaps the most dependable way of keeping abreast of the world of books would be to supplement one's own vigilance with a circle of well-loved and well-read friends whose weaknesses you know and who know you well and who may say from time to time, "—— ought to read this," and then recommend it or, better still, buy it for you. But such friends are as rare as the books that can change one's life.

Beyond that, we are each alone with our reading. And, in the last analysis, there is really no better way than to follow one's nose, or leave it to God, or abandon one's choice to whatever other metaphor one's reading and experience lead one to prefer.

(2,600 words)

EXERCISE 17

Answer the following questions briefly without referring back.

1. The author lists five different sources of bibliographical information to be found in this book. Name three of them.

    (1 mark for each)

2. Describe in your own words the reader's attitude to book reviews that the author suggests as the most realistic and fruitful.

    (3 marks)

3. In addition to libraries, book reviews, and the suggestions for further reading incorporated in this book, the author mentions some other aids in the choice of what to read. Describe two of them.   (1 mark for each)

4. Answer either part of this two-part question.
    a. What is the decimal classification of this book?
    b. In which decade did Dewey first publish his system of decimal classification?   (1 mark)

5. What does the chapter tell you about the subject of the following reading extract?   (1 mark)

Check your answers by applying skimming techniques to this chapter. When you have calculated your score, note the main headings under which the chapter was constructed. Then turn back to the paragraphs describing the decimal system of classification and, using skimming techniques again, *draw up in a simple tabular form the class numbers and descriptions of as much of the system as you are given, leaving gaps for those classes not referred to in the chapter.*

The full relevance of that exercise should become clear as you read the next section of the book which, if you are still willing to follow the instructions, you will meet after a week's break for other reading.

Now prepare to read the following extract at an increased speed. You have already been told a little about it; and a few moments' reflection should remind you that you have been thinking about its general subject matter quite a lot in the past few minutes. Allow half a minute for skimming through it to assess what it is about and discover its outline. The comprehension exercise is a multiple-choice recognition test.

READING EXERCISE

The Reader's Pilgrimage

BY LIONEL MC COLVIN

A course of non-purposive reading is not unlike a good conversation: it may start with immortality and end with the culture of sweet peas or with laundry bills, or it may be the other way around. And, as washing and sweet peas and immortality are all part of the same all-embracing topic—life—it is fitting that in a conversation they should be related even by haphazard links to one another. The charm of conversation lies in this free-wandering inconsequence.

In general reading the best method is that of following up each new line of thought as it is disclosed and pursuing it as long as its fascination holds or until a greater attraction is offered. To plan a course of reading beforehand is undesirable—unless, of course, you have a definite objective. If you say, "I will read first this, then that, and then the other," you make reading a self-imposed duty rather than a compelling pleasure. Set off, instead, with an inquiring mind, resolved "to get to the bottom of it," but without ever saying what "it" is, and you will be happy. In reading there is always something around the corner.

How are *you* to know what you will enjoy until you meet with it?

Just one example of a reader's pilgrimage (as indicated by a list of books he had read): He evidently began with a pamphlet on the United Nations project, and the topics about which he next read were, in this order, the causes of war, the biology of war (the "man is a pugnacious animal and is bound to keep on squabbling" idea), the social life of animals (to see if there was anything in the theory), the social life of primitive man, primitive religion and magic, the wanderings of prehistoric peoples, the archaeology of England, the old churches of England, the work of the craftsmen of the Middle Ages and their guilds. Now he is dipping into the works of William Morris and, probably, the cycle of his thoughts will take him next to socialism, thence to internationalism and so back to his starting-point. These literary explorations have a knack of running in circles, returning home at intervals, but pursuing their course without any conscious plan.

Our reader might not know a great deal about any of the themes he touched upon, but in the sum total of his inquiries he has learned much more than he would from any regular systematic course, since all the while he has read only because he wanted to find out more about the things which appealed most to him. As psychologists and educationists are well aware, we remember best those things we most *like* remembering.

Courses of study are not, of course, condemned. On the contrary, if you find a course which you can pursue to the bitter end without losing interest you will be well advised to gain the combined advantages of systematic reading and sustained enthusiasm. Similarly, if, through want of experience or because your circumstances make study difficult, you find it a help and an aid to concentration to have your route planned out beforehand, by all means adopt a course. Don't, however, commit yourself to *too* long a course or to one which is too advanced, and don't be perturbed if you find you want to fly off at a tangent and read something else.

One little matter might be mentioned in passing: Reference has been made to a "list of books read." Many readers keep such a record. It is very useful to people who read books which are so machine-made that their only distinguishing mark is the title; it prevents their wasting their time rereading books which at the first reading made so little impression that they are now completely forgotten. It is quite bad enough to read them once. Otherwise there is little point in lists. You know what you have read and what you haven't, and if you keep a list there is always the danger of making a fetish of it—by finishing books you don't want to read simply in order to be able to enter them up. Quite a few *do* behave so stupidly.

But whenever you make a note of anything, no matter what it is, always add to it the name and author of the book from which it is noted with its date and edition. You might want to use or to follow up and amplify your notes and unless you know the source the notes are useless.

To refer again to "interest reading." Occasions when books can make the other things you do more interesting are innumerable, if you will only look for them. As there will be, it is hoped, some who read this book who have not yet begun to use books fully, here are a few suggestions as to how the first steps might best be taken. You—those of you who are on the threshold of the book world—probably read novels of a fairly popular character, scan the newspapers, and occupy your time with some form of work and a hobby or two.

Let these—your novels, newspapers, work and hobbies—be your starting-point. Is there anything you enjoy that you could enjoy better with the help of books? Is there anything you do that you could do better with books? Do you ever feel that your curiosity is aroused, that you would like to know more about this or that, but you don't quite know how to satisfy your interest? Yesterday you wouldn't have bothered. You would have said: "I wonder . . . ?" "Why should . . . ?" "Is that true?" "How can that be?" And left it at that. Today you cease to be content. You try to find out. You realize now that all the loose ends *can* be sorted out and tied up, if only you take a little trouble. You know now that you can't leave the matter so imperfectly explained, and that, if you turn to books, there is no excuse to remain uninformed. Yours is an "inquiring" mind, and you use it.

From: *How to Use Books* (1948)
(1,000 words)

EXERCISE 18

Choose the best answer to each question.

1. A lively conversation compares with a course of non-purposive reading because they are both concerned with:
    a. a variety of subjects haphazardly linked;
    b. an interest in life;
    c. pleasure rather than duty;
    d. sweet peas and immortality.
2. A planned course of reading is:
    a. the best way to learn a lot;
    b. undesirable without a definite objective;
    c. a self-imposed duty;
    d. of no value whatever.
3. The attitude of the inquiring mind should be:
    a. to remember that there is always something new around the corner;
    b. to treat reading as a compelling pleasure;
    c. to get to the bottom of something indefinite;
    d. to avoid making excuses for remaining uninformed.
4. Unplanned reading is likely to:
    a. teach one little about any single subject;
    b. develop a grasshopper mind;
    c. lead one on a rewarding pilgrimage;
    d. pursue what in retrospect will be seen to have been an exploratory course of its own, returning home at intervals.
5. The things we remember best are those which:
    a. we most like remembering;
    b. we have taken the trouble to learn;
    c. come from books we enjoy reading;
    d. are encountered in literary explorations.
6. The writer's advice about keeping a list of books read is to:
    a. beware of making a fetish of it;

141

    b. do not do so unless there is always a danger of unintentional rereading;

    c. avoid finishing books for no other reason than entering them up;

    d. not bother because there is no point in it.

7. Whenever we take notes, the writer says, we should:

    a. beware of making a fetish of it;

    b. do it systematically;

    c. ensure that they are subsequently readable;

    d. note also details of the source.

8. We may suppose that the writer would answer a reader's question about what to read next with:

    a. Anything that takes your fancy.

    b. A good novel, to see where it leads you.

    c. What, among your interests, has aroused your curiosity lately?

    d. Try a basic book on an unfamiliar subject.

9. A good guess would be that the author of the extract is a:

    a. librarian;

    b. journalist;

    c. novelist;

    d. psychologist.

10. The main idea of the extract is:

    a. If we follow our noses through our reading, intuitively, without much of a conscious plan, we shall enjoy our books and learn much more.

    b. Systematic courses of study have some value if they are not too long and can be sustained with enthusiasm.

    c. The reader who embarks on a pilgrimage of literary exploration will gain much valuable and unexpected knowledge.

    d. To keep a list of the books we read and make notes as we read them will provide a valuable "diary" of the way we have acquired our knowledge.

When you have checked your answers against those on page 301 and skimmed back through the passage to check, if necessary, where you went wrong, put this book aside for a week and re-

turn to your general reading, employing all the techniques you have learned so far.

If you feel confident enough to extend the scope and challenge of your reading still further, here are some suggestions of the direction you might take from the personal into the collective.

SUGGESTED PRACTICE READING (PART III)

Dennis Gabor	*Inventing the Future*
Richard Hoggart	*The Uses of Literacy*
Lewis Mumford	*The Culture of Cities*
Arthur Koestler	*The Lotus and the Robot*
Raymond Williams	*The Long Revolution*
Hans Zinsser	*Rats, Lice and History*

PART IV

LEARNING

·10·

Remembering

Is YOUR MEMORY good or bad? Most of us, I think, would reply that it was poor to bad, though some might add that it was moderately good for a few things. It is usually other people who are the ones with the excellent memories, seldom ourselves. For we know how much we forget. And among the things we forget is how much others with apparently good memories also forget. But whatever we say—unless we already know something about the psychology of learning—we are likely to answer the question wrongly. Is your memory good or bad? The right answer is: neither. For you have no memory at all. There is no such thing.

We have our memories, certainly. But they are not stored in a place called The Memory, which can be improved or tidied or enlarged or trained. It is important to know this because all the stories of phenomenal feats of memory are like those myths about page-at-a-glance readers: they help to make ordinary idiots like you and me think of prodigies and geniuses as being of different stuff from ourselves and existing, like gods, somewhere Out There in the Unattainable. And we believe, and repeat the myths, and so far abrogate our humanity as to worship. We are all born with genius for something. Some survive.

Many prodigious feats of remembering have been recorded in the past but of course only recent, living examples have been properly investigated by psychologists. Consider the feats of some medieval kings planning invasions and you may wonder whether they owed their power to little more than their ability to remember. They were often illiterate, and there were only Roman numerals. How *do* you calculate in your head a small

item like the number of food wagons, each with a capacity of
CXLIV haybags, required to feed DCCC horses making a sortie
into Scotland that you expect to last XXVIII days, when each
horse requires III bags of feed every V days? When at last you
have done the sum, and you find you have forgotten to feed the
draft horses, no wonder you decide to commandeer from farmers
on the way. Today we know that calculating geniuses have an
imagination that sees relationships between groups of digits that
most of us would not perceive, and where we might have an
average memory span of seven digits, they have one nearer to
twenty.

Napoleon was said to have had a phenomenal memory, but
further investigation reveals that it worked mainly for military
matters and in other ways he was as forgetful as anyone else.
He might well have forgotten his own language in time if he had
been forced to retreat from Moscow eastward far enough. . . .
What more myths and miracles would be elevated to everyday
human terms if we could examine those who associated with
them? Did the British parliamentary reporter Woodfall really
memorize speeches verbatim, or did he simply pay enough attention when he was listening to be able to write detailed paraphrase
versions which, when no one took written notes, were better
than anyone else's recollection? What of all the scholars of the
past who bewildered people with apparently encyclopedic
knowledge stored in their memories? Did they really have any
more knowledge available at any given moment than a well-
trained undergraduate sitting for his degree? Today we know
that abnormal feats of remembering can conceal other surprisingly subnormal qualities. A modern investigation of an American youth with a remarkable memory for the names and birth
dates of everyone he met, revealed that this was almost his only
interest in life. He thought, as a child might, that height is the
determinant of age, so that faced with any two people he
thought the taller one was older, even though their birth dates,
which he knew, proved otherwise.

Clearly, whatever we have been calling The Memory all this
time is something much more complex than we supposed. The

present-day hypothesis about it is that when we experience any-thing, some parts of that experience are permanently recorded in the brain as memory traces and that these traces have something to do with biochemical changes in nerve cells in different parts of the brain. Subsequently, by a process about which virtually nothing is known, parts of those traces can be retraced and we recall elements of the experience, thus creating a new experience that reinforces parts of the old traces and establishes some new ones. But recalling functions haphazardly and unreliably, as every lawyer knows; and thus before anything can be said to have been remembered, it must be recognized as an accurate recon-struction for immediate purposes of the original record. Even recognition can be unreliable, as innocent men picked out in identity parades can testify. It is all too easy for us to fulfill our subconscious wishes of how things might have been by convinced recognition of a faulty recollection. The greater the effort we make to recall something, the more likely becomes a false recog-nition of it.

Such, then, is the range of separate processes that constitute the act of remembering, and which are all emulsified in the popular idea of the faculty of memory. They are, in short, the four Rs of registering, retaining, recalling, and recognizing.

So if, hitherto, you have been thinking that you have a bad memory, and you are now willing to concede that it is more meaningful to say that you have difficulty in remembering cer-tain things, then you must ask yourself which of the constituent processes of remembering are most in need of improvement.

Of course there are differences between one individual and another in the ability to remember, and they cannot all be elimi-nated by cutting the prodigies and memory men down to their proper size. Some improvement can be effected by realizing the normal human limitations of the faculty and then under-standing its components so that work can be applied to those susceptible to improvement. You are already doing much the same kind of thing with your reading processes. But a good deal of poor remembering, like a lot of poor reading, is part of the visible tenth of an iceberg of psychological disturbance, the amelioration of which lies far beyond the reach of a book like this. I can tell quite a lot about my students' lives from what they reveal to me of their reading and other behavior at my classes, but I dare not tell them. Anxiety, for example, is a powerful factor in poor remembering, as it is in poor reading, and it cannot be by chance that the most extensive and frenetic research of recent years into ways of improving both reading and remembering has been done in America. You can read it all up, elaborately dull experiments on hapless students and other animals, recorded in minute detail and ponderously discussed in numerous wordy books by worthy worriers, most of whom have succeeded in discovering little more than new ways of proving a statement made toward the end of the last century by the Harvard psychologist whom I have actually seen described in a book by one of his compatriots as "short, full-bearded William James." James said that all improvement in memory consists in the improvement of one's habitual methods of recording facts.

In other words, unless we register better to start with, there is nothing to be done about the other three Rs of remembering. It is sheer dishonesty to say we *forget* the name of someone to whom we have just been introduced when in truth we made no effort to remember it in the first place and were probably hardly listening. An experience that leaves no trace leaves no trace.

But if an experience has been adequately registered, and we can presume it therefore to have been retained, then a little may be done to improve recall and recognition. If you have difficulty with recall, try to re-create actually or in imagination the exact situation in which you experienced the thing you are trying to remember. You may encounter it by association. If that is not successful, beware of trying to think too hard, and think instead about other things and your recollection may come, as it were, by stealth. If that fails too, and you have reason to think it is something you ought to be able to recall, then try constructing a hypothesis like this. Suppose part of you wanted to forget it. If so, what useful purpose might you have been fulfilling by thus hiding it from yourself? You may still not succeed in remembering, but you may discover something interesting about yourself in the attempt, and the discovery may help to prevent a similar lapse in future. If you have reason to think that you recognize recollections unreliably, try something similar. Ask yourself how far your recognition is telling you the way the experience really was and how far it might be telling you the way you wish it could have been.

Once again, then, we are forced back to considering how we register our experiences and what constitutes an adequate record. We find that registering for remembering falls into two general categories. One is to learn the experience; and a proper discussion of learning methods needs a chapter to itself. The other is to respond to it.

Optimum response involves awareness of all one's sense impressions at any given moment of experience. At this moment, you are experiencing these statements of mine. I am leading up to the end of a chapter and if you skimmed it well to begin with you should have an idea of whether it ends with a climax, on a rising note or a dying fall, or merely with the quiet completion of a discussion and a full stop. You may expect from your reading thus far to be stimulated, amused, angered, irritated, bored, or merely indifferent to my words. And as you experience them and your feelings about them you may have other thoughts: irrelevant, distracting ones, perhaps, or reflections upon what I am saying that amplify or modify or connect with ideas you have already, and so aid your understanding. You are also seeing the printed words and their relation to the page and the book as a whole. Around the book, your peripheral vision will be registering other things—shapes, colors, textures—and if you look up from the book there will be much more to see. At the same time, your body is in a certain position. You can feel the weight and texture and temperature of the book, the seat under you, the floor or whatever is supporting your feet. You can hear certain sounds, the turning page and perhaps a passing car. A good deal of other noise, maybe. And there are smells: the air, cigarette smoke, food, perfume, a human body.

To be conscious of all these impressions would, of course, be as distracting to your reading as thinking all the time about how your eyes are moving across the page; but to be aware with some part of your waking mind of what is happening is as important as knowing what the components of your reading processes are. Optimum response to any experience is equally unnecessary and probably undesirable, but when you need to recall some prominent part of the experience, then it may be by reconstructing the apparently irrelevant impressions that you will succeed. For recall need not be, and seldom is, an exact reproduction of the original. It is much more often a gradual imaginative reconstruction of fragments into a new, coherent, and applicable whole. And those fragments will be the fragments of active responses.

Hence, if you say that you have a bad memory, you may be saying more than that you have difficulty in remembering the things you failed to notice, or things you have no particular interest in. You may be saying that some of the things you try to remember were inadequately registered while you were below par: first thing in the morning, late at night, during illness or depression or headache or hangover or indigestion or intoxication or premenstrual tension and so on.

You may register almost everything inadequately if you are the victim of incessant noise, or if you subject yourself daily to the indignity of repetitive subhuman labor at a conveyor belt, or if you are the passive receptacle of pop culture, the square-eyed televiewer, the do-it-not-yourself expert, punch-drunk from advertising, stiff from commuting, barren from ugliness, cold from loneliness. You may even register almost nothing of anything because you have your being in a private fantasy world of pulp novels, bad films, advertising, vicarious violence, and nightmare sex. There are such people, who can remember almost nothing but their accidents and operations. They are the zombies, the morons, the sick and the dead. They are the dead beats, the no-hopers, the organization men, the cogs in the machine. They are the mental and emotional cripples of the twentieth century, the effects of every cause, the uniforms, the stuffed shirts, the statistics, the ciphers, the isotypes. They are the conformists, the obedient, the patient, the meek who inseminate the earth. They are the fodder of priests and patriarchs, the spawn of bureaucrats, the backs on which dictators climb; the politician's floating vote, the capitalist's profit, the salesman's commission. They ask no questions and ignore no regulations. But they deform their children and eat their mates. Their lineaments are present in each one of us: they hinder us from learning and defy us to grow.

(2,200 words)

Answer the following questions briefly without referring back.

1. Describe in your own words how the author explains the prodigious memories of famous men that we sometimes read about.
(2 marks)
2. List the four Rs of remembering with a brief description of each.
(½ mark for each)
3. What, in your own words, did William James say about improvement in memory? (1 mark)
4. List at least eight of the states of mind described by the author as being the cause of inadequate response to experience and a consequent limitation of learning ability. (½ mark for each)
5. What do you think is the relevance to the improvement of your reading techniques of the final paragraph of the chapter? (1 mark)

Check your answers to all but the final question by skimming back through the chapter. If your speed or comprehension score were lower than recently, I hope you are not surprised or discouraged. This was probably the most difficult chapter you have read in this book so far. The subject matter may have been even more unfamiliar; certainly the style was more complex and the sentences and paragraphs more involved. Moreover, the final paragraph was deliberately provocative in order that you might experience the way that your concentration may be confused or your comprehension reduced by reading material that arouses your antagonism. There is your answer to Question 5.

Be on your guard against such provocation in future. The mature reader can detach himself from involvement with his material if it is necessary. There need be no reduction of efficiency with either provocative or boring material if the reading of it is regarded as a simple matter of applying techniques.

Now give yourself a chance to restore your speed and comprehension by romping through the following easy passage and comprehension test.

READING EXERCISE

Datas, the Memory Man

BY FRED BARLOW

In June 1901 a fresh arrival in the entertainment world was the occasion of much speculation. The name of this new attraction was W. J. M. Bottle but it was as "Datas" that he rapidly became publicly known. As the name indicates, Datas specialized in dates. He claimed that the power of memorizing was a natural gift and in proof of this he expanded this power to such an extent that in the particular sphere of his operations he eventually reached a stage almost of infallibility.

Datas was born on July 20, 1875, at Newnham, Kent, where his father kept a small shoemaker's shop. As an infant, he was very delicate and was unable to walk until he reached his sixth birthday. It will be readily understood that the education of a young sickly child of poor working parents, who had a family of eleven to support, left much to be desired. By the time he had received sufficient schooling to enable him to read, the family removed to London and at the age of eleven Datas was working as a newspaper boy. Some eight months later he became a parcel boy at Lordship Lane station and remained there for three years. There followed a short period as errand boy and in November

1891, at the age of sixteen, he obtained employment at the Crystal Palace Gas Works. For a period of five years he was occupied in various ways at the gas works, eventually landing in the black-smith's shop as a striker, for which he was paid twenty-four shillings a week.

From the time he was able to read, Datas began habitually to commit items of information to memory with the object of repeating them afterward at leisure. From memorizing shopkeepers' names he got to cabbies' and policemen's numbers and then to reading Lloyd's newspaper. Writing of himself, Datas said: "Paper in hand, I would sit down on a little stool in a cozy corner by the fireside, and, my head resting against the chimney piece, I would concentrate all my attention on the matter I wished to learn. I soon exhausted Lloyd's, and, though continuing to read it weekly, went further afield. A copy of Tussaud's calendar of events came into my possession. The mention of famous names therein whetted my appetite for works of history and adventure."

This process of acquiring information was carried on in the little spare time that was available and it would appear that Datas took particular care to ensure that each impression was sufficiently vivid to enable him to retain it indefinitely and to recall it at will. It was not until after he began his stage career that he knew anything of mnemonics, but what he describes as "mental pictures" were undoubtedly of this nature, as witness: "Suppose I am asked the date of the Great Fire in London. I give the correct answer—1666—and immediately there rises before me a panoramic scene, as it were, of that calamity, from its start in Pudding Lane, to its finish in Pie Corner. The picture that is thus marvelously and so expeditiously drawn for me is one of my own fashioning entirely. The pencils are Nature's and the materials are the suggestions conveyed to the optical nerves by the facts hidden safely away in my mind. In what precise manner they act I know not. Suffice to say, I have the vision, and it materially assists me in narrating my version of the facts, acting as an all-powerful mentor. When in the future you are called upon to answer any questions, endeavor to call up at the same time some 'mind pictures,' for you will find their help of immense value.

Remember that failure is the result of a weak mental impression due in the first place to lack of concentration of thought on the subject matter you are endeavoring to commit to memory. Make up your mind always to create the strongest impression you are capable of creating and eventual success will not be wanting. To me, it is now all the same, whether it is a matter of trivial or great importance. Practice has enabled me to store and reproduce each fact, mentally and visually; with practice, lengthy and constant, you can do the same."

This is how Datas described the events of a day in June 1901 that launched him on the successful career of a memorizer: "I had been working on the night shift, from ten o'clock till six and reaching home about six-thirty, I went to bed. By midday I was up again, had dinner, and then took a walk to the Crystal Palace, where fate had much in store for me. While taking a little refreshment, I overheard two gentlemen discussing the date of the finish of the great Tichborne trial. Neither knew the correct date so I ventured to give this. Finding how surprised they were at my knowledge, I felt encouraged, and continued with a number of dates of events in English history, etc. Quite unnoticed by me, a third gentleman was a listener to our conversation and when I had finished my long string of dates, he quietly came up to me and put the momentous question: 'Would you like to go upon the stage?' He then and there took me to the Standard Music Hall, Victoria, where I gave my first performance."

The new form of entertainment became an immediate success and Datas left the gas works for the stage. He traveled throughout the British Isles and eventually acquired a world-wide reputation. During his performances, many curious and unusual questions were put to him and it is said that only on rare occasions did he fail to give a correct or satisfactory answer. As in mnemonics, Datas claimed that what he described as the "law of association" was the only real help in memorizing. He goes on to say: "One idea begets another; therefore, when memorizing one idea, kill two birds with one stone, and also memorize the corresponding idea. It may be that you will not at once discover the associated idea, or ideas. Here you will again perceive the necessity for a searching analysis of your subject matter. Suppose you wish to remember the date of the opening of the first railway line in England. Instantly the figure of George Stephenson arises before you. You recall the date of his birth, etc., the year of the great financial railway bubble, the opening of the Mont Cenis and Simplon tunnels, the dates of notable collisions, etc. A host of things come to mind, the mine of recollection fired by the magic word 'railways.'

"Where you have ideas which are, so to speak, unconnected, it is essential that in order to commit them to memory successfully, you should establish an intermediary idea as a connecting link, an idea which although not directly associated with either one of the two ideas you wish to memorize, is nevertheless indirectly associated with both so that in remembering either, the link manifests itself which binds the two together. You wish to remember Newton—gravitation, the link is the word 'apple.' You say to yourself an apple falls from the tree to the ground; falling is an act of gravitation. Who watched a similar action and noted the result?—Newton. You also have an extra aid by reason of a certain sort of apple being named after the great scientist."

Datas insisted that all questions put to him should be brief and definite. His replies, while giving the dates asked for, frequently included additional information associated with the replies. For example, if he were asked: "When was Big Ben set up at Westminster?" he would, in addition to the actual date, include other items of interest concerning Westminster and Big Ben. . . .

It should be placed on record that when asked how he was able to remember dates so accurately, Datas would frequently claim that he had no idea how it was done. Nor could the usual arrangements obtaining at a music hall be described as anywhere approaching "test conditions." When inviting questions in the ordinary way, these would be fired at him from various parts of the building so that, to some extent, he had a choice from which to make his selection or to ignore awkward questions. It is also quite possible that to increase the entertainment value of his show a "stooge" or "stooges" were employed. To such a question as "When was Kruger vaccinated?" his answer "On March 15, 1826 —and it took in four places—is that right, sir?" scarcely ever failed to bring down the house. This does not affect the genuine nature of his gift of which there was no question.

On one occasion the Lord Chief Justice of England was an occupant of the stalls. He put three questions: "When was the *Utopia* wrecked?" "When were the Corn Laws repealed?" and "When did Mr. Low propose to put a tax on matches?" Datas did not know until afterward who was his questioner. After his "turn," however, while in the dressing room, his Lordship visited him and congratulated him, stating that the correct answer had been given to each of the three queries. On another occasion, Sir Edward Clarke put a series of difficult questions to which Datas gave the correct replies.

A lengthy notice in the *Evening News* said of him: "The dark, well-knit young man who is appearing under the *nom du théâtre* of Datas at the Palace is a human Haydn's Dictionary brought up to date. For six weeks he has answered, quick as thought, all sorts and kinds of questions on subjects of historical or public interest. He predicts nothing, but forgets nothing that he has ever heard or read. . . ."

Datas did not confine himself to a knowledge of world-wide events. His acquaintance with the local history of the towns he visited was equally thorough. When visiting a fresh town this was his procedure: "I would first visit the police headquarters, where I could generally obtain a great deal of information regarding famous crimes and criminals associated with the place, big accidents, and so forth. Then I proceeded to the fire station to learn all that I could about important fires that had occurred in the neighborhood. The remainder of the time I would fill in by inspecting local cathedrals, churches, museums, etc., from all of which I managed to extract a great deal of valuable information. A few hours spent in the manner described used to suffice to give me all the history of the place I wished for."

From: *Mental Prodigies*
(1,700 words)

EXERCISE 20

Choose the best answer to each question.

1. When did Datas begin to memorize things?
   a. Before he could read.
   b. From the time he could read.
   c. Before he left school.
   d. While he worked as an errand boy.
2. He was:
   a. an only child;
   b. one of a large, poor family;
   c. an orphan;
   d. a foundling.
3. He left school when he was:
   a. eleven;
   b. fifteen;
   c. old enough to read;
   d. still unable to read.
4. He first appeared on the stage:
   a. during his apprenticeship;
   b. in his middle twenties;
   c. at the age of forty;
   d. during a works concert.
5. Datas was first discovered by a man of the theater:
   a. in a public house;
   b. dispensing information in an open-air restaurant;
   c. while taking refreshment at the Crystal Palace;
   d. in the blacksmith's shop at the gas works.
6. How did Datas explain his ability to memorize dates?
   a. By his interest in doing so.
   b. By reading all he could about the places he visited.
   c. By association of mental images.
   d. He could not explain it.
7. To increase the entertainment of his shows, Datas:
   a. answered questions about local events;
   b. identified famous people in the audience;
   c. probably planted stooges in the audience;
   d. gave additional information that was not asked for.

8. The writer of the passage implies that Datas was:
    a. a fraud;
    b. a freak;
    c. a simple soul;
    d. a genuine prodigy.
9. We may infer that Datas was:
    a. a poor working lad who made good;
    b. a born entertainer with a gimmick;
    c. an undiscovered intellectual;
    d. a genius.
10. The main idea of the extract is:
    a. anyone with a bit of luck and a determination to train his memory can make a fortune;
    b. mental prodigies are to be found in all walks of life;
    c. anything can be memorized if you use a system;
    d. in any consideration of prodigies of memory, it is worth knowing something of the personality and self-confessed methods of an Edwardian music-hall phenomenon called Datas.

·II·

Understanding

THE CRITERION OF EFFICIENT LEARNING is that after a long interval the matter learned can be applied as effectively as necessary to new tasks. Simple memorizing has very limited value in that it is no help in applying the knowledge to new tasks. The only learning worth the name, in fact, is learning by understanding; and the fuller the understanding the easier learning becomes. That, in brief, is my case in this chapter and a dominant theme in this book. In other words, imaginative reconstruction is better than literal reproduction; and that way learning can be an everyday source of pleasure.

Most deliberate learning is done for a specific limited purpose and the material is forgotten when the purpose is fulfilled. This is perhaps as well with a great deal of stuff that people subject themselves to learning. As any actor with experience in weekly repertory knows, a new part has often to be learned while the part learned last week is in rehearsal and the part learned the week before is being performed in this week's run of the play. It might be thought that after a week of rehearsals and seven or eight performances, a part would be remembered for months and the dangers of confusion between plays become such as to make someone enter with "Who's for tennis?" in the one drawing room comedy that does not contain the line. By the same token, one would expect any actor pinioned for years in an interminably long-run play to remember his lines all his life. But this is seldom the case. The professional actor forgets as easily as he learns, because he learns only for a limited purpose. If he were engaged for a return performance years later, he could relearn his part quite quickly; and he might be able to recall most of a part without relearning if he changed into the same costume and walked onto the same set among the same cast and someone started the play off again.

The forgetting of some of our deeply rooted skills can sometimes be surprisingly thorough, especially if there is a drastic change of environment. A student of mine, an attorney, once told me of an experience of his mother, who returned to visit relatives in her native Russia after thirty years in England speaking nothing but English. After ten days there she could not remember enough English to send a cable home to her children giving the date of her return. It was an exceptional lapse, of course, perhaps with traumatic overtones, and if the old lady had made up her mind to imagine her English environment vividly enough, she might have succeeded in composing the cable. It is possible that her return to a world of her youth which she had tried to forget during her exile was shock enough to annihilate the years between, when she had started her life afresh without building it upon the foundations of an acknowledged past. Strange forms of damage can be wrought in the personality by attempts to bury the past.

Similar experiences in milder forms are fairly common, such as the surprise of how much of a foreign language you can forget in your own country or of how easily you can remember it when you return to the foreign environment. The explanation may be that, reasonably enough, the foreign language was learned with a limited purpose that did not extend to speaking it at home.

Many potential examinees study with only the limited purpose of passing the exam. If they know it, there is little wrong in doing so, since so many examinations are mere initiation rites that bear no relation to the postgraduate life for which one has supposedly trained. Motorists are not taught to drive; they are taught to pass the driving test by learning to perform a certain pattern of movements known to be acceptable to the examiners. When they pass, they have to learn anew to drive in everyday conditions, for if they do so in the way that got them through the test they would be a nuisance to everyone on the road.

Examples could be multiplied from countless other formal examinations, and any unsubdued graduate of anything will recognize the process. In a world of too many people, most of them fearful and few with the courage to arrive at and act upon an independent judgment, the certificate is as indispensable a proof of ability as it is of a respectable marriage, or as a passport is proof of another's identity, or as a peace treaty used to certify international amity—all further examples of superstition about the printed word.

If he is honest, the certified graduate probably knows that his position is not unlike that of the ex-lunatic certified sane and now able to boast himself more demonstrably sane than anyone without a certificate of sanity. After months and even years of narrow study, undertaken less for its own sake than for the piece of paper certifying it, the examinee eventually proves what? At best, that he could pass the exam. He may, in passing, as it were, also demonstrate his conformity, his willingness to engage with futility, and his tenacity in sticking to his last of boredom, all qualities still valued in our post-Victorian world. He will also experience a sense of relief, a few psychosomatic disorders, and, if he is lucky, the insight that anything undertaken for any sake but its own is the best incubator of anxiety there is. Then he will begin to learn what he is supposed to have been educated for.

One constant in all the equations of learning is that effort and inefficiency increase in proportion with the lack of interest in the learner. If learning is to be efficient, there must be a desire to learn and an intention to retain for a long time. That is the first principle of efficient learning.

The second principle is that the experience, or the material to be learned, must be invested with meaning, and the meaning must be the learner's meaning and not that of any other authority or party to the experience.

Hence the third principle of efficient learning is that all learning must be acknowledged as the learner's own experience, even when the experience of others is being learned. In other words, it must accord with what we already know, and thus seem reasonably likely.

Then all that remains is the question of study methods, and we shall examine those in the next chapter.

The first experimental studies in learning were conducted during the early eighties of the last century by a young philosophy tutor attached to Berlin University called Hermann Ebbinghaus, who had a curious obsession. Entirely alone, using himself as both experimenter and subject, he spent six years of his late twenties and early thirties working with characteristic German thoroughness at the self-imposed task of planning, executing, and evaluating a series of experiments which involved him in memorizing lists drawn from a collection of about 2,300 nonsense syllables, each syllable formed by placing a vowel between two consonants: NAC : MIJ : WOL : REH : TEG : WOH : SES : ROF : SIK : LEM and so on (for example) for thirteen or sixteen syllables. They were, of course, German nonsense, so that they were pronounceable by a German tongue, and they were built up phonetically, so that a sound like KÖSCH could have been included.

During the course of all his experiments he memorized thousands of such lists. He would group six or eight lists together and then read each list aloud at a precise rate of 150 syllables a minute, measured by the ticking of a watch, and sometimes count the number of repetitions by means of buttons on a string. When he could repeat a list twice without error, he would allow fifteen seconds to record his learning time and proceed in the same way with the next list.

One of his most important experiments involved him in learning twice over 163 groups composed of eight lists of thirteen syllables. When one batch of 104 syllables had been mastered, he recorded his total learning time and then, after a given interval, relearned them in the same way until the same standard had been reached. There were seven different intervals of twenty minutes, one hour, nine hours, twenty-four hours, two, six, and thirty-one days. Each batch of eight lists was relearned only once, and at each relearning the saving in learning time was noted.

By a stroke of genius he calculated that the proportion of the original learning time taken with the relearning was equivalent to the proportion of the material forgotten in the interval. From the seven tables of figures he compiled, it is possible to plot a graph of which the horizontal axis represents the time intervals and the vertical axis represents the amount remembered. Thus Ebbinghaus has been rewarded by the privilege of being able to hand down to posterity the Ebbinghaus Curve of Forgetting and with it a little book, published in 1885 and called *Über das Gedächtnis*, which has become a classic in psychology not only because the experiments were so thorough that other psychologists have since been able to duplicate them with essentially the same results, but also because it recorded the first attempt to study the higher mental processes by scientific method.

A few moments' thought about what the Ebbinghaus Curve looked like will probably make the illustration of it at the end of this chapter (page 178) superfluous. Anyone who thought about it, indeed, could doubtless have told Ebbinghaus the same, thus saving him all that trouble. He himself wrote:

> It will probably be claimed that the fact that forgetting would be very rapid at the beginning of the process and very slow at the end should have been foreseen. However it would be just as reasonable to be surprised at this initial rapidity and later slowness as they come to light here under the definite conditions of our experiment for a certain individual, and for a series of 13 syllables.[1]

The important thing is that Ebbinghaus proved it conclusively, and in doing so added another item to the poignant annals of the lengths to which people will go to be first.

His experiments with nonsense, moreover, have provided a criterion for all subsequent research into learning, for they represent a learning and forgetting ability pretty close to the nadir of efficiency, only to be succeeded by someone for whom the task had no interest and the material no significance. Ebbinghaus, of course, fulfilled all three principles of sound learning,

---

[1] Hermann Ebbinghaus: *Memory, a Contribution to Experimental Psychology* (1885), translated by Henry A. Ruger and Clara E. Bussenius (Columbia University Teachers College, New York City, 1913); paperback edition, with an introduction by Ernest R. Hilgard, published by Dover Publications, Inc., New York.

otherwise he could never have stuck it so long. He reduced meaning to a minimum with his lists, but in time they must have developed some meaning for him, even if he succeeded in preserving the pure nonsense of the syllables themselves.

The Ebbinghaus logarithmic curve has been regarded by some psychologists as the only curve of forgetting, but conditions have been created that induced a rise after an initial fall as, for example, when less is remembered immediately after learning than after a longer interval. There are other exceptions, too, usually occurring at random, such as temporary forgetting and reminiscence.

Most experiments in learning have been directed toward discovering the conditions of perfect learning and so produce a curve of no forgetting, a sort of teacher's philosopher's stone curve. Ebbinghaus himself discovered some conditions that helped to flatten out his curve. Instead of ceasing to learn his lists after two accurate recitations, he continued to learn them, overlearning them, and found a substantial reduction in the amount of forgetting. He also found that he needed to allow a 12 per cent increase of his relearning time if his relearning exercise was timed to take place at the end of the day or when he was otherwise fatigued.

Ebbinghaus learned nonsense by rote. Other experiments have shown how learning becomes easier when meaning is introduced, easier still when the meaning is enhanced by association with wider meanings or experiences, and easiest of all when an underlying principle is understood.

Consider the simple example of nonsense syllables given above: NAC : MIJ : WOL : REH : TEG : WOH : SES : ROF : SIK : LEM. Clearly, it would be easier to learn them if each were inverted: CAN : JIM : LOW : HER : GET : HOW : SES : FOR : KIS : MEL. Now most of them form recognizable words. But if an arrangement is imposed on them we find: HOW : CAN : JIM : FOR : GET : HER : MEL : LOW : KIS : SES. As a meaningful sentence, the ten syllables are more memorable still, but as it stands the sentence belongs to no apparent context. "How can Jim forget her mellow kisses?" Who is Jim? Who is the girl? Or was it his mother? And why does he want to forget? Or does it mean that he can never forget? If so, can it be because he has efficient learning techniques?

The sentence as it stands, then, can only be learned by rote. There are methods of improving rote learning, which can be discussed with other study techniques, and there are occasions when rote learning, at some early stage in the process, is the only kind possible. Solo musicians and actors must learn by rote at some time; so too, alas, must many examinees, who are so often tested on how much they have memorized instead of how well they can organize and present their knowledge.

Simple memorizing is used much too indiscriminately as a learning method, perhaps as an odd form of laziness (among teachers or students) because it demands less imagination than more efficient forms of learning. It might almost be described as false learning to distinguish it from true learning, for "true" learning means learning for life; and simple memorizing is no help when it comes to applying knowledge to new tasks.

One very popular aid to memorizing, which attempts to shorten the chore of rote learning and to form a link with understanding, is that of mnemonics. The four Rs of remembering are a kind of mnemonic. "Thirty days hath September . . ." is a mnemonic that many people still need to recite before they know how many days a month has. Examinees, as one would expect, make the greatest use of them, and their usual form is that the initial letters of a group of names to be reproduced in a certain order are composed into a sentence with the same initial letters to each word. Medical students have dozens, remarkably obscene but not particularly ingenious. The initial letters of Lovely French Tart Sits Naked In Anticipation, for instance, are also the initial letters in the correct order of the names of the nerves entering the eye socket from behind. (From the left or the right?)

The qualities of a good mnemonic are ease of memorizing and immediate association with all the data to which it relates. Very few fulfill both these conditions. Complex mnemonics sometimes fulfill the latter condition but demand a lot of rote learning;

simple mnemonics usually fulfill the former condition, but a good deal of additional knowledge is often required to complete its associations. The names of the nerves entering the eye socket from behind have still to be learned, and they are difficult words. Students of mine in medical practice, who can usually recall two or three of their medical student mnemonics, assure me that they have never used them in practice, although they think they were a help in passing their finals and so demonstrating their ability to memorize. In practice, the knowledge is available to them whenever circumstances demand it, either because it has been learned by frequent use or because they can turn to a reference book at their elbow.

The mnemonic that my students most commonly produce exemplifies the characteristics and limitations of simple mnemonics very well, if I may labor the point for another paragraph. It is a familiar one: Richard Of York Gained Battles In Vain. The connection is not historical, of course, for nonsense associations are part of the point of mnemonics. So firstly it is necessary to remember that it relates to the order of the colors of the spectrum. Sometimes it is expressed as a single word, "Roygbiv," or a man's name, "Roy G. Biv," easy enough to relate to the spectrum, provided that the colors from red to violet are always arranged from left to right. In spectrum analysis indeed they may be, but I would need to turn to a reference book to confirm it. Some confusion has arisen since I heard the word "Vibgyor" used in this connection, and therefore the mnemonic has not equipped me for making much practical use of it. If I wanted to paint an imaginary landscape with a rainbow, how then could I use the mnemonic? Is the upper side of the arc red or violet? I have usually assumed that it must be violet because I have imagined, in what may well be a mistaken attempt to *understand* the refraction of sunlight, that since the rainbow appears opposite the sun, and the curve of its arc changes with the angle of the sun, it must be a kind of projected halo of the sun. This would suggest that the warmest color, red, is on the inner curve of the bow. On the other hand, Doubt has said, perhaps an inversion takes place with the refraction, as when light passes through a lens and (I suppose) a prism. But I have generally adhered to the idea of direct projection, and now, since seeing a rainbow while I have been writing this chapter, I shall continue to do so. For I have verified that I am wrong, and I can hardly forget that. Richard's vain battles should not be written from left to right but from top to bottom. Otherwise, one must stand him in golden armor, bright sword aloft, at the end of the rainbow where the pot of gold is. The left-hand end.

For me, Richard can stand where he likes. I can remember from everyday use the words infrared and ultraviolet, which I know to be wave lengths at either end of the spectrum, and on that knowledge I can *reconstruct* the rest from my understanding of how colors blend: red must pass through orange before it becomes yellow, and so on. Next, I must remember to look up a book on spectrum analysis—and not by a knot in my handkerchief. Now I really want to know for use in my next lecture on remembering.

The mnemonic method of learning is open to a still more serious indictment, in my opinion, with its hugely elaborated use as the basis of those widely advertised memory systems offering expensive courses in memory training. I have no doubt that, given diligent students, the memory schools do produce the results they claim. Some people may well think it a useful skill to be able to memorize every item of a long shopping list; but in our house we write down whatever we need at the moment the need arises, and the twice-weekly shopping expedition is made with such a list. Others, with a need to impress the impressionable at parties, may like to do so by demonstrating feats of memory, or even to make an entertainer's living with their skill. One can understand it, if the alternative is the gas-works smithy. A superficially more general function of the skill would be to remember the names, occupations, and other vital statistics of everybody one meets after the first meeting.

Such feats are done and can be learned to be done, but they all depend on the rote learning of an adaptable mnemonic system. The more adaptable the system, the more intricate it is, and the more tedium of rote learning is involved. Once a system has been learned, it must be continually and vigorously applied in the way that we use our multiplication tables, which we remember not so much because we memorized them well at school, as by our frequent everyday use of them.

Memory systems in general rely as much as any other kind of learning on the basic principles of desire to learn, intention to retain, and adequate observation. Then they make elaborate use of the laws of association mostly through visual imagery and always through private nonsense. Their exponents emphasize that one's pictorial associations must be as ridiculous as one can make them. Logical associations simple enough to remember, they argue, are likely to become confused in time with other logical associations. Nonsense, however, is unlimited, and each piece of nonsense is made to serve only one purpose. Hence there is no danger of confusion, as you will see from the following example, created to illustrate a fairly elaborate use of such a system.

Each digit from naught to nine is accorded a phonetic consonant value similar to those of shorthand alphabets. Phonetic T and D, for instance, are one, and a mnemonic is used to remember the fact, because the downstroke of the T resembles the figure 1. P and B are nine, because p is a nine reversed and b is a nine inverted. M is three, because of the similarity of the letter m with the roman III. Next, each phonetic is supplied with a vowel to make a one-syllable word. Tea, bee, ma. Combinations of digits are formed by combining phonetic consonants, so that 13 gives TiMe, 91 gives PoT, 913 gives BoTToM, and so on. Once a word is chosen to represent a given number it is never changed, and neither is the mental image used to visualize it. It must always be the same tray laid for tea, the same outsize bee, your own mother, an archetypal bottom.

The entire list, from one to a hundred, or a thousand if you are so inclined, has to be learned by rote and used as often as possible. Now, suppose you needed to remember a list of 93 people, their names, telephone numbers, and interests. Number 39 is Sir James Thomson, stamp collector, of Hampstead 1113. You have chosen MoP for 39, so you must first visualize Sir James, as you remember him, mopping a vast floor with your standard mop. To associate the name with the face, you remember that James sounds like "shames" and, since this is your standard association for any James, you see this one shaming a group of expert charwomen with the efficient way he mops. They are all saluting him, which is the way one chooses to remember to call somebody "Sir." Sir James's surname is Tom's son. Tom was the piper's son, and Tom's son must have been the piper's grandson. Hence it must not be the piper who is shaming the saluting charwomen by mopping the floor. He is marching up and down, kilted and caterwauling, leaving dirty footmarks on the freshly mopped floor, with his son, a half-sized piper, walking and wailing in father's footprints, possibly piping on a pig. The man mopping the floor is a minute, quarter-sized, bald-headed piper with foreign stamps stuck all over his pate. Sir James's most prominent feature, in your observant eyes, is his baldness, and if on that noble pate you always visualize his stamp collection, how can you ever forget his hobby?

Ordinary memory, the experts will assure you, will prevent your thinking of Subject 39 as Colonel Tom Jameson a bald post-office worker. For his telephone number, you could have him mopping against TiMe, measured by your standard clock on the wall, with a still more minute figure (your standard ToT) sitting on one of its hands, eating a huge HAM. If you should think his number to be HAM 1311, and ordinary memory fails to supply the fact that you are wrong, you make only one wrong call. To be quite sure of making no mistake, you can identify Subject 39 with Hampstead 1113 by the link system, thus: the MoP is cleaning a huge HAM, another HAM is supplying a stool for your ToT, and another ToT sits on the hand of your standard TiMepiece. Perhaps you would care to try it out by ringing Sir James's number and telling whoever answers about the pictures in your mind, and how you propose to learn the remaining 92 subjects by similar methods. . . . (In fact, it happens to be the number of Hampstead Police Station.)

And by the way, if you are likely to forget that that particular batch of people were 93 in number, you should blow them all up with a BoMb.

It is easy to see how such a flexible system can be adapted to any contingency, and how an expert in the use of it could be introduced to two or three hundred people in an evening and remember all their names. It may be important to you to impress people with your remarkable memory for their names. It may even be your lot to have frequent dealings with those who are impressed by such monumental trivialities. I myself always carry a notebook, and I would far rather an acquaintance thought on meeting me that my name was Norman Mailer than to visualize me heavily in debt (owin') with spiders spinning their webs between my glasses and the books which have taken the place of my ears. And if I meet a man outside a psychiatric clinic, I want to know the man, not the stunts emanating from a nonexistent memory that he has been training like a weight lifter for years. Human relations are subject to enough distortion without deliberately increasing it.

By now it must have become apparent that I have no system, as such, to offer for either reading well or remembering. Both interrelated processes respond best to common sense and common confidence. It is not common sense to expect to remember everything one reads after only a single reading. To skim and read once ensures better understanding; and it is your understanding, not the ability to remember, that all the exercises in this book have been designed to test. Understanding equips the reader to decide how much it is necessary to retain for subsequent recall, and more often than not all that matters is knowing where information is to be found when required. To skim, read once, and skim again, should ensure enough retention both to fulfill this purpose and to achieve the kind of understanding that absorbs the meaning into the body of one's usable knowledge. More specific and detailed retention can only be acquired by the application of proper study techniques.

Reflection after reading should therefore be directed along the lines of a mental comprehension test, answering such questions as the following:

What connection has this with what I already know?
What do I remember that bears on it?

What is its significance?

What of it?

With more practical material, such as the techniques described in this book, it is important to ensure that one understands how they work, how they can be used, what else can be done with them.

Finally, there is no better check on one's own understanding than having to explain it all to somebody else.

(4,250 words)

EXERCISE 21

Choose the best answer to each question.

1. The foregoing chapter connects with what you already know by virtue of its:
   a. common sense;
   b. confirmation that there is no panacea for remembering all you read;
   c. explanation of the title of this book;
   d. implication that efficient remembering can only be achieved by a lot of very hard work.
2. The significance of the chapter is that:
   a. common sense and confidence, properly applied, will enable one to learn anything one chooses;
   b. widely advertised memory systems are a waste of money;
   c. mnemonics are all right for limited purposes, but are useless when it comes to understanding;
   d. learning by heart is false learning.
3. The best way to make use of the information given in this chapter is to:
   a. realize one's own undeveloped ability for learning;
   b. embark on a course of study;
   c. read as widely as possible;
   d. remember it.
4. When something has been properly learned it can be:
   a. applied when needed;
   b. recited by heart;
   c. remembered indefinitely;
   d. explained to somebody else.

5. The author is opposed to most examinations because they are:
   a. no proof that the knowledge they test can be applied in practice;
   b. easy for the crammer and difficult for the plodder;
   c. as silly for rational people as initiation rites;
   d. essentially tests of a willingness to conform.
6. The mnemonics one learns at school, in the author's view, are:
   a. amusing and easily remembered for a long time;
   b. never used in adult life;
   c. all right for getting through exams;
   d. confusing to one's adult understanding.
7. The author's purpose in describing memory systems as he does is to:
   a. make fun of them;
   b. protect his readers from wasting their money;
   c. show that they work in certain circumstances;
   d. show that observation made for the purpose of creating nonsense associations does not promote better understanding.
8. The best way to ensure that one has understood something is to:
   a. learn it properly in the first place;
   b. ask oneself questions about it, relating it to existing knowledge;
   c. write out a summary of it;
   d. explain it to somebody else.
9. The author's system for reading well and remembering is:
   a. a matter of applied common sense and confidence;
   b. to skim, read once, and skim again;
   c. useful as long as one keeps up one's reading;
   d. not a "system" at all, in the sense that it might be patented, like a memory system.
10. The main idea of the chapter is:
    a. Something better than examinations must be devised before students can be said to have learned their subjects.
    b. If things are learned by understanding, they can always be recalled well enough to be applied when needed.
    c. Rote learning is no help when applying knowledge to new tasks.
    d. There is no system or short cut to developing a better memory.

The World of Books

"Great land of sublimated things, thou World of Books!" cried H. G. Wells; but any reader curious enough to consult the section devoted to books in the United Nations Statistical Yearbook for 1962 may well be struck by the way great lands sublimate things into their world of books. Statistics are compiled by UNESCO every year to show the number of books (by titles) produced in various countries, and it is especially valuable to find that the titles are separated into their different categories, thus revealing to perceptive analysis a number of significant trends.

The most striking fact at first glance is that although Britain is the largest producer of books in the Free World, with a total in 1961 of 24,893, Russia produced three times as many, and tops the world poll with the fantastic figure of 73,999. Japan comes third with 24,223, followed by West Germany with 21,877, the United States with 18,060 and France with 12,705. Among the smaller countries, Czechoslovakia is shown to be the most prolific with an output of 9,728 books, followed closely by Holland with 9,010. Both countries narrowly escaped being overtaken by India, with a total of 8,967, her lowest for the past three years. Both in 1959 and 1960 India produced more books than either Holland or Czechoslovakia.

A startling picture of national preoccupations is revealed when the totals are broken down into different subjects. Fiction accounts for the largest single group of books in 32 of the 69 member countries listed. Of the remainder, all but nine had their largest figure in the social sciences, and among the exceptions were Russia, Poland, Czechoslovakia, Hungary, and Romania, all of whom published more books on the applied sciences than any other subject. The important countries with highest figures in the social sciences included all the other Communist countries except East Germany, together with West Germany, Austria and Portugal.

In fiction, Britain was well in the lead with 8,615 books, followed by Russia a close second with 8,581. Well behind came the United States (5,759), West Germany (5,294), with Japan (5,015), and France (4,928) wrestling for third place.

Russia was so far ahead of the field in 1961 with books on the applied sciences, that all the other countries were also-rans. Her total was 37,073. She was followed by Britain with 4,024, and then by Czechoslovakia (3,564), Japan (2,902), and Poland (2,331), all scraping home before the United States, who managed to produce a mere 2,329 books in this field. The Americans, in fact, only narrowly escaped being overtaken by West Germany and Portugal. Russia also heads the list in philosophy with 577 books against Japan's 567, the U.S.A.'s 565 and Britain's 541. The Communist satellites evidently had other things to think about. Hungary, for example, produced only 20 books on this subject.

Only one country produced more books on religion than any other subject, and that was Ireland, with 67 religious books out of a total of 257 titles produced. Among the other countries, the picture of religious publications is divided much as one would expect, with the Western bloc at one extreme—Britain (1,443), West Germany (1,438), and the United States (1,290); and the Communist countries at the other—Russia (355), Poland (112) to Bulgaria (4), and Albania (1). The ideological rack on which our tortured world groans is more plainly evident in figures such as these than in any of the books they represent.

(560 words)

EXERCISE 22

Answer the following questions briefly, referring back to the text where necessary. Do your best to answer each question before passing on to the next.

1. What is your opinion of the article?
2. What statements in the article helped you to form your opinion?

Understanding

3. Why did you arrive at that opinion?
4. What fact in the article did you find the most surprising?
5. Why?
6. What possible explanations could there be of this fact?
7. What other facts did you find especially interesting; and why?
8. Can you think of any explanation for them?
9. Do you think the tone of the article is pro-Soviet, anti-Soviet, or neutral?
10. What statements led you to this conclusion?
11. What picture of life in Communist countries do you derive from the article?
12. What statements provide you with the evidence?
13. What impression of life in the United States do you gain, and why?
14. To what do the figures refer?
15. What is the definition of a "title"?
16. Are paperbacks included?
17. Are second and subsequent editions included?
18. In what language or languages were each country's books published?
19. Are translations from other languages included?
20. Are monographs and other publications for specialized circulation included?
21. Are pamphlets and periodicals included?
22. Were all the books published for sale?
23. What differences, if any, do these considerations make to the impression given?
24. How were the figures collected?
25. How were they compiled originally?
26. Is the system of classification the same in all the countries concerned?
27. What differences, if any, do these considerations make to the conclusions to be drawn from the figures?
28. What, in essence, is the writer of the article saying?
29. Is the final sentence of the article justified by the given facts, and why?
30. Is there anything else that it is important to know, and if so, what?
31. What is the significance of the statement that Hungary produced only 20 books on philosophy, and why?
32. What can be demonstrated by the use of statistics?

33. What can be proved with statistics?
34. In what kind of publication do you think the article appeared and at what sort of reader was it aimed?
35. In what circumstances might it have been written?
36. What is the relevance of the opening quotation?
37. Have you any other observations about minor details, and if so, what are they?
38. What might be the effect over many years of casually reading hundreds of articles with the tone and qualities of this one?
39. What is your opinion of the article now?
40. What is the purpose of this exercise?

See page 165 for a footnote to the article.

CURVES OF FORGETTING

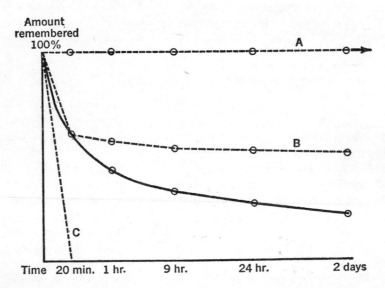

The continuous line is the Ebbinghaus Curve. Broken lines represent:
A. The teacher's philosopher's stone curve
B. The curve after reciting the same thing again and again without further relearning
C. The zombie curve

·12·

Studying

So MANY STUDENTS pass through school and university learning little but techniques of hoodwinking examiners into admitting them through the various check points with which the authorities capriciously encumber their paths, that one begins to question whether those who try to govern our lives really believe all they say about education. So few students learn to learn, which is the best that any school could do for them, that one might not unjustly ask whether the compulsory system we all pay for is not more truly one of indoctrination in docility. For if it were successfully educational it should surely produce more people capable of running their own lives and forming their own judgments. Of course, if it produced too many, the powerful would be left with too few subjects to control. Perhaps it is even worth asking how high the price really is that we pay for our free educational system.

Certainly the violent competition and attempted asexuality of normal school life have as little to do with educating social beings as the effort and misery of cramming have to do with learning. And if learning and study are not stimulating and enjoyable, it is because they are being done wrongly. Wrong study may be too much study, inefficient study, or study for the wrong reasons.

The faults of our educational system begin in the cradle and persist until maturity has been achieved. One of its consequences is that for the first principle of efficient learning an incentive must be found to replace the element of desire.

Our desires are the finger posts by which we find our individual ways to wisdom and fulfillment. Those who have lost their way through allowing their signs to be obscured by the fogs of guilt and faintheartedness blunder along the paths of rectitude kicking the curbs of duty and bully others into following their example to help them preserve the illusion that they have not lost their way at all, with the result that most of us lose touch with our desires quite early in life.

Hence, it is usually necessary to have an incentive to learn and, in the absence of one, to create one. It may be for something trivial, like the need to earn another hundred pounds a year in a "better" job; or for something important, like enriching an Italian holiday by being able to talk with peasants; or for something ignoble, like beating the other fellow.

So first and always ask yourself why you want to study, and try to ensure that your reasons can override whatever idle temptations may be generated by natural laziness.

Next, make use of your studies in a practical and interesting way from the time you begin them until, if ever, you have no further use for them. It is for this reason that I have insisted on the importance of spells of other reading between the chapters and sections of this book. Many of the students who enroll for courses in efficient reading are surprised that a minimum of an hour's reading a day should be required throughout the course, as if they expected to learn to read without reading. Any who are disappointed with their results invariably confess that they would have done better if they had done their homework. By that time they have understood the value of continuing use of an acquired skill or knowledge, and I can only hope that they will be diligent enough to apply and develop after the course whatever techniques and attitudes their interest in it enabled them to retain. It is of course vital that each stage in the acquisition of any skill should be practiced and applied between lessons, so that problems can be clarified and errors rectified as they occur or at the following lesson. Practice and study independently of the teacher and alone with the subject must take place at as early a stage as possible and errors must be discovered before they become an indelible part of the memory traces.

The same principles apply to learning by rote. Consider the amateur actor. He has a desire or an incentive for learning his part, though I have never been able to fully understand what it is, having watched some hundreds of amateur theatrical productions and met some dozens of their players. He will certainly learn his part more easily and remember it better if he supplements his need for drama in his life by expending his energies down at the church hall rehearsing and helping to make scenery instead of reciting it over to himself in an armchair at home until he thinks he has it. Simple memorizing and recitation are not to be excluded, however, but he will be best advised to learn his part in the order in which he will have to speak it and not by picking out the longest speech for learning first and then memorizing the easier ones, or vice versa, leaving the most difficult till last. It may seem less rewarding at first, but in the long run it would be more efficient to learn the entire part in one act straight off and then turn to the next act. Ideally, if the part is not too big, it should be memorized straight through the play from the rise to the fall of the curtain. Similarly, it is more efficient to memorize poetry by taking the poem as a whole, if it is not too long, rather than memorizing one stanza at a time. Anything of greater length should be divided into its natural parts, each as long as the learner can tackle.

The actor should try to manage without the script as soon as possible, but not so soon as to encourage "ad libbing," whether reciting on stage or in bath, and errors should be corrected against the script as they arise. If he wants to remember his part for a long time, he should not stop learning it as soon as he thinks he has it, but overlearn it, reciting and checking with the script at gradually increasing intervals. Although a certain amount of indirect overlearning takes place while the actor makes use of what he has learned during the performances of the play, his limited intentions are inapplicable to the value of overlearning.

A better example of the value of overlearning is provided by the language student, whose desire to learn is usually supported by the concomitant desire to retain for a long time. He may well increase his incentive and put his studies to immediate use by finding a girl friend whose native tongue he is learning. Later, he may overlearn indirectly by visiting the country of his second language as well as directly by taking his grammar book with him and continuing to study it in spare moments, eliminating errors in conversation as soon as possible after they arise.

Throughout these stages of learning, the good language student will be consciously using all his senses. Sight and hearing should be interlinked whenever possible in all learning, but especially when learning a new vocabulary, which is always first experienced as nonsense and therefore easily subject to following the Ebbinghaus Curve. This is partly why I insist that even the most efficient readers need to sub-vocalize a certain amount of their reading.

Most people are predominantly visualizers, but the images they visualize most easily are more likely to be pictorial than verbal. Hence the additional conscious use of the auditory memory should help with the memorizing of words and anything else studied from books. Auditory memorizers form a sizable minority who can learn more easily from lectures than from books. They are also likely to be quick to learn the superficial conversation of a new language, but when discussing ideas or reading the literature they may meet more difficulties than the visualizer. The auditory learner can stimulate the use of his visual memory by writing things down, for words can often be recalled partly from their sound and partly from the appearance of the page, handwriting, and color of pencil or ink in which they are noted. Language students are often sensibly advised to carry a batch of cards with foreign words and phrases noted at one end and their equivalents in their native tongue at the other. New words are added to new cards and spare moments can be spent sifting through the pack and checking one's knowledge of their contents, withdrawing them as they are learned. The same device, using words and their meanings, is equally sound for increasing a vocabulary in one's native language or special field of study.

The act of writing things down is also valuable because it employs the motor senses as well: those memories that predominate in the learning of partly physical skills like typewriting, dancing, sports, or playing musical instruments; where, again, the use of other senses can greatly assist learning. Many simple drills performed by simple people are best learned by verbalizing the actions aloud, the simplest and most sickening example with depressing associations for so many of us being the concerted shout of "Hup, two, three!" Here, too, some roots may be found of the illusions created by the practice of rituals. . . .

Musicians with the task of memorizing an entire repertoire are an example of one group of learners who need to marshal all the relevant senses. Auditory learners may be able to memorize music more easily than visualizers, but both can do it better if they associate the bodily movements they make to produce the music with the music itself, and to continue associating them both when they read the music and when they "recite" it in imagination. The visual memory of what the music looks like will assist the visualizer just as the sound of it is recalled by the auditory learner.

But the mere juxtaposition of sense images at all stages of study is worth little without understanding. And understanding implies meaning. Where there is no obvious meaning, it must be sought; and if none can be found, perhaps a rhythm can be discovered. A good deal of scripture, especially Oriental scripture, is written rhythmically in its original language as an aid to rote learning and subsequent incantation. Where neither meaning nor rhythm can be discovered, then there may be a case for inventing a mnemonic, if not for asking whether the material needs to be memorized at all. A note in a pocket book is often just as good.

Paderewski, who as a young schoolboy could compose and improvise, could not memorize music until a teacher induced him to analyze the structure of a work independently of the piano, discussing the composer's intentions, understanding its rhythms and accompaniments, its moods and tones and how they were achieved.

Music is not quite so abstract as it seems, and neither is anything else. If some objective meaning cannot be extracted from study material, a subjective meaning has to be imposed on it. And with most of what we study, meaning can be both extracted and imposed, by systematic organization and the conscious association of new knowledge with what we know already. The exercises at the end of this chapter involve more than may be immediately apparent, for the act of reorganizing study material by condensation and tabulation, and the preparation of graphs and diagrams, involve all the processes of efficient learning.

Efficient learning, remember, means an appreciation of all the relevant applications of a single concrete example. That is why I have laid such emphasis on the importance of following the instructions in this book. For if you can learn by understanding all its contents and examples, you will also understand and apply to maximum advantage every kind of encounter you have as a reader with the written or printed word.

There is one indispensable element of the learning process that I have considered so far only in passing: the organism doing the learning. Clearly the efficient operation of that organism matters as much as the efficiency of the techniques it applies; in other words, our health can affect the efficiency of everything we do. For health read condition; and by condition I mean every state of the human organism from the acute to the chronic: that is, from momentary enthusiasm to youth and from momentary fatigue to old age. It must also be added that I mean both mental and physical condition, since popular thinking still insists on separating the two; and this condition is influenced more or less equally by our dietetic lives (including our caffeinic, alcoholic, nicotinic, and pharmaceutical intakes), our working lives, our use of leisure and our sleep, our sexual lives, the air we breathe, the things we look at, the noise we endure, the thoughts we have, our human relations, and—to reintroduce a phrase you will be meeting again—our underlying philosophy. I am fortunately not concerned, in this book at any rate, with guiding readers toward efficient living by discussing these factors in detail, though I have good reason for thinking that an all-around improvement in our reading ability has unpredictable repercussions in other departments of our lives. The totality of the individual organism, and, by extension, the unity of a species, implies that any real improvement in one sphere may be expected to result in improvement in others. Hence, however we specialize, we ought never to lose sight completely either of the intimate connection between our specialty and the rest of life, or of that between our way of life and the efficiency of our performance in any department of it.

There are, however, three matters closely associated with reading and studying that are worth discussing briefly here. They are fatigue, concentration, and aging. Further reading in all these subjects is recommended to anyone with reason to be especially concerned with them.

Fatigue can be momentary or prolonged and the result of any of a huge variety of causes. Its common factor is that it reduces the efficiency and increases the effort of whatever we are trying to do. If we have to draw on reserves of energy for emergency work, we may have to pay dearly for it. The commonest kind of fatigue associated with reading and learning comes of doing the same thing for too long at once. The coffee break is as important for the student as it is for the truck driver. There is a limit to the length of time that any of us can usefully concentrate upon one thing and it is foolish to try to ignore the fact. A few moments' change of activity may be rest enough in many circumstances, and from it we can return to the main task refreshed. The semiconscious lighting of a cigarette or pipe which many people say helps them to concentrate may really be providing them with a minor change of activity. Perhaps they could reduce, if not eliminate, their smoking if with every cigarette or fill of a pipe they asked themselves why they were doing it. If they took a short walk or a cup of coffee instead, or looked out of the window, or talked to someone, or made a telephone call, or merely daydreamed for a while, they might well find that it was enough to supply the concentration that had begun to flag. If we could regulate our lives to working for shorter periods, allowing more freedom to individual needs for rest and the individual demands of every piece of work, we might all work a good deal better. When I advise reading a book at a sitting, therefore, I do not mean a completely uninterrupted one. When a student is ad-

vised to forget his studies and enjoy himself on the night before
an examination, the advice is sound enough although the anxiety
generated by the examination usually prevents its being taken.
All study should be set aside briefly at the first signs of fatigue,
and this applies especially to mechanical memorizing, when the
drills should be kept short and the rests to do other things
adequate. The short-term avoidance of fatigue, together with
sufficient sleep, should prevent prolonged exhaustion, even after
long spells of exceptionally hard work.

This advice must be prudently balanced against the problem
of concentration. Wandering concentration is not necessarily a
sign of fatigue; it may be a weakening of the inclination to work,
which may have to be ignored or may need a renewal of incentive or a reorganization of working conditions. But given efficient
reading techniques, curiosity, and the other elements of efficient
learning, the concentration should improve of all but the most
scatterbrained. Although the amelioration of extremes of anxiety
may need the services of a psychotherapist, we can do a lot for
ourselves by consciously and systematically worrying out our
minor anxieties before starting work, or completing any task left
undone that may be disturbing us. Some minutes should always
be allowed for warming up at the beginning of a day and after
meals, during which time there may well be a reluctance to work,
wandering concentration, and other symptoms of pseudo fatigue.

One form of wandering concentration that troubles many
people is the train of thought set rolling by some provocative
statement or idea. It need not be avoided altogether, because it
may well be a necessary means of associating new knowledge
with the old and thus an essential part of comprehension and
learning. But many readers overindulge it as an only partly conscious habit, and for some it can become the positive vice of
arguing with the author's every statement. Any degree of it, of
course, will reduce the reading speed, and too much of it can
result in poor comprehension. The habit can be corrected by
becoming fully aware of its existence so that it may be employed
deliberately—but only after first paying the author the courtesy
of hearing him out. The vice might perhaps be purged by writing

down all the argumentative points as they arise, and then arguing with one's own arguments.

The greatest value of well-ordered questions and reflections is that they support the change that should take place in our learning methods as we grow older. All our functioning tends to become slower with age, but it need not lead to reduced efficiency in reading and learning. Students of mine past middle age who are faced with having to free themselves from the reading habits of a lifetime can be expected to take longer to show an improvement. But in general I have found them tenacious, thoughtful, aware of the fuller implications of basic principles, and, ultimately, able to make a permanent improvement. What research has been done on the effects of age upon learning ability is really much more inconclusive than popular imagination would have it. Old dogs can be taught some new tricks but they will probably have to be taught by new methods. Evidently, as breadth of experience replaces rapidity of functioning, different methods of presenting material are needed, different elements of the learning process must be emphasized and explored, and different criteria of learning must be offered.

(3,000 words)

EXERCISE 23

Without referring back to the text, write a summary of the foregoing chapter covering its main points. Mark your results as you do the following exercise.

EXERCISE 24

Using skimming techniques as much as possible, go through all of the foregoing section on learning (each of the last three chapters, but not the reading extracts) and make notes for study purposes of all the important points. Do the task as quickly as you can, but beware of making your notes so brief that they are incomprehensible after a few days. Make them in such a way that you could refer to them usefully years hence. Include in them a list of a dozen to fifteen rules for learning and memorizing. When you have finished, copy them out again, spreading them over large sheets of paper in an arrangement that makes them meaningful to you and easy to learn. Then rearrange all your other notes in tabular or diagrammatic form.

Do not read any more of this book for at least a week. If your other reading is progressing well, here are some suggestions for further reading, chosen as "basic" books which may suggest a profitable field in which to plan a formal course of study.

SUGGESTED PRACTICE READING (PART IV)

Mortimer J. Adler	*How to Read a Book*
Hannah Arendt	*The Human Condition*
Jacob Bronowski and	
Bruce Mazlish	*The Western Intellectual Tradition*
Selig Hecht	*Explaining the Atom*
Claire and W. M. S. Russell	*Human Behaviour*
H. G. Wells	*Outline of History*

A simple example from one of the livelier series of learning experiments, this one demonstrates the value of understanding principles.

Given five equal squares, change the position of three sides to make four equal squares. All sides must be used and no sides must be doubled.

TASK A   TASK B

One group of subjects were told what to do and given ten minutes to solve Task A. The few who did so were unable to solve Task B and after eight days had forgotten the solution of Task A.

A second group were told what to do and given Task A for two minutes. No solution. Task B was given for two minutes with no solution. Then the solution of Task A was shown as illustrated, but it was no help in solving Task B. Four of the same subjects were tested a week later and only one could solve Task A in two minutes.

A third group were given Task A and told the principle for solving it. The five squares are composed of only sixteen lines because some squares share a single side. To make four squares of the same sixteen sides, they must be arranged so that each side limits only one square. Those who understood the explanation quickly solved both tasks and after eight days most of them immediately solved them again.

(Adapted from *Organizing and Memorizing* by George Katona, Columbia University Press, 1940.)

PART V

AGGRESSIVE READING

·13·

Newspapers

MUCH OF THIS BOOK was shaped and written in an isolated village on the coast of a Greek island where I lived for a month in the summer of 1963 until I could endure the noise of its couple of hundred human and animal inhabitants no longer. For nearly two months, in fact, I did not see an English newspaper; and I never succeeded in learning to read Greek. But by word of mouth I was briefly apprised of three events: a nuclear test ban treaty, an earthquake, and a notorious suicide. What more would I know, I wonder, if I had stayed at home with the papers?

When Henry Miller visited Greece before the war, he too observed the absence of newspapers, and in that part of his frenzied fiction entitled *The Colossus of Maroussi*, he recorded it thus:

> The absence of newspapers, the absence of news about what men are doing in different parts of the world to make life more livable or unlivable is the greatest single boon. If we could just eliminate newspapers a great advance would be made, I am sure of it. Newspapers engender lies, hatred, greed, envy, suspicion, fear, malice. We don't need the truth as it is dished up to us in the daily papers. We need peace and solitude and idleness. If we could all go on strike and honestly disavow all interest in what our neighbor is doing we might get a new lease on life.

Well, perhaps. One sees his point, despite the pointlessness of the "if everyone" argument. (If we could all read more widely and urbanely we might understand our neighbor better and get a new lease on life. But we all never will; not at least this side of the visionary's future.)

There is something, however, in what Henry Miller says. Newspapers do give us a distorted and fragmented picture of life, trafficking as they do only in the extremes of drama, violence, and disease. It would be difficult to imagine them otherwise, though I confess I do sometimes toy with a dream of having enough money to run a newspaper that presents a balanced perspective of a community's life, giving as much prominence to the lives of those who dwell harmoniously and creatively among us as to the deeds of the powerful and the failed.

With the stark world picture we get from the papers, underscored by the other media of mass communication, it is almost impossible not to feel continuously whipped into a lather of anxiety about what has happened to someone else, what is going to happen to ourselves, and what might be going to happen if. And this anxiety, moreover, helps both to darken the picture and aggravate the habit of newspaper reading.

For with most of us it is a habit; and if we define a habit as any persistent practice which controls us, then it is one we would be better off without. This is not, I hasten to add, a case for eschewing newspapers altogether. Far from it. My purpose is to suggest ways of keeping them in proportion so that, given their proper place in the framework of a literate life, selectively read and perceptively evaluated, they can be used to deepen our understanding of the world we live in.

Modern life would probably not be possible without them, in any case. Once, after a period of three newsless months, I remember having felt that in a few more weeks I might have begun to miss them. I recall the widespread distress of the British newspaper dispute of 1959, when lending libraries ran short of books, fish and chip fryers had to buy brown paper, and we were all thrown back upon the restricted news coverage of the B.B.C. So, having established that newspapers are indispensable, let us examine some of the means by which they might be accommodated more prudently into our lives.

As with any other kind of printed matter, there are three ways to reduce the time spent reading the papers: to produce fewer of them; to read them more rapidly; and to read less of each one. Modern economics and television are helping with the first; your quicker reading ability ought to be helping with the second; and by the time you have finished this chapter, you should be well equipped to make good use of the third.

If you pride yourself on being adequately informed after a daily hour or two of reading your morning paper from first page to last, it should be possible to be no less well informed by the time you rise from the breakfast table. It need take no longer than ten or fifteen minutes to assimilate the contents of any single daily paper, perhaps with a few extra minutes set aside on some days for the occasional feature of special interest. A second daily, if you take one, should require still less time; and the weeklies need take only a little longer.

Of course, if you happen to enjoy reading almost every word of your paper, let me not disturb your pleasure. Though I may privately question your priorities, my only immediate concern is that you should be aware that you are merely entertaining yourself and that you do not try to justify your devotions in some loftier way. At least one popular newspaper king is on record as saying that the mass-circulation daily is a medium of mass entertainment, and no one needed telling the same of its Sunday counterpart.

As every journalist knows, any single issue of any paper is as ephemeral as marsh gas; only in accumulation, when the dust in which they are born has begun to settle on files of them, do they fit into a context of history, and their facts take on the shape and value of knowledge, the substance of memory. Turn out some old newspapers one day and see how much of their contents has any meaning for you. Better still, let me demonstrate my point with one of the exercises at the end of this chapter, in which you will be asked to recall and jot down everything you can remember from yesterday's paper.

What my case amounts to is that since no one, not even the most dedicated student of current affairs or the most vigilant critic of the press, could be expected to find more than a small proportion of the contents of any newspaper memorable, meaningful, or even noteworthy, it is more sensible to select, deliberately and methodically, only what interests you, and perhaps occupy the time saved by ignoring the rest with reflection on the significance of what you happen to find significant.

Newspapers are designed to help you with this, because they are aimed to interest all of the people some of the time. Separate pages or sections are usually set aside for features, finance, foreign news, fashion, the home, the arts, opinion, sport, and so on. The reader knows roughly what to expect on almost every page; beyond that, remember that decoration is only part of the function of headlines. The front page and the tops of the inside news pages are usually reserved for what subeditors consider to be most "newsworthy"; but the reader should be on his guard against allowing his own sense of proportion to be too much influenced by the news values of the press. News sense is as subjective as a sense of humor; and there may be more rejoicing in your heart at one filler paragraph about an unmarried mother finding a husband than with several columns with banner headlines about the breeding of royalty.

So the presentation of a newspaper is helpful only so far. For still finer sifting, you must use your skimming techniques and remember three further points which should help you to save both time and any last dregs of worry that you may be dealing with your paper too summarily and missing something vital. The first is an extension of the use of anticipation, when all your relevant knowledge of the subject about which you are reading is mustered for an attack on the material, arming you with the questions you want it to answer. We shall discuss and practice the method in the next chapter, for it is applicable to a wide range of material in addition to newspapers. The second technique to remember is one that employs a further element of newspaper presentation, and the third involves cultivating an attitude toward your newspaper reading that I call sophisticated and my brethren of the press would call cynical.

One of the first lessons every cub reporter must learn upon entering the trade is that the introductory paragraph of any news story he writes must contain the basic facts of the whole event, the who, what, where, and when, and if possible the why and how, together with its most "newsy" fact. (This is the start of the "inverted pyramid" structure discussed in Chapter Eight.) Of course, if ever the introduction, with sometimes the first few lines of the second paragraph, does not tell you all you need to know, the rest of the article is usually there to be read.

If, for any reason, you have ever been featured in a newspaper, did you feel that the result represented you faithfully? If anyone you know has had a similar experience, did they seek to repeat it? If you have ever read a newspaper report about something of which you have expert or intimate knowledge, was it correct in every detail? If the answer to any of these questions happens to be in the affirmative, do you take it for granted that it should be so? If, on the other hand, the answers are negative, did you seriously expect otherwise? Do you think that journalism ought somehow to contain a higher proportion of men and women of integrity and competence than any other occupation? If so, why? Because it bears a high degree of responsibility? But who invests it with all that responsibility? Or because it is a highly paid profession? In fact, it is not. There are big financial rewards at the very top, and high prices charged for them; but, as with most other branches of the entertainment industry, from just below the top downward the rewards are relatively poor and the job looks more exciting from without than from within.

Let us examine some of the simple mechanics of the job in order to understand a little of what can happen between a happening happening and a description of it appearing in print, always bearing in mind, of course, that no two people ever have exactly the same experience, whether they are watching it, hearing it, recalling it, reporting it, or merely reading it.

Recall, for a working example, the Australian soldier whose reading went with the wind. We have already considered how he might have been shown to have a reading rate amounting to eighty words a second; but between this rather commonplace fact and its dissemination in the *Guardian*, what happened? Here is the paragraph again, with its yesterday's dateline.

GONE WITH THE WIND?

Brisbane, September 20

An Australian soldier who took a 13-day course in "quick reading" can comfortably read *Gone with the Wind* before breakfast or Shakespeare's complete works in about two days—at 80 words a second—an army spokesman said here.—Reuter

First of all, what event are we reading about? The soldier settling down before breakfast to devour *Gone with the Wind*, or simply his demonstrated ability to read eighty words in every second? Neither, surely. All we are told is that an "army spokesman" said he did those things. But who was this gray eminence announcing the feat? How well did he know the soldier, or the business of "quick reading"? From where did he get his information? From the soldier himself, from the soldier's reading tutor, or from someone with an interest in selling a quick-reading course? We are not told. In what context did he report it? Was he giving a talk about the methods and results of quick-reading courses, was he lecturing authoritatively on some of the achievements of army education in Australia, or was he chatting informally about the increased pace of life in the modern Australian army, throwing out an odd piece of hearsay as an amusing example, without expecting it to be taken too seriously? Then to whom was he speaking? Evidently, among others, to a reporter. One of Reuter's own staff? Unlikely, unless the event was of national interest. In a place the size of Brisbane, the news agency would probably depend a good deal upon local reporters telephoning news to a head office, hoping to make some extra money from "linage," so called because payment is made for each line used. Hence the reporter may have telephoned a fuller report of the army spokesman's speech, which was cut by a Reuter subeditor before it was cabled to London. Suppose we give both the reporter and the gray eminence the benefit of all the doubt the paragraph raises. If neither of them was versed in the intricacies of adult reading behavior, as we are, is it not possible that the speaker said something more like this?

. . . and one soldier who took this thirteen-day course, it might amuse you all to know, is said to be reading at a rate of—er—four words in one-twentieth of a second or, if you prefer it, eighty words a second. And if that figure doesn't mean very much, either, you might say that he could comfortably get through a book like *Gone with the Wind* at this rate in a hundred and four minutes—before breakfast, as it were—and if he had a couple of days or so to spare, he could romp through the complete works of Shakespeare.

We have already observed that many more words are used in speech than in writing, so would it not be a fair paraphrase if the reporter condensed the speaker's words and telephoned something more like this from his notes?

After a 13-day course in quick reading, when he was able to read at a rate of 80 words a second, a soldier could comfortably get through a book like *Gone with the Wind* before breakfast, or Shakespeare's complete works in about two days, according to . . .

It is a long and rather badly balanced sentence, so a busy Reuter subeditor in Sydney or London could be forgiven for rearranging, punctuating, and refining it by deleting the few superfluous words remaining:

An Australian soldier who took a 13-day course in "quick reading" could comfortably read *Gone with the Wind* before breakfast . . .

At any stage during this long series of communications, one of the key words, *could,* could easily have become changed to *can*—or, if the speaker had said *could have read,* it might as well have become *can read.* The shorthand outlines are very similar, so perhaps the reporter misread his notes. The Reuter news telephonist might have misheard, the subeditor might have misread, the telegraphist might inadvertently have changed or omitted the word. And if none of these things happened, there remain the normal hazards of the *Guardian*'s printers and proofreaders and, last of all, the reader himself, with his good will and accuracy. (In case it should be thought that I have misquoted the paragraph, be assured that I have the original cutting in my possession.)

Throughout this series of suppositions, moreover, I have taken for granted that everyone concerned, from the army spokesman onward, acted in good faith and was normally sober, conscientious, responsible, and efficient at his job; that the reporter could write good shorthand, that the telephone line from Brisbane was working at its best, that the news telephonist was not distracted by background noise or someone bringing him a cup of tea, that all the subeditors who handled the story were efficient readers, and that no one was trying to work at a pace twice as fast as is humanly feasible. Indeed, perhaps they arrange things so in Australia. . . .

It is possible, of course, to subject every paragraph in every paper to a similar scrutiny, or "probe," as the papers themselves would have it—perhaps every printed word everywhere. Sometimes it may be important enough to do so, as lawyers well know, but one cannot treat every communication one receives as if it said, "The enemy is dancing on a wet plank; send three and four-pence." (This message was sent by word of mouth from man to man along a fighting line and originated as "The enemy is advancing on the left flank; send reinforcements.") One must take some things on trust. Hence I would not like to be credited with asserting that everything we read in the papers is wildly and willfully untrue. A little may be, for although not everything is sensationalized and probably nothing is completely unauthenticated, stories can be colored to make them more "readable" or amusing, to place the surprising or improbable in an everyday context with which the reader can identify himself:

Motorists driving home in the rain through Tokyo's rush hour yesterday jammed on their brakes when they heard a woman's scream . . .

Jean-Pierre Lavalle went home to his luxury flat in Algiers last night and took off his coat in the tiny black-and-gold hall. It had been a hard day at the office. . . .

I remember a notorious report in the London *Daily Express* at the time of the disappearance into Russia of the British diplomats Burgess and Maclean. "Mrs. Maclean smiled," the paper declared, although the reporter had talked to her only on the telephone. More news than we realize is gathered by telephone, with all the limitations it imposes on accurate communication, and one can often read news items in which a pretty piece of description or an intrusive "human angle" might as easily have been supplied by the reporter's or subeditor's imagination as by "objective" fact.

I was once walking in Fleet Street with a professional acquaintance after he had entertained me to an expense-account lunch and pocketed a copy of the bill which the waiter had volunteered to increase, fictitiously, for the deception of my colleague's firm's accountant. My host hailed a well-known columnist and congratulated him on a series of features he had recently sent back from abroad, describing the adventures of an elaborate circulation stunt arranged by his paper. "Ha," he laughed over his shoulder as he hurried on, "you must hear the true story sometime."

I have only once known a reporter admit to inventing an eyewitness's comment to enliven a dull report, adding a fictitious name and vague address. But perhaps one could argue that even the manufactured "news" item, the sensationalized trifle, the photographer's stunt of a Godiva on horseback in Piccadilly Circus, hastily photographed and bundled into a coat and a Jaguar before the police awake to what is happening, all have their own perverse measure of the truth.

The words *Fact is sacred; comment is free* are supposed to be chipped into the heart of every newspaperman. But between the heaven and hell of fact and comment stretches a vast misty limbo of selective description, in which brightness is sacred, imagination is free, and the sole commandment is "Thou shalt give the public what it wants."

Ever since I was a very young journalist I have found my face set against the dogma that what the public wants should be the criterion of good journalism. No journalist has ever succeeded in persuading me that he knew who the public was, let alone what it wanted. And every journalist I ever knew, however noble and resonant the sound of his justifications, seemed to me to be merely pleasing himself. There is a significant contradiction between the view that newspapers are influential, educational, an indispensable contribution to progress and the common good, bastions of freedom, blabs of blab, and the persistent refusal of those who hold this belief to address themselves to anyone other than the lowest common denominator of thirty years ago. It has, I am sure, something to do with an assumption that circulation is synonymous with the number of readers, and a confusion between readership and influence. If the influence of popular newspapers is in decline, perhaps it is because those who produce them have become so caught up in the high-speed, ulcer-making vortex of circulation, competition, man biting dog and dog eating dog, that they have lost sight of who their readers are and failed to notice that they have had a little influence, contributing to a slow process of mass education through which the average literate citizen has become a little less easily deceived, more demanding, with standards a little higher, and a slightly greater ability to ignore hidden persuaders and manage his own affairs.

And there are dangers in any loss of identification by newspapers with their readers. For in spite of all the screaming and thundering, the vicarious drama and fomented indignation, the lather of anxiety and the ceaseless titillation of moribund appetites, there are still times when the vigilance of the press, which needs to be as persistent as that of the public health authorities toward the biological plagues and epidemics that lurk always in our midst, is all we have to warn us that our social health, our few joys and freedoms, can always be savaged or overrun by Grundys and bureaucrats, jackboots and judges, and all those other omnipresent and once-human miseries whose existence is so fearful and joyless that their only rest can be found after making everyone else more enslaved and terrorized than they themselves. It is not for nothing that one of the first acts of any totalitarian government is to silence or muzzle the opposition press.

My point, as it has been by implication throughout this book, is simply that the printed word everywhere, and especially in newspapers, ought to be taken with a spoonful or two of the salt of that urbanity of likelihood, that worldly wisdom of reasonable expectation, that comes from wide and efficient reading, balanced by a creative use of personal experience. One last warning word. If, when you toss tomorrow's paper aside as you rise from the breakfast table, you think of canceling your order with your news agent, as I have been disturbed to discover some of my evening students have done after a display of my mode of newspaper reading, please ask yourself one question. Have you been reading me now as uncritically as once you read the papers?

(3,650 words)

EXERCISE 25

Choose the best answer to each question.

1. The chapter you have just read was:
   a. a scurrilous attack upon the press;
   b. a libel on the integrity of journalists;
   c. an attempt to provoke the reader into examining his habitual attitudes to newspapers;
   d. a lighthearted discussion of something most people take too seriously.
2. The efficient newspaper reader, the author asserts:
   a. reads papers mostly over other people's shoulders;
   b. is well informed about current affairs in a few minutes of daily reading;
   c. tosses his paper aside after breakfast;
   d. treats everything he reads with suspicion.
3. Every reader of newspapers, the author implies, either makes use of techniques like those described, or could profitably train himself to do so.
   a. There are no exceptions.
   b. Except journalists.
   c. Except professional critics of the press.
   d. Except students of current affairs.
4. A realistic aim of those who produce newspapers is to:
   a. interest some of the people all of the time;
   b. entertain all of the people all of the time;
   c. interest all of the people some of the time;
   d. give the public what it wants.

5. The author quotes Henry Miller:
   a. with approval;
   b. as an extreme viewpoint worth consideration;
   c. to illustrate the joys of living in Greece;
   d. to show how hostile some people can be toward newspapers.
6. We can conclude that the paragraph about the Australian soldier's reading ability:
   a. ought never to have been printed like that;
   b. was unavoidably mangled beyond recognition;
   c. sounded improbable, so should have been read with judgment suspended, pending further evidence;
   d. was a good example of the way things get distorted.
7. The anecdotes about journalists' behavior are intended to show that:
   a. there is every reason to be on our guard against reading our papers uncritically;
   b. journalists are only human like the rest of us;
   c. some journalists are corrupt and irresponsible and the reader cannot know which;
   d. the author has experience of what he is talking about.
8. The author argues that newspapers are:
   a. concerned mainly with the violent and sensational;
   b. in spite of many understandable shortcomings, valuable watchdogs over our liberties;
   c. invested with too much responsibility by all their readers;
   d. concerned to give the public what it wants.
9. One may infer that the author's view of Kipling's lines:

   > He hath sold his heart to the old Black Art
   > We call the Daily Press

   would be that they are:
   a. unreasonably hostile;
   b. tragic but true;
   c. perceptive and sympathetic;
   d. an understatement of the truth.
10. The main idea of this chapter is:
    a. A cursory but methodical skimming and reading of the papers is enough to keep us informed, especially as the conditions in which they are produced make it inadvisable to take them too studiously.
    b. A newspaper is not worth reading past breakfast time

because the reader has no means of knowing how much of it is accurate or reliable.

c. If there were no more newspapers, the loss would not be so very great providing we ourselves are vigilant in the protection of our liberties.

d. A daily paper requires no more than ten minutes' reading because large sections of the press have lost touch with their readers who, although still comparatively ill-educated, deserve more respect for their intelligence than they get.

The following three newspaper articles should be read at top speed, much faster than anything you have read in this book so far. Try to double your present speed, paying only scant attention to details of comprehension. This is the only time that I shall suggest allowing speed to take precedence over comprehension; but such an experiment at this stage may help you to break through some remaining inhibitions or consolidate your confidence. As the questionnaires following each passage are very simple, the exercises may also stand as illustrations of the kind of material that I have described as being used in "rapid-reading" schools to delineate students' progress.

Remember to spend half a minute skimming through each article before you begin it, getting an idea of its structure and anticipating its subject matter. The first article is 600 words in length and the others contain 900 words. You should aim to spend less than two minutes reading each, and try to take each one quicker than the one before.

READING EXERCISE

Strength Out of Misery

BY D. W. WINNICOTT

The term "depression" has a popular as well as a professional psychiatric meaning. The two are much alike.

The affective state of depression carries with it hypochondria and introspection. The depressed person is therefore aware of feeling awful and also aware to an exaggerated degree of heart, lungs and liver, and of rheumatic pains.

It is clear that depressed people suffer, that they may hurt themselves or end their lives, and that some of them are psychiatric casualties. I believe, however, that depression also has value because it has within itself the germ of recovery.

Depression, like mourning, tends eventually to finish its job. The built-in tendency to recover also links depression with the maturing process in infancy and childhood.

In the beginning the infant is the environment, and the environment is the infant. By a complex process the infant separates the environment from the self. A complex interchange between what is inside and outside now begins and continues throughout the individual's life.

In the course of emotional development, *ego structure* and *strength* gradually become a fact, and the new individual becomes less and less dependent on the environment as he moves toward independence. At first the ego has strength only because of the support given by the adapting mother.

There now comes a stage at which the child has become a unit, becomes able to feel "I AM." The child has now an inner psychic reality and is capable of containing the strains and stresses that arise in the course of living: he has *become able to be in a depressed mood*. This is an achievement of emotional growth.

The prime cause of the depressed mood is a new experience of destructiveness and of destructive ideas that go with loving. This necessitates internal reassessment, and it is this reassessment we see as depression.

Unconscious hate is locked up somewhere in all this. Perhaps the difficulty is in accepting such repressed hate, even though the depressed mood implies that hate is under control. It is the clinical effort of the control that we are seeing as the depressed mood.

The personal inner psychic reality has a complex and everchanging organization, and the resolution of a mood is a matter of the rearrangement of good and bad elements in the inner reality.

Depression coming on, continuing and lifting, indicates that the ego structure has held over a phase of crisis. This is a triumph of integration.

It is no good offering cheer to a depressed person or jogging the depressed child up and down, offering sweetmeats and pointing to the trees and saying, "See the lovely shimmering green leaves." To the depressed person the tree looks dead and the leaves are still. Or there are no leaves and there is only the black and blasted heath and the barren landscape. We only make fools of ourselves if we offer good cheer.

On the other hand a really good persecution may make a difference—threat of war, for instance, or a spiteful nurse in the mental hospital, or a piece of treachery. Here the external bad phenomenon can be used as a place for some of the internal badness, and produce relief by taking over the inner tensions. But one can hardly prescribe evil.

But one can help a depressed person best by adopting a principle of tolerating the depression until it lifts spontaneously, and by paying tribute to the fact that it is only the spontaneous recovery that feels truly satisfactory to the individual. The individual is often a stronger person than he or she was before becoming depressed.

Observer
May 31, 1964
(560 words)

EXERCISE 26A

Choose the best answer to each question.

1. Depression, according to the writer, is invariably associated with:
    a. both popular and psychiatric ideas;
    b. a crisis;
    c. hypochondria and introspection;
    d. the maturing process in infancy.
2. He argues that depression has value because:
    a. its sufferers are not all psychiatric casualties;
    b. it helps one to be aware of one's heart, lungs and liver;

    c. it contains the germ of recovery, which may result in the
        individual becoming a stronger person;
    d. it can happen at any time in one's life.

3. When a child becomes depressed, it is most often best seen as:
    a. the beginning of a complex interchange between the ego
        and the environment;
    b. a stage in the process of growing up;
    c. a warning that he may become destructive;
    d. a sign that the mother has withdrawn her support at the
        wrong moment.

4. What outwardly appears as depression, the writer argues, is
really:
    a. the result of an attempt to control the destructive feelings
        that arise in a period of internal reassessment;
    b. an exaggerated awareness of internal organs and rheumatic
        pains;
    c. a triumph of integration;
    d. a hypochondriacal condition.

5. The resolution of a depression is a matter of:
    a. attaining a sense of one's own psychic reality;
    b. projecting one's internal tensions onto an external bad
        phenomenon;
    c. getting one's feelings of hatred under control;
    d. successfully rearranging the good and bad elements of one's
        inner world.

6. Depression tends to finish its job, the writer says. In this sense he
compares it with:
    a. mourning;
    b. loving;
    c. recovery from illness;
    d. an outburst of anger.

7. The writer suggests that the best way to help a depressed person
is to:
    a. cheer him up by pointing out that the world is not such
        a bad place;
    b. shock him with a threat of persecution;
    c. tolerate the depression until it lifts spontaneously;
    d. remind him that he will feel better when it has passed.

8. One may infer that the writer is:
    a. a minister of religion;
    b. a psychoanalyst;

    c. a philosopher;

    d. a women's magazine writer.

9. One may suppose that the article was published in order to:

    a. analyze a common problem found in medical and daily life;

    b. help the reader to understand himself and others better when passing through a difficult period;

    c. tell people that they usually do the wrong thing when they try to help the depressed;

    d. throw new light on an old subject.

10. The main idea of the article is:

    a. Depression is such a widespread phenomenon that it is important to find some good in it.

    b. The onset and eventual resolution of a depression are the outward manifestations of a period of internal reassessment often resulting in the individual becoming a stronger person.

    c. There are times in life when cheerful behavior is foolish.

    d. Whenever one succeeds in passing through a depression, one is justified in asserting "I AM."

READING EXERCISE

What It's Like to Attend a Hanging

"I always loathed and detested the whole business," said the former British prison governor, "so emotionally I'm an abolitionist. But honestly I don't know what the alternative is. Life imprisonment is the most dreadful thing. I could never stand the long-term prisoners. A man gets institutionalized: he can't decide anything for himself any more. Everything slows down for the last couple of years of a long sentence.

"There's no doubt at all, of course, that hanging's no deterrent. That's the stupidest argument there is. If anyone comes to me with that one, I tell them, 'It's a deterrent for you. But you're a normal person and you're not likely to commit murder anyway. Murderers are abnormal.'

"Most of them want to be hanged, you know. A murderer accepts his fate. He's apt to be an exhibitionist, anyway. He asks if his name's in the paper and that sort of thing. But hanging a spy is a different matter. It can be pretty messy because he'll fight. He's a normal man, you see.

"I remember having to tell one man he'd been reprieved. Do you know, he went for me. Really attacked me. Took him weeks to get reorientated afterwards, once he knew he had to live. He managed it all right eventually, as far as I know.

"The first hanging I ever attended was when I was an acting governor. I must say I was surprised at myself. I suppose I'd made up my mind to it, because there was no shock, no after effects at all. But the governor, he was in a dreadful state. Last person you'd expect: one of the old school of governors, you know, ex-Guards officer and all that. A tough, hard man, he was—but he needed a couple of brandies before he could go through with it." The retired governor laughed heartily.

"I had to visit the man twice a day, and I didn't like that a bit. I had butterflies all the time. I told the chaplain how I felt, and he gave me a lecture about it. The parsons don't mind a bit, you know. Like the officers, such as the engineer who sees that the lever's working the bolts properly. They don't mind a hoot. Among themselves they call it 'topping.' I saw a couple of them come away laughing. No one minded except the governor.

"The officers used to give me the impression that it was all part of the job. Anyone who couldn't stand it wouldn't go into the Prison Service in the first place. Like the governors. There are plenty who don't like it, even one or two Quakers. I don't know how they manage. I suppose they find it's a duty and get on with it."

The ex-governor explained that the effect on the prisoners was different: an atmosphere he hated. But he was talking of the days when prisoners were confined to their cells during executions. Nowadays their working routine is not interrupted. The burial within the prison walls is carried out during the dinner break.

"I don't think they should hang people in prisons at all," said the ex-governor. "If they must do it, there ought to be an abattoir. But it would be very expensive, and I suppose there'd be an outcry about that."

He told me about the rehearsals with a sack beforehand, the

careful estimates of the length of the drop in relation to the condemned man's weight and height. "No, it's not just the hangman's estimate. Everyone has a go at it." He emphasized the care taken to see that death—usually by fracture dislocation of cervical vertebrae—was instantaneous. "The heart may continue beating for up to twenty minutes," reported a Commission on Capital Punishment, "but this is a purely automatic function."

The ex-governor did not describe how the waxed hempen rope, one inch in diameter and between fourteen and twenty-two feet long (depending on the prison), was fitted to an adjustable chain hung from an overhead beam, and secured at the correct height by a piece of thread that breaks with the fall. I already knew how two prison officers stand by the double trap door to hold the victim as he stands on a chalk mark across the division of the trap, that the assistant executioner's job is to pinion the legs while the executioner places a white hood over the head and secures the leather-covered noose in position by a sliding ring with the knot drawn tight under the left lower jaw.

There were other minute details I wanted to know, like the appearance of the execution chamber, the depth of the pit, whether the sun shone in the window, or the most harrowing moment of the obscene ritual.

"Oh, I can't remember now," said the ex-governor cheerfully. "I remember the trap door seemed to take up most of the floor space and I had to stand by the wall. It's all over so quickly, you know. The hangman and his assistant go into the condemned cell, the man's hands are pinioned behind his back, then one-two-three-four-five-six" (he counted in pairs of seconds) "—and bang! It's all over. I think the man's head disappeared below the floor, and then the doctor hopped down the steps into the pit to make sure he was dead." The body is left hanging for an hour.

"Afterwards Pierrepoint came up and asked me, 'Do you agree, sir, that it was done most expeditiously?' That was the way he had of talking, you know. 'I could have done it a little quicker, sir, but I hope you will agree it was quite expeditious and efficient.'" It was the same Albert Pierrepoint who told the Commission: "It's sacred to me."

"One thing I will say," said the ex-governor finally, "I can't think of a better way of getting rid of a man if you have to. It's most efficiently done."

Time and Tide
May 23, 1961
(900 words)

EXERCISE 26B

Choose the best answer to each question.

1. This article appears to have been written by someone who:
   a. believes that capital punishment should be abolished;
   b. believes it should be retained;
   c. cares neither way but thinks it worth discussing;
   d. wants to see an alternative to life imprisonment.
2. The speaker quoted is:
   a. a retired prison governor;
   b. a retired prison warden;
   c. an acting prison governor;
   d. a former member of the Commission on Capital Punishment.
3. Hanging, according to the speaker, is:
   a. better than life imprisonment;
   b. a deterrent to others;
   c. no deterrent;
   d. an obscene ritual.
4. Most murderers, according to the speaker:
   a. put up a fight;
   b. would do it again if they had a chance;
   c. want to be hanged;
   d. fight if they are told of a reprieve.
5. Prison chaplains, according to the speaker:
   a. hate hangings more than anyone;
   b. seem not to mind a bit;
   c. speak of it as "topping";
   d. take it as part of the job.
6. In the speaker's opinion, executions should be carried out, if at all:
   a. during the dinner break;
   b. as efficiently as possible;

    c. in a special abattoir;

    d. without the other prisoners knowing.

7. The hangman Pierrepoint told the Commission that:

    a. the job was sacred to him;

    b. he disliked the job, but someone had to do it;

    c. he could do it a little quicker;

    d. he left the body hanging for an hour.

8. The speaker's manner while he talked to the author of the article seems to have been:

    a. helpful and cheerful;

    b. vastly amused;

    c. angry and indignant;

    d. coldly scientific.

9. One may infer that the details of hanging method and materials are included in the article because they are:

    a. sensational, making it more worth reading;

    b. a way of indicating the ritualistic nature of the practice;

    c. instructive, and too few people know them;

    d. worth remembering.

10. The main idea of the article is:

    a. Hanging may be an objectionable procedure, but it is necessary.

    b. Hanging is the most efficient way of getting rid of a man if you have to.

    c. Not everyone with experience of working in a prison wants hanging retained.

    d. Hanging is a barbaric ritual which most civilized countries have abandoned, and some alternative to capital punishment must be found.

READING EXERCISE

Reading at the Double

BY COLIN MARES

When highly educated industrialists, businessmen and senior Government officials, headed by the Lord Privy Seal, find it necessary to go back to school to learn how to read effectively, one is justified in wondering how this situation arises.

PART FIVE: AGGRESSIVE READING

According to a 1956 report, which remains largely true today, one school-leaver in four, in England, is a backward reader (the position in America is even worse).

In fact, most people adopt a way of reading that is far below the level of speed and comprehension at which they might read pleasurably and efficiently. By developing certain physical skills the adult reader can be made to use his reading potentialities to the full, thereby increasing his speed, creating greater efficiency of comprehension and considerably less fatigue.

WORD GROUPS

Good reading is basically a process where word groups form thought units which, in turn, are put together for comprehension. Training is therefore given in keener perception to develop the ability to interpret large word groups. Eye movement is reduced and eyespan is increased by improving the use of the peripheral vision.

Mechanical aids, though not essential, are used in the development of these largely physical skills. The tachistoscope—a machine for flashing digits, words and phrases on a screen at speeds varying from one second to one hundredth of a second—is one. Another, the reading-rate controller, or reading accelerator, moves a shutter down over a page revealing each line to the reader at a speed that can be exactly regulated to his needs. Reading films are also widely used.

One important characteristic of slow and inefficient reading is the habit of saying words silently to oneself while reading. Until this sound barrier is broken the speed at which a person reads can rarely be much faster than his speed of speaking.

"Regression" is another word frequently used in reading courses and much work is done to cure the common habit of letting the eyes return to words and phrases previously read.

But, in the best courses, probably more time is devoted to other essential skills. These include making the student proficient in picking out the central idea of each paragraph and in separating main ideas from less important details. Both general and specialized vocabularies are developed and skills such as "skimming" (the selective skipping of non- or less-essential matter) and "scanning" (searching for specific information) are also taught.

Reputable reading courses always stress the need for a flexible approach to reading, with emphasis on the use of varied reading techniques for different purposes and at different levels of complexity. They also stress that reading without adequate comprehension is completely useless.

On the evidence available, the old-time advice to "read it slowly and carefully" appears to be completely misleading. Careful reading does not have to be slow, and slow reading is frequently ineffective, fatiguing and time-wasting.

To achieve "quicker reading" the British Institute of Management runs regular courses, and several industrial firms such as Leyland Motors and the Carborundum Company, as well as a few technical colleges, offer similar courses largely for people in managerial and executive positions.

The Staff College of the National Coal Board has been running courses since 1958 and claimed in 1960 that after nine hours of instruction spread over six weeks some students had attained reading speeds of 3,000 words a minute.

In sharp contrast a voluntary course for Foreign Office officials aims modestly (and perhaps diplomatically) only to emulate the Prime Minister's reported reading speed of 500 words a minute.

COMPREHENSION TEST

And in America, most universities, colleges, business concerns and government departments offer their students or executives some form of training. Numerous reports claim that reading speeds of several thousand words a minute can be attained but these claims depend for their validity on the definition of "reading."

This usually implies the apprehension, not necessarily of each individual word, but certainly of each group of words. So far as this definition is concerned it is a physiological impossibility to read at more than 800 or 900 words a minute though there must be some modifications depending on the complexity of the material and the comprehension required.

It is also notable that whenever demonstrations of really fast reading speeds are given, the comprehension is never properly assessed.

Very high speeds invariably refer not to reading but to "skimming" and "scanning." There is nothing new about these techniques and they have been used effectively by many people who have never heard of "quicker-reading" courses.

These criticisms do not invalidate the fact that reading courses provide an essential service. The quality of a person's mind depends largely on what he reads and what he is capable of reading. The teaching of reading should not stop at the mechanics of the subject. Learning to read should be a continuous and never-ending process, not only to enable people to deal with the complexities of modern life but also for the satisfying pleasure that efficient reading gives.

Sunday Telegraph
May 30, 1962
(900 words)

EXERCISE 26C

Choose the best answer to each question.

1. The proportion of school-leavers who are backward readers is said to be:
    a. one in ten;
    b. half;
    c. a quarter;
    d. 75 per cent.
2. Reputable reading courses, according to the writer:
    a. develop largely physical skills;
    b. claim reading speeds of 3,000 words a minute;
    c. stress flexible reading and adequate comprehension;
    d. are given to industrialists, businessmen, and senior Government officials. ˙
 3. The schools and colleges mentioned in the article offer courses like those described mainly for:

a. backward readers;
b. people in managerial and executive positions;
c. people who are willing to revolutionize their reading habits;
d. industrialists, businessmen, and senior Government officials.

4. The validity of claims of reading speeds of several thousand words a minute, according to the article, depends on:
   a. a special definition of "reading";
   b. long and arduous practice;
   c. the use of the reading accelerator;
   d. a variety of mechanical aids.

5. Careful reading, the writer of the article says:
   a. does not exceed 800 or 900 words a minute;
   b. is old-time advice;
   c. implies good comprehension;
   d. need not be slow.

6. Very high speeds, the writer says, invariably mean:
   a. something that is physiologically impossible;
   b. disreputable reading courses;
   c. skimming and scanning;
   d. an extensive use of the tachistoscope.

7. The most likely reason for the Foreign Office officials aiming only to emulate the Prime Minister's reported 500 words a minute was that:
   a. they were taking a reputable reading course;
   b. it would be undiplomatic to read faster than the P.M.;
   c. the Prime Minister at that time was an ex-publisher, and publishers know what efficient reading is;
   d. by the nature of their work, Foreign Office officials ought to read extra carefully.

8. The average untrained reader with little knowledge of the subject of the article ought to read it:
   a. at top speed;
   b. with reasonable care;
   c. with suspicion because it may be inaccurate;
   d. as if it were authoritative.

9. One may infer that the author of this book would regard the article with:
   a. gratitude;
   b. mild approval;
   c. disapproval;
   d. incredulity.

10. The main idea of the article is:
    a. Many quick-reading courses claim very high speeds, but the reputable courses emphasize flexibility and good comprehension.
    b. Because reading is such an important part of an educated life, the courses that teach people to do it more efficiently are providing an essential service.
    c. When people like the Lord Privy Seal need to be taught to read effectively, one wonders what has happened.
    d. Most people adopt inefficient reading habits and a great deal can be done to improve them.

PRACTICE EXERCISES WITH NEWSPAPERS

1. Make a note of all the facts you can remember from yesterday's paper. Do not expect to jot them down all together in about ten minutes; think about it for a couple of hours while you are doing other things and make your notes as you remember, observing, if you can, anything that may have prompted you to remember. When you have recalled all you can, skim through the paper and check, observing what you omitted and what prominence was given to what you remembered.

2. Repeat the exercise on this morning's paper. Then do it again tomorrow with what you remember of the same paper, observing whether you are recalling what you read, what you wrote, or what you found on checking back.

3. Read tomorrow's paper, employing the techniques and attitudes discussed in the foregoing chapter. Try to do so without thinking that you are going to test yourself later. Then before you settle down to read the next chapter, repeat exercise 1 just above noting whether your methods helped you to recall more or less.

4. Take any two different newspapers of the same date and compare them in such a way as to note:
    a. three news items in each that do not appear in the other;

b. three facts or figures that differ significantly between one paper and the other;

c. three examples of comment or opinion that contradict each other about the same event;

d. three items appearing in both papers in which description is used in such a way as to color your impression of the event, differently in each case, while adding little or nothing of importance to your knowledge;

e. one news report that corresponds in every important respect with the report in the other paper.

5. Take any copy of any paper and find in it:

a. three quotations attributed to an unnamed "spokesman" or other gray eminence implying that they represent the supposed views or expert knowledge of some legal abstraction, e.g., the Bell Telephone Company or the U.S. Marines;

b. three examples of the news item artificially "worked up" from almost nothing, or of "informed" speculation or prognostication about something which has not yet happened, leaving you as wise as you were beforehand (albeit perhaps a little more worried);

c. three pieces of information that make you feel your day has been brightened by acquiring them, and that the world is not such a bad place, after all;

d. three facts or ideas which, if you had not read them, would have left you more ignorant or in any significant way worse off than you are now, having read them;

e. any statement made in such a way as to reveal the writer's presumption that you, the reader, would share one or more of the following attitudes:

    i. you are a Christian;

    ii. baseball is the national pastime;

    iii. American is best;

    iv. the Russians are wrong;

    v. murderers must be executed;

    vi. criminals must be punished;

    vii. everyone wants to make money;

   viii. cats/dogs/zoo inmates are lovable creatures;
    ix. morals are in decline;
     x. adultery is wrong.

Repeat these exercises *ad lib.* on a variety of different newspapers whenever you read about a proposal to improve the standards of journalism or any attempt to persuade you to take your favorite daily more earnestly.

·14·

Reports

My task in this chapter is nothing less than that of reminding you of everything you know. Not just everything you know about reading, but everything you know about everything. If you have ever reflected upon your own ignorance, no doubt you have been shaken by its extent. But the greater our sense of ignorance, the greater our body of knowledge probably is; and perhaps we may usefully take heart from that paradox and begin cultivating a discreet consciousness of what that knowledge amounts to. By doing so, we may use it more effectively to increase it.

However little you actually know, it is still a staggering amount. To have acquired this book and read its first page alone implies a body of knowledge always available to you which, ordered and written down, would fill a small library. Let us begin to list that knowledge. You know at least one language and you can read it and recognize it in print at a glance. If you have been using this book properly, you will have an idea by now of what a formidable achievement that is. You can handle at least one nation's currency; you can count; you can measure up to a certain quantity, down to a certain quantity, and with a certain degree of accuracy. You can count in several archaic systems of measurement if you live in the English-speaking world, but perhaps you need to be a foreigner to have an idea of what a formidable achievement that is. You probably know what a library and a bookshop are, and how to reach at least one of each. You may well know the difference between a book, a journal, a magazine, and a newspaper; although of course there are some people, whose experience and decisions have chanced to be different from yours, who do not. That knowledge alone took you several years of steady learning to acquire. Shall we say between five and eight?

All this knowledge, and a great deal more, was engaged before you even opened this book. How much went into choosing this book in the first place? How much into the decision to read it? How much more was required to understand the first page? Perhaps I need not try to detail any of it; the point is made. All of it, of course, is knowledge that you take for granted, much of it passing under the name of experience. And in this basic sense, life would hardly be possible if the entire history of every act, from breathing onward, were apparent upon performing it. Self-consciousness can be reduced to absurdity, if not insanity, like everything else.

But although we must take most of our knowledge for granted, there are many everyday acts and experiences which would be ineffective or meaningless if we did not consciously muster to our aid some part of our existing knowledge. Experience becomes knowledge when it is evaluated; and only as knowledge is it consciously usable. It may be by virtue of trained reflexes that you can change gear while motoring without thinking about it, or through habit that you opened and began reading this book from the beginning; but you would be a remarkable student if already you can change gear while reading without ever thinking about it, and mistaken if you say you can appreciate the Australian soldier's alleged feat without consciously recalling something from your existing body of knowledge. Dare I disinter the Australian soldier again? Yes, why not? He is already part of our experience. What would his feat have meant to you if you had never heard of *Gone with the Wind*, if you believed that the Sonnets were Shakespeare's complete works, or if you thought that everyone breakfasted only on the first of every month?

A persistent underlying theme of this book has been the truism that we perform everything with a competence directly related to our knowledge of what we are doing, and that, in the long run, the more we know about how we do anything, the more efficiently we do it. Even breathing or circulating the blood, as some adepts of yoga and other religious disciplines will assure us, can be brought under control and so done more efficiently. But most of us are satisfied with the moderate autonomic efficiency of these and similar functions for a sizable part of our expected lives, because the run toward performing them better is too long and single-minded, and we have chosen instead to devote our energies to other more social skills and disciplines. But whatever our choice, it is invaluable to know how we read and learn, in order to do both more effectively, and the value of preparing to read anything by mustering all the facts relevant to it from our existing knowledge is that it helps us to read more quickly and easily still.

To that end, therefore, it is not only necessary for me to administer a corrective to the superstition that words are sacred and to the consequent widespread humility toward the printed word that regards it by right as more authoritative than the testimony of a friend or than any knowledge communicated to us by any other means. It is also important to inculcate an attitude of cooperation between reader and author, a relationship in which the reader takes a more active role than his accustomed one, attacking the author's work in such a way as to demand that he answer the questions the reader's existing knowledge has enabled him to pose.

Reconsider for a moment your last timed reading passage. Suppose you had actually come across it in the *Sunday Telegraph*.

What's this? *Reading at the Double.* Another piece on that subject? Looks like it. I wonder if it's more believable than that gimmicky one in—what was it? Should be; it's the *Sunday Telegraph*. And Colin Mares . . . yes, he's usually pretty dependable. Well, what's his angle on the subject? Rapid reading, or quicker comprehension? It's not long enough to tell you much, certainly not how to do it. Probably it's just information about what's being done. Let's skim through it and see. . . .

Businessmen back to school—school-leavers—backward readers —most people below efficient—good reading is—mechanical aids (oh, yes) films—saying words—regression—the best courses (yes, I see) reputable reading courses—without adequate comprehension is completely useless—British Institute of Management, National

Coal Board, Foreign Office (ah, British, of course)—America (mentioned briefly)—800 or 900 words a minute (but does he say how that is possible? Must read it for that)—very high speeds— criticism (ah!) satisfying pleasure that efficient reading gives. . . .

Now what else do I want to know? What mechanical aids does he mention? How are they regarded? What are the best courses? Where do they hold them? Only in Britain, I guess. With what results, then? High speeds or better comprehension or both? Is it likely to tell me where I can find the best course in America? Probably not . . .

I see. . . . Yes. . . . Yes . . . yes . . . oh, yes . . . improving peripheral vision—tachistoscope . . . yes . . . yes . . . reading-rate controller . . . yes . . . I see. Ah, the central idea of each para- graph—separating main ideas from less important details—skim- ming and scanning—a flexible approach to reading—different pur- poses and at different levels of complexity. Um, yes . . . yes . . . oh yes. . . .

And so on. You have much the same attitude, I suggest, when you read anything in your own special subject, though you may not have thought of it like that before. If you are a gardener, you will do it with gardening books and seed and bulb catalogues; if you are a photographer, it will be photographic magazines and books on special subjects like portraiture, lighting, filters; if you are a motorist, perhaps it is a road-test report, or the motoring page of your newspaper; if you are a doctor, it will be all that scientific publicity about pharmaceutical products, and ought to include selected parts of the *Journal* of the American Medical Association. If you have been reading such material in this way all along, then take confidence from the knowledge that you have not been skimping your reading.

In fact, you have probably been reading, if you but knew it, in the same way as those prodigious, legendary readers we have all heard tell of, who are supposed to have been able to read a page at a glance and remember every word. The next time such a claim reaches your notice, try to examine it closely. Find out if the claimant can read any book on any subject like that, or whether his ability is restricted to subject matter in which he is already an expert. Then try to discover what he is really remembering. Is it every word verbatim, or a few salient points arranged in a context of something he already knows by heart? And does he merely repeat a few disconnected facts, or can he show that he understands the meaning and emphasis of what he has read? The danger in such claims, you see, lies not in their failure to be literally true, but in the kind of image that appears from a few of the facts repeated without a proper understanding of them. The consequence is that people like you and me begin to think that there are two kinds of reader: prodigies that we can never hope to emulate, and miserable dunces like ourselves who have to read a book or take a course before we can read and absorb a little more efficiently than a child. Whereas in truth the only likely difference is that the prodigy's gluttony for knowledge from books, or his obsession with his specialty, have led him to stumble upon a commonplace reading technique which the rest of us have to learn more slowly by analysis.

The main problem in handing on the technique to others is to demonstrate it so that it is universally employable. Everyone's experience is different, everyone's body of knowledge unique. I cannot hope to do more than elucidate some principles and supply a specific example from which further techniques may be deduced.

The first principle is that just as a specialist can make use of expert knowledge to attack material on his own subject, so the layman can employ general knowledge to attack material of general interest. We are all both experts and laymen.

In the previous chapter I suggested some ways of using certain methods of newspaper production to change the techniques and attitudes with which they are read. But in addition to this, whole areas of newsprint can be attacked or eliminated by the use of an ordinary intelligent background of current affairs. If you read in your paper one day about a Russian action intended to offend the United States, do you really need to read a report a day later telling you that the U.S. Government has protested? If you are interested only in the verdict of a trial, do you read through a long report of the case before discovering in the last line that it was adjourned? And if a jet airliner crashes, and no one you know was likely to be traveling in it, are you any wiser for reading that all the passengers and crew were killed and that bodies were dragged from the wreckage—unless you happen to recognize a name as you skim through the list of the dead? It is, of course, a disaster by definition, but it is hardly more extraordinary or significant than a road accident, except that more people are involved and the chance of survival is virtually nil. People are dying all the time: at the rate of 600 an hour from starvation alone. Death is news only to the bereaved.

I must stress again that I am not advising against reading newspapers. Every news report has importance and meaning for someone. I am simply citing some crude examples of the way an efficient reader might use his general knowledge to eliminate what is meaningless to him, spend more time on what is important, and, with anything significant that he picks out on the way, usefully expand his body of knowledge. If you are still in doubt about the wisdom of this apparently ruthless ragpicking of newspapers, ask yourself the next time you are absorbed in one whether your interest is adding to your knowledge or merely indulging some idle lust, like passing the time, taking yourself out of yourself, vicarious violence, or righteous indignation. I am making no judgment of such indulgences; I am only reiterating my thesis that the efficient reader knows why as well as what he reads.

As with news reports, so with longer articles in magazines of general interest, whatever height of brow they are aimed at, and so too with all reports. Reports and magazine features can be grouped together in this context because they have one significant quality in common: they seldom say very much. Reports are unlikely to be aimed to anyone without a special knowledge of their background and a specific reason for reading them. They are seldom the work of professional writers, and in consequence they contain a good deal of extraneous verbiage and minor detail which, although relevant, can be safely ignored by the reader who knows it already or wants only limited information, such as conclusions or recommendations. Magazine features are more often written professionally, and their use of words ought to be economical. But because they are usually aimed at a general readership and their length is restricted by factors other than their subject matter, they will contain less information. The demanding reader, seeking satisfaction of an individual curiosity, is likely to find most of his questions unanswered, although some new ones may be provoked. For those answers, he must turn to books.

Books are susceptible to the same mode of attack, once the reader is armed with the three basic questions:

What do I already know about this?
What is it likely to tell me?
What more do I still want to know?

Then he finds out, noting what is confirmed, remembering how his expectations are contradicted (simply because they are contradicted), and using all his reading techniques in the process.

(2,350 words)

EXERCISE 27

Answer the following questions briefly.

1. What, in your own words, is the author's main point in the foregoing chapter? (2 marks)
2. How is the discussion in the chapter related to its title, *Reports?* (2 marks)
3. What role does the chapter encourage the reader to perform? (1 mark)
4. What is meant by the statement: "We are all both experts and laymen"? (1 mark)
5. What does the author suggest is the most likely explanation of the alleged ability of some great men to read a page at a glance and remember every word? (2 marks)
6. Name one of the ways in which the author distinguishes between reports and magazine features. (1 mark)
7. What have they in common? (1 mark)

Check your answers by skimming back through the chapter.

EXERCISE 28

For this exercise you must pretend that you have in your hands a copy of a British Government Blue Book, in this case the Report of the Committee on Weights and Measures Legislation as presented to the British Parliament by the President of the Board of Trade in May 1951 (Cmd. 8219). It is a closely printed paperback of 148 pages, or about 100,000 words, which would take a good reader from three to four hours to read thoroughly from beginning to end. Your task is to find out the most important things it has to say in about ten minutes.

An extract from the Report follows these instructions and you are going to read it as fast as you possibly can. It is therefore necessary to prepare yourself for the attack, so that you know exactly what your purpose is in reading it. Government reports and similar documents, as you may know, are usually simply and clearly arranged and often surprisingly well written. They tend to be much less dull to read than one perhaps expects. A glance at the contents page of any report of a Royal Commission or Select Committee will show toward the end a summary of recommendations relating to the body's terms of reference: those recommendations that so rarely make any difference to our legislation until so long after they are made that their origins are forgotten and they are platitudes on the lips of the man in the street interviewed on television. The Report of the Committee on Weights and Measures Legislation, we find, is no exception to any of those rules. A glance at the five-page Summary of Recommendations shows that most of the fifty recommendations relate to details of the laws about weights and measures and the sale of certain commodities. Only one of the fifty paragraphs of the Summary is so important as to affect all of us throughout the English-speaking world. In comparison with it, all the other recommendations are insignificant:

2. *The Government should take steps, in concert with the Commonwealth and the U.S.A., to abolish the imperial system of measurement in favour of the complete adoption of the metric system over a period of about twenty years (21–26).*

Paragraphs 21 to 26, we find, are part of Chapter 2 of the Report, "The Adoption of the Metric System," and this is the chapter which, we can safely estimate, contains the meat of the entire Report. It is the chapter reproduced here, and which you are going to read at top speed.

It is 3,000 words in length; hence, at an initial skimming rate for our purposes of 1,500 words a minute, two minutes should be allowed to ascertain what ground is covered by the chapter. Turn now to page 231 and skim the complete passage for structure and main ideas against a measured two minutes. Then turn back here and read on, answering the following questions without further reference to the passage, but with particular reference, where necessary, to your existing knowledge. As in the original, the spelling is, of course, that of British English. It should not delay you. The efficient reader is not deterred by such trifles, because he is not restricted to reading words and letters individually.

1. Which one of the main constructions of a chapter or article does this one follow?
2. How is each main element of the structure related to the subject?
3. What is the chief difference between, say, measurement of money, length, and weight in Britain and the U.S.A. on the one hand and the continent of Europe on the other?
4. Jot down the names, or a couple of the units, of as many tables of measurement in use in Britain as you can think of: e.g., inch—mile, penny—pound, etc.
5. Do the same with any continental tables you know for the same things.
6. Taking the world as a whole, would you say that the majority of people used our system or the continental one?

7. What size majority would you imagine?
8. What historical reasons do you think there might be for there being these two main systems of measurement?
9. What do you think would be the main advantage of our adopting the continental system of measurement?
10. What other immediate advantages can you think of?
11. Are there any long-term advantages that could accrue after the suggested twenty-year period for the adoption of the continental system?
12. What do you think would be the main disadvantage of such a change?
13. What other immediate disadvantages can you think of?
14. Are there any disadvantages that would still be apparent after the twenty-year period over which it is proposed the change should take place?
15. Can you think of any compromise solution that might avoid most of the disadvantages of such a change?
16. If such a compromise were adopted, what disadvantages would remain?
17. Why do you think the twenty-year period was recommended?
18. Would the change be difficult to accomplish administratively?
19. Why?
20. Would it be expensive to accomplish financially?
21. Why?
22. Can you think of anything else that would add to the cost of the change?
23. Government committees of this kind, as you know, gather evidence about their subject largely from representatives of various organizations. Can you think of any likely organizations or interests who may have given evidence to this Committee to help them form their conclusions?
24. Which interests do you think might have supported the proposal to change?
25. Which interests do you think might have opposed it?
26. Why do you think those interests took the line they did?
27. Do you think the Committee's main recommendation concurred with the majority of the evidence that was given them?
28. Why do you think nothing has been done about the recommendation?
29. Has anything happened recently, and, if so, what, to suggest that

the Committee's recommendation has not been completely shelved?

30. What is your opinion of the Committee's recommendation?

Whether you have been able to answer or guess the answers to all these questions or not, try to read the following extract in seven and a half minutes at the longest (i.e., 400 words a minute). A more appropriate time would be five minutes, a rate of 600 words a minute. Time yourself reading it in the usual way, and, in doing so, use all the reading techniques you have practiced so far: anticipating where possible, reading rapidly through unimportant parts, answering the questions you have already posed, and reading carefully anything that seems especially important. Remember, before you begin, that you are about to read a British publication, so at times, of course, the spelling will be unfamiliar as well as some technical terms and turns of phrase. Prepare yourself for this likelihood and, if you are truly reading for meaning, you ought not to be delayed. Flexibility of this order is essential in our modern shrinking world. Your attitude should be an aggressive one, actively involving you, and demanding that your questions are answered. Now, READ AS FAST AS YOU POSSIBLY CAN.

The Adoption of the Metric System

13. There are at the present time only two principal languages of quantity in general commercial use throughout the world— the metric system and the imperial system. The units of the latter were fully established in Great Britain in their present form by the Weights and Measures Acts of 1824 and 1878 and are, of course, those most commonly used in everyday transactions in this country. This system is, however, the official domestic system today only in the countries of the Commonwealth and in the U.S.A. Most other countries of importance have adopted the metric system since its introduction in France in the early years

of the nineteenth century; and recently certain countries of the Commonwealth have taken preparatory steps towards abandoning the imperial system in favour of the metric.

14. It is, however, hardly correct to talk of the "imperial system" in quite the same way as one talks of the "metric system." The latter forms one compact, closely defined and universally recognised system of measurement under the guidance of an international body consisting of representatives of all the countries subscribing to its activities; whereas the imperial system is really a conglomeration of units which have in the past been found convenient for particular types of measurement and which have, over the years, been linked together to form a rough whole. Under the umbrella heading of the imperial system, there are five different systems of weight and three of capacity at present lawful in Great Britain. The countries of the Commonwealth, in general, use these same units and base their values on the Imperial Standards kept in London; but the U.S.A. on the other hand defines its yard and pounds in terms of the International Metre and Kilogramme and has different values for many of the other units—for example, a ton which is about 10 per cent lighter than the imperial ton and a gallon which is about 20 per cent smaller than the imperial gallon. There is, moreover, no internationally recognised body responsible for the imperial system which can in any way compare with the International Metric Conference, so that there has been virtually no tendency for the countries using the imperial system or variations of it to come together to establish and maintain a greater degree of uniformity.

15. The metric system, therefore, has many advantages over the imperial. It is entirely decimal, whereas in the imperial system one has to work in such numerical steps as 14 (pounds to the stone), 16 (ounces to the pound), 3 (feet to the yard), 437½ or 480 (grains to the ounce) and so on, in a manner that can only be learned by rote. From its earliest days the metric system appealed to technicians and scientists on account of its ease of calculation; and there is no doubt that, coupled with a decimal system of coinage, it offers many benefits to traders in respect of their day-to-day calculations, costings and invoices. There was conse-

quently for many years a pressure inside those countries which used only the imperial system for the permissive use of the metric system as well; and for some time the metric system has been fully legal in this country and can be freely used as an alternative to the imperial. Similar provisions apply in most other "imperial" countries; and there is no doubt that great inconvenience would be caused if the metric system were now to be made illegal. The real problem facing Great Britain and these countries, therefore, is not whether to adhere *either* to the imperial *or* to the metric system, but whether to maintain within their boundaries two legal systems of measurement or to establish world-wide uniformity by changing over completely to the metric system and abolishing the imperial.

16. It has been suggested to us that a possible compromise would be to decimalise the imperial system, so as to obtain one of the major benefits of the metric system whilst retaining the historically valuable associations of the imperial yard and pound and enabling much of the existing weighing and measuring equipment to be kept in use. We consider, however, that the confusion and inconvenience of such a step would be only a little less than that which would be caused by a complete change to the metric system, without conferring in return the advantages of world-wide uniformity. Certain improvements can and should be made in the imperial system if it is to continue to exist; but we are convinced that, if a major change is to be made, it can only be towards the full adoption of the metric system. We have therefore considered it our duty to make enquiries as to whether the continued existence for use in trade in this country of two distinct systems of measurement is a source of inconvenience and waste and, if so, what remedial steps should be taken.

17. Before, however, recounting the evidence we have received on these points, we should like to summarise what might be called the "external" factors in this problem. First, the metric system is used by the overwhelming majority of countries in the world, representing the great proportion of the world's population; and there is no indication that the trend towards its universal adoption has been reversed. On the other hand, it is in the field

of international trade that the benefits of uniformity of measurement come fully into their own; and at present about half, if not more, of the world's trade is conducted in the imperial system, owing to the predominant trading position of the Commonwealth and the U.S.A. Secondly, it is obviously illogical for there to be two separate systems in a world which is, from the trading point of view, becoming rapidly smaller; and the advantages of a decimal system are such that it is highly unlikely that any country not now using it would adopt the non-decimal imperial system. Alternatively, it can with some justification be maintained that the actual units of the imperial system are more convenient for everyday use than the metric and that, for many trading purposes, a quantity can be stated more concisely in imperial terms than in metric and consequently with less chance of it being misunderstood. Thirdly, the part to be played in international affairs, over the next few years at least, in respect of supplies of defence equipment etc., by countries using the imperial system, particularly of course the U.S.A., is likely to increase considerably; and it is even possible that "metric" countries may be associated with a standardisation of equipment which will be based on the imperial units. But such a process would tend to accentuate both the slight differences between the American and British fundamental standards, which we examine in the next Chapter, and the major differences between some of their units of measurement.

18. The external picture is therefore far from definite; and the evidence we have received from various bodies in this country is equally inconclusive. The Federation of British Industries has stated that there is a tendency towards a greater use of the metric system in industry but has urged that the present free option between the two systems should be maintained, as any compulsory change would entail considerable expense and re-organisation. The Association of British Chambers of Commerce, on the other hand, has for many years advocated the complete adoption of the metric system and has represented to us that its members would not object to the ensuing cost of re-equipment. Of the 100 or so other associations representing manufacturers, traders and professional, scientific and technical bodies from whom we have

received evidence on this issue, about half a dozen have advocated the adoption of a policy of a long-term transition to the metric system; the rest have stated that there has been little tendency on the part of their members to use the metric system and have not favoured any alteration to the existing position. Sample enquiries undertaken on our behalf by a number of women's organisations reveal, as might be expected, that a very substantial proportion of the purchasing public is likely to be against abolition of the imperial units in most common use; and the local authorities' associations have advocated the retention of the imperial system, with the exception of the County Councils' Association which has maintained that this will only perpetuate what it considers to be a waste of machinery and man-power. Virtually all the bodies which have recommended the complete adoption of the metric system have suggested that a transition period of something like twenty years would be needed; and the Decimal Association, a body devoted to the abolition of the imperial system in this country, has furnished us with detailed suggestions of how the Government and public trading bodies could assist in the transition period.

19. It is obvious that, in the face of these conflicting external factors and the mixed evidence we have received, we can record no recommendations which can be claimed either to afford an easy practical solution or to reflect the wishes of all those who have made their views known to us. In such a situation, the arguments of those who advocate the retention of the present free option between the two systems appear strong indeed. If one system is in fact better than the other, the contention runs, then it will gradually come to be used by everyone and the question will have solved itself in a manner satisfactory to all; and if not, it proves that people have found one system to be more suitable for some purposes and the other for other purposes. There is little doubt that purely by a counting of heads the great majority of evidence we have received falls within this category.

20. Nevertheless, as our Enquiry has proceeded, we have come to doubt the validity of this argument for two reasons. First, a policy of allowing a gradual and voluntary change to a system

which can claim to be "better" on general grounds may well cause the disadvantages of transition to be far greater than they would be under an ordered change within a definite time limit; and some of our evidence has revealed how gradual a move away from inconvenient to more suitable units can be, attended all the while by the double disadvantage of the prolonged use of the old units by the more conservative elements and the obligation thereby imposed on others to be acquainted with, and perhaps actually to work in, two systems. Secondly, in the case of the continued use of two systems each of which appears to be the most suited to a particular sphere, not all persons may be agreed as to which sphere is which, with the result that the two systems may here and there be used for the one purpose, with the same confusion as above. More important, the element of human inertia is often ignored; and the contention that a separate system is suitable for particular purposes may often be based on an assessment in which the real long-term advantages of a change to complete uniformity are obscured by the probable immediate inconveniences of the disturbance.

21. Bearing all these arguments in mind, we have come to the unanimous conclusion that the metric system is, in the broadest sense and in the interests of world uniformity, a "better" system of weights and measures than the imperial; that a change from imperial to metric for all trade purposes is sooner or later inevitable; that a continuance of the present option to use either the metric or the imperial until the inevitable comes about will cause in the long run more inconvenience than an ordered change within a specified period; and that the long-term advantages which would flow from an organised change in the near future would far outweigh the inconveniences of the change itself. We therefore recommend that the Government should straightway take the steps which we outline below with a view to abolishing within a definite period all use of the imperial system in Great Britain and to establishing the sole use of the metric system for all trade purposes.

22. We would, however, make two important provisos. First, any change of this nature should only be done in concert with

those countries of North America and the Commonwealth which base their units on the yard and the pound. For the United Kingdom to move out of step with these countries with which it does so much of its trade would only be to exchange one set of inconveniences for another at the expense of great domestic disturbance. Secondly, the internal convenience of a decimal system of measurement could not be adequately realised unless at the same time the coinage was decimalised. The whole argument of the greater ease of commercial and domestic calculation falls largely to the ground so long as the steps of the coinage are not decimal also. The coinage is outside our terms of reference; and we therefore make no recommendation about it. We note simply that the abandonment of the imperial system, if it is to be undertaken, should be accompanied or preceded by the decimalisation of our coinage.

23. We have found it difficult to obtain any very relevant evidence as to the way in which other countries have overcome the difficulties of transition; but we believe it to be true that most of the countries which were early in adopting the metric system were previously using a multiplicity of local units of weight and measure and actually made the change at a time when the trading community had not become integrated to the extent which it has today. The change-over must, therefore, have appeared in their cases very often as being a welcome rationalisation of a confused situation, and as being only a part of a process of the breaking down of local barriers to trade, and the building of a single trading community within the nation.

24. The practical disadvantages of a change-over to the metric system fall into two main groups: those associated with the ordinary internal and external trading activities of the country, which mainly appear as the need to replace weighing and measuring equipment and to re-educate traders and consumers in the use of a new system; and those particularly associated with the engineering industry, which would require to re-equip itself not only with measuring equipment but also with tools, gauges, and so on, to make metric sizes, and which would have, during any transitional period, very serious problems on the maintenance of stocks

of spares and replacements and might during this period suffer a certain amount of trading loss in consequence. The former difficulty could, we believe, be very largely overcome by a suitably planned programme of education and by placing the actual period of turnover at a time when the necessary equipment would not be a serious burden on the country's economic capacity. The latter presents more problems, particularly since the engineering industry is continually elaborating and renewing its equipment and since, in whatever way the actual period of turnover is planned, there is bound to be some additional capital cost of equipment and double stocks of spares and therefore some advantage during that period to the countries already on the metric system, so far as international trade is concerned.

25. The evidence we have received leads us to believe that a complete change to the metric system could not be effected in under twenty years without considerable dislocation. It would have to be inaugurated by full discussion between the Government, industry and commerce as to what the transition period should in fact be and as to what practical steps should be taken during this period to facilitate a smooth and steady change. It would, for example, be desirable for the Government to have power to require particular industries and trades to convert completely by given periods, within the framework of a previously agreed plan and in the light of the availability of new metric weighing and measuring equipment. Also compensation might have to be paid in certain cases and could in others be used as an incentive to achieve speedy change-overs in particular sectors of the economy.

26. To sum up, we recommend that the imperial system should eventually be abolished in favour of the metric and that the change should be preceded by:—

  a. discussion with industry and commerce to determine the period of transition

  b. agreement with the Commonwealth and the U.S.A. for simultaneous change on their parts

  c. a lengthy process of preparing the general public for the change *d.* the decimalisation of the coinage

e. the preparation of schemes for the compulsory change-over, trade by trade, during the period of transition, with provision for compensation wherever necessary.

27. We realise that this recommendation is contentious in the extreme; and we have therefore considered it also to be our duty to examine the imperial system of weights and measures with a view to suggesting what improvements are needed. Accordingly, in the following Chapters we recommend certain changes in the definition of the basic units of the imperial system, the establishment of a scientific body to continue the process of improvement as and when needed, the elimination of a number of minor systems and units within the imperial system and the eventual creation of one single imperial system of weight and measure capable of being adapted to meet changing trade requirements. We would say here, however, that we are so convinced of the desirability of these improvements and of the relative ease with which they can be brought about that we would advocate their immediate adoption irrespective of whether our recommendation in this Chapter in favour of an eventual transition to the metric system is accepted or not.

(3,000 words)

Check your comprehension of what you have just read by answering the following questions as briefly as possible without referring back to the text.

1. With what two languages of quantity is the extract concerned?
2. What parts of the world use the system in use in Britain?
3. Why is one system more compact than the other?
4. How many different systems of weight are in lawful use in Britain?
5. How many systems of capacity are in lawful use in Britain?
6. What, if any, is the chief difference between the system used in Britain and that used in the U.S.A.?
7. Which system is subject to international control?
8. What change is recommended by the Report?

9. What is the chief advantage of the change?
10. Which of the two systems can be legally used in Britain?
11. What compromise has been suggested?
12. What is the Committee's opinion of such a compromise?
13. Which system seems likely to be universally adopted?
14. What indications are there of the change taking the opposite direction?
15. Taking the world as a whole, which system is predominantly used for trading?
16. What is the advantage when trading of the system used in Britain?
17. What does British industry want to be done?
18. What do the Chambers of Commerce want?
19. What proportion of the other associations which gave evidence to the Committee were in favor of the change recommended?
20. What is the attitude of women to the matter, as far as it can be ascertained?
21. What argument is used by those who advocate preserving the status quo?
22. What is the essence of the Committee's case against this argument?
23. Was the Committee unanimous about its recommendation?
24. What is suggested about Britain adopting the recommendation unilaterally?
25. Was the Committee asked to make recommendations about coinage?
26. What is the suggestion about coinage?
27. What has happened in other countries where changes similar to those recommended have been made?
28. How long does the Committee visualize would be required to enforce its recommendation?
29. What are the two main groups into which the practical disadvantages of the recommendation fall?
30. What problem is associated with the first of these groups?
31. How can it be overcome?
32. What problem is associated with the second of these groups?
33. How can it be overcome?
34. Why do you think British industry views the matter as it does?
35. What does the Committee think should be done to facilitate the implementation of the recommendation?
36. Which organization would be most wholeheartedly in favor of the recommendation?

37. What, in principle, does the Committee suggest should be done if the recommendation is not adopted?
38. What has been done so far in Britain to adopt the Committee's recommendation?
39. What has been done elsewhere since the Report was published to adopt the recommendation?
40. What is the underlying philosophy of the extract?

Use skimming techniques to mark your answers, allowing a mark for each one correct. Then divide the total by four to give a mark out of ten to compare with your other comprehension scores.

Full marks on the test would indicate a thorough comprehension of the entire extract in detail and some knowledge of its topical context. If you have read it at anything like twice your present average speed, limiting your demands of the extract in order to do so, you should not expect full comprehension. A total of twenty-four or twenty-five correct answers is a reasonable result from such a reading technique, unless you already know a good deal about weights and measures legislation.

You have not, of course, read and assimilated the complete Report, but in a few minutes you have spent on this extract from it, you may agree that you have assimilated a good deal more of it in less time than would have been possible by more usual reading methods.

·15·

Factual Books

Books as thinking machines—their arrangement—the reader's needs—programed learning—children's books for adults and adult books for children—freedom from the limitations of books —methodical preparation for reading—techniques of attack— skimming to studying—categories of books and how far to penetrate them—a basic question for all readers of all books.

A BOOK is a machine to think with. Dr. I. A. Richards commenced authorship with those words at the start of the preface of what became his best-known work, *Principles of Literary Criticism* (1924). The statement was patently a challenge, and I repeat it here with a similar intention but for a much narrower purpose. If all its implications were thought out and realized, schools and examinations as we know them at present would disappear, teachers would begin to teach and cease being inglorious bartenders pumping measures of bitter fact into empty vessels, and the idiotic divisions between art and science, and work and play, those nineteenth-century barriers on the barbs of which the coattails of our culture are still impaled, would be seen for what they are, gimcrack political expedients.

In the present context, a book is a machine to think with in much the same sense as newspapers, magazines, and reports are. The differences are mostly those afforded by length: a book can permit its thinking to spread wider and deeper. The mode of attack is essentially the same as that described in the previous chapter, and there is no book, from classic novel to autodidact's manual, which is not better assimilated by employing it.

The reason for books being assembled and bound so that they start at page one and end at page x is a convention connected with production and distribution and not necessarily with the needs of their readers. From a reader's point of view alone, all books should be loose-leaf and printed on one side of each page in such a way that the reader can spread the pages out on the floor and reassemble those he needs to read in whatever order he desires. He would often want, of course, to reassemble many books in the order ordained by the author. All but the most eccentric would want to read novels, for instance, most other narrative books, and some philosophical dissertations, at least once in the author's order; and most well-devised self-teaching books are best studied methodically from page one seriately to the end. Some books, of which this is perhaps an example, would take so much time and foreknowledge to rearrange for individual needs that the author's arrangement is probably the most convenient one.

The idea of loose-leaf non-fiction is impracticable and unnecessary, but that there is a need for some application of its underlying principles is shown by the growing popularity of programed learning. The film strips projected onto the screens of teaching machines are made so that, in effect, the student assembles the "book" to meet his own needs; and if only they were typographically designed for efficient reading and the students who have to use them were first taught to read efficiently, the public expenditure on them might begin to be justified.

Traditions of book production and distribution are unrelated to the convenience and needs of readers in other ways. In the field of non-fiction, for example, there is the usually unbridgeable gulf between children's books and adult books. If the authors of books for older children were encouraged by the prospect of an adult edition to write also with young adults in mind, and others of limited reading experience wanting basic knowledge; and if the authors of adult books were encouraged more often by the prospect of a children's edition to write with the clarity and enthusiasm of the author of a good book for older children, several benefits would ensue. I can think of three immediately. There would be fewer unreadable books on both sides of the gulf; teachers of backward adult readers and foreigners studying English would have less difficulty in finding books both adult in subject matter and simple in language; and members of the younger generation might have less justification for asserting that their elders are out of touch with them. The more general educational advantages are incalculable.

During the later part of my career in journalism, it became clear to me that I had been writing for the mature twelve-year-old mind; and I would not be surprised if any intelligent and curious high-school senior who has survived his schooling would find much to interest and stimulate him in this book. What his experience may not allow him to realize is the need for techniques of efficient reading and processes of selection and elimination. At sixteen, every word of the newspaper can be interesting.

I know of two distinguished occasions in recent years when the gulf was bridged, once in each direction. Rachel Carson's *The Sea Around Us* was first published for adults and later in an illustrated edition for children, and *The Little Prince*, by Antoine de Saint-Exupéry, was first published for children and sold widely to adults. Two well-known fairly recent books have established themselves independently of the gulf: Bertrand Russell's *The Wisdom of the West* and J. R. R. Tolkein's *The Lord of the Rings*. But of these examples the children's books read by adults are fiction, and in that field the gulf is less pronounced. Indeed, time tends to fill it in altogether. Were the tales of Hans Andersen and Jules Verne, the Alice books, *Lorna Doone, The Wind in the Willows, Kidnapped*, intended for adults or children? One of the fates that tend to overtake some authors after a generation or two is that they come to be thought "suitable" reading for children or, fate worse, suitable books for high-school English courses. Thackeray, Dickens, George Eliot, and Scott are still read, I am told, by people who have left school, although one would expect them to be more often recommended by surveillant aunts to bright ten-year-olds. I expect Wells, Bennett, and Sinclair Lewis are succumbing to a similar fate, but Samuel Butler, who has hardly been overtaken by the times as yet, has probably escaped the aunts' attentions. If Lawrence and Huxley escape for a little longer, who comes next? Hemingway, I predict, who will one day be read as I once read Percy F. Westerman, and perhaps the early works of Colin Wilson. Well, why not an illustrated edition of *The Outsider*? It is amusing to speculate so, but it is a digression.

My concern is to elucidate some general principles and provoke some individual attitudes via which a developing reader might free himself from the limitations of such things as the form, presentation, classification, and style of factual books, and develop a free-ranging awareness of how such books might best be exploited.

Although they are not loose-leaf, all factual books can be read in whatever order the reader desires. Techniques of skimming and structure analysis should initially ascertain the author's arrangement and intentions before the reader decides firstly whether he wants to read the book at all and next whether his own arrangement imposed upon that of the author will be a better way for him to assimilate it.

All the elements of a book's presentation should be observed before starting to read it: its title and author, dust jacket, size and weight, its publisher's imprint and blurbs, the quality of its paper and typographical design, its publication date and printing history, its author's other works, and perhaps also its published price, which might indicate the kind of sale its publisher allowed for. Such observations may not reveal much, but they will orientate you in relation to the book and set your anticipative processes to answering the question: What is it likely to be about?

The printing history will tell you whether the edition is up to date or, if it is the kind of book that is always topical, whether its popularity has been such as to demand several reprintings. Next, the type and quality of any illustrations will reveal something more: whether the book was expensive to produce, as colored plates would suggest, or whether its line drawings, illustrative or merely adorning, were intended for readers who were expected to be specialists, laymen, children, or morons.

The items of an index should tell you a little more by putting you *au courant* with the character of the language and terminology, the scope of the subject matter, and the thoroughness with which the book was intended to be studied. A bibliography or list of references will place the book into a wider literary context, but full appreciation of this might require a widely experienced reader.

A quick reading of any introduction and author's preface (which should be reread with more care once the whole book has been read) ought to equip you with enough extra knowledge of the purpose and scope of the book to make the contents page a meaningful guide to which chapter or chapters form its core. Remember that whatever its length and however minute its detail, the structural rules for a book are essentially the same as those for an article, or a series of related articles.

The indications given by the contents page should be confirmed by skimming through the likely key chapters, by which time—ten to fifteen minutes after first opening the book—you ought to know enough about it to decide whether you need to analyze it or study it, read it fully, or merely pick the meat out of it. If you want only the meat, your purpose will usually be met by a quick attack on the key chapter and then an even quicker comparative reading of one or two related chapters, noting as you do so how they are constructed and using any structural similarities between them to assist the speed at which you confirm or amplify both your expectations of the book as a whole and the more specific information gained from the key chapter. If the author should have provided synopses as chapter headings, as I have with just this chapter for an example, make all the use you can of them to increase the efficiency of your attack. The process of evisceration in any case need seldom be the work of more than half an hour.

When you decide to read the entire book, rather than merely take the meat out of it, you will find it helpful to write down the main idea of the key chapter after your first skimming of it. Then do the same after skimming each of the other chapters until you have synoptic notes covering the entire groundwork of the book. With that much basic knowledge it should then be possible to read and assimilate the whole book quite quickly in whatever order is suited to your needs. Such a reading is best done pencil in hand, marking off key passages in the margins and underlining important minor points; or, if the book's ownership forbids marking, page numbers and brief references of a word or a phrase may be noted on a flyleaf or bookmark. For here, after finishing the book, will be found the skimming aids to any further task of studying, learning, or annotating.

At any stage in this progression, from reading the title to analyzing the detail, a book may be set aside or abandoned. Most books may well be abandoned at an early stage; many others, especially those on one's own subjects, can be quickly gutted and earmarked for reference. Plenty of others, formidable in their detail and impersonal precision because they are written by specialists to withstand the critical analysis of other specialists, need not deter the non-specialist reader from sifting out the conclusions and the author's estimates of their significance. All too many more are unnecessarily verbose, like the majority of American textbooks, which often seem to me as if they were written by clever but insecure people desperately needful of proving their own cleverness to equally anxious readers, perhaps the products of high-speed reading courses, who read so carelessly and digest so poorly that each strong piece of knowledge must be padded out and reiterated in several varieties for fear of perforating their mental ulcers. Experiments on average American readers have shown that a few ideas expressed in a thousand words are more easily comprehended than the same ideas expressed in two hundred. Hence there is a case for long-windedness, though not for long-wordedness. There is a better case for teaching people to be better readers and to demand better writers. At another extreme, there has lately been issuing from some American publishing houses a kind of corrective. This is the serious digest, for which a couple of hundred verbose and indigestible textbooks and a handful of lively and stimulating ones have been gutted, cleaned, minced, dehydrated, sterilized, and predigested, till they have the flavor of having been prepared for babies. They are none the less useful basic books which deserve to be quickly assimilated like vitamin pills to supply the energy and direction for further reading in the subject. Their taste may thus be ignored. A good deal of the American background reading to the subjects covered by this book is to be found in one or other of these forms, so that one has a choice, for example, between having to read something like this:

> When Ebbinghaus (1885) conducted the first quantitative study of associative learning he found that his curve of retention was roughly logarithmic in form and proceeded to postulate a mathematical formulation of his principle. . . .

and something like this:

> Twentyish, bespectacled Hermann Ebbinghaus, who was to become one of the first giants of experimental psychology, plodded through his recitation of 104 nonsense names and ticker-tape abbreviations for the seventeenth time that day. . . .

Specialists and students may have to learn the details of dull books, and laymen may want to study great books, but however far a reader penetrates a book the task will be better done by a methodical attack such as I have described.

But whatever and however you read, there is one fundamental question to which you should be demanding an answer, irrespective of any other more personal questions your individual needs may arouse. It is a more basic and less precise question than: What is the author saying? I submit that it is a question which every reader of everything asks with some part of his mind, albeit too often a dark and inaccessible part. I believe it should be brought consciously and deliberately into the forefront of the reader's mind and answered as articulately as possible. The answer will not only unify and explain the most rambling book. It will also supply even a relatively inexperienced reader with a standard of evaluation and a meaningful enlargement of his reading experience. Long after the facts of a book have been absorbed into a body of general knowledge or lost beyond all but capricious recall, the significance and value and tenor of the work can continue to be associated with its title and author if the reader, no matter whether he skims or studies, answers as he does so one question: *What is the underlying philosophy?*

(2,400 words)

EXERCISE 29

Without referring back, write a summary of the foregoing chapter, including in it, if possible in the correct order, all the stages of preparation and attack described in the chapter. Then allow yourself two minutes to skim through the chapter again and correct your summary accordingly. When you have finished, check carefully back through the chapter, correcting your summary where necessary and assessing your comprehension score. Finally, ensure that you have copied out a numbered and correctly ordered list of all the stages of attacking a book. Use the list for the following exercises.

PRACTICE EXERCISES WITH BOOKS

1. Using this book, go through the stages of preparation up to the point at which you would start skimming, writing down your observations briefly as you go. Your notes should be evaluative rather than factual; e.g., dust jacket—tasteful, formal, arty, gimmicky, or whatever; size and weight—average. And so on.
2. What is the underlying philosophy of this book?
3. Repeat those two exercises with any other book, then skim through it chapter by chapter in any order that seems appropriate, jotting down the main idea of each chapter as you go. Then read each chapter as fast as you possibly can, beginning with the most important and filling in the background with the others until you think you have extracted

as much of the book as you would have done if you had read it in your old way before embarking on this course of study. When you have finished, read it again in the old way, noting where it makes new additions to your knowledge.

4. Repeat those three exercises with other books until you fully understand the technique and are confident in your use of it.

5. Continue to practice reading books aggressively and to some purpose by evolving a formal course of study in any challenging subject with which you are unfamiliar. Most people know of at least one subject that they have often wanted to study but somehow never had time for, or always thought too formidable. Now is the time to meet the challenge and demonstrate to yourself how a combination of curiosity and efficient reading techniques can help you to extend your mental horizons and add immeasurably to your self-confidence. Read at least a dozen books on the same subject methodically and intensively, starting with two or three "basic" books and gradually concentrating on more specialized works. If you need help beyond the advice in Chapter Nine, consult your librarian and a specialist bookseller.

You have now reached the end of your basic course of study in efficient reading that you began, if you have been following the instructions, not less than six and a half weeks ago. By now, you should have a sound and adaptable basis on which to develop your reading; one which, if you continue to read widely and responsively, should last you the rest of your life.

Your result on the timed reading passage on page 251 is to be compared with your result on Exercise 4 (the article called "Pot"). I have not attempted the unnecessarily difficult task of finding a passage of comparable caliber and I would therefore expect most readers to find it and its comprehension test more difficult than the newspaper article. Your speed and comprehension score ought nevertheless to be higher than they were on Exercise 4, and if they are you may justly conclude that your

Factual Books

progress has been better than the figures suggest. In any case, it is your subjective assessment of your progress that counts in the last analysis, not the figures.

When you have done Exercise 30, look up your reading rate in the table on page 314 as usual and check your answers against those on page 301. Compare your comprehension score with that for Exercise 4. If it is lower, or still below 80 per cent, you need to do much more reading, more discussion of what you have read, and more comprehension of all kinds. Find the difference between your reading rates on the two tests, make a fraction of the difference over your rate for Exercise 4, and multiply it by 100. This will give you your percentage increase (or decrease). Here, if you need it, is the formula:

Let your reading rate for Exercise 4 be x; and your rate for Exercise 30 be y; then your percentage improvement in reading speed is:

$$\frac{y - x}{x} \times 100$$

READING EXERCISE

The Different Types of Reader

BY C. S. LEWIS

Already in our school days some of us were making our first responses to good literature. Others, and these the majority, were reading, at school, *The Captain*, and, at home, short-lived novels from the circulating library. But it was apparent then that the majority did not "like" their fare in the way we "liked" ours. It is apparent still. The differences leap to the eye.

In the first place, the majority never read anything twice. The sure mark of an unliterary man is that he considers "I've read it already" to be a conclusive argument against reading a work.

251

We have all known women who remembered a novel so dimly that they have had to stand for half an hour in the library skimming through it before they were certain they had once read it. But the moment they became certain, they rejected it immediately. It was, for them, dead, like a burnt-out match, an old railway ticket, or yesterday's paper; they had already used it. Those who read great works, on the other hand, will read the same work ten, twenty, or thirty times during the course of their life.

Secondly, the majority, though they are sometimes frequent readers, do not set much store by reading. They turn to it as a last resource. They abandon it with alacrity as soon as any alternative pastime turns up. It is kept for railway journeys, illnesses, odd moments of enforced solitude, or for the process called "reading oneself to sleep." They sometimes combine it with desultory conversation; often with listening to the radio. But literary people are always looking for leisure and silence in which to read and do so with their whole attention. When they are denied such attentive and undisturbed reading they feel impoverished.

Thirdly, the first reading of some literary work is often, to the literary, an experience so momentous that only experiences of love, religion, or bereavement can furnish a standard of comparison. Their whole consciousness is changed. They have become what they were not before. But there is no sign of anything like this among the other sort of readers. When they have finished the story or the novel, nothing much, or nothing at all, seems to have happened to them.

Finally, and as a natural result of their different behavior in reading, what they have read is constantly and prominently present to the mind of the few, but not to that of the many. The former mouth over their favorite lines and stanzas in solitude. Scenes and characters from books provide them with a sort of iconography by which they interpret or sum up their own experience. They talk to one another about books, often and at length. The latter seldom think or talk of their reading.

It is pretty clear that the majority, if they spoke without passion and were fully articulate, would not accuse us of liking the the wrong books, but of making such a fuss about any books at all. We treat as a main ingredient in our well-being something which to them is marginal. Hence to say simply that they like one thing and we another is to leave out nearly the whole of the facts. If *like* is the correct word for what they do to books, some other word must be found for what we do. Or, conversely, if we *like* our kind of book we must not say that they *like* any book. If the few have "good taste," then we may have to say that no such thing as "bad taste" exists: for the inclination which the many have to their sort of reading is not the same thing and, if the word were univocally used, would not be called taste at all.

It is worth noting that the same difference of attitude is displayed about the other arts and about natural beauty. Many people enjoy popular music in a way which is compatible with humming the tune, stamping in time, talking, and eating. And when the popular tune has once gone out of fashion they enjoy it no more. Those who enjoy Bach react quite differently. Some buy pictures because the walls "look so bare without them"; and after the pictures have been in the house for a week they become practically invisible to them. But there are a few who feed on a great picture for years. As regards nature, the majority "like a nice view as well as anyone." They are not saying a word against it. But to make the landscapes a really important factor in, say, choosing the place for a holiday—to put them on a level with such serious considerations as a luxurious hotel, a good golf links, and a sunny climate—would seem to them affectation. To "go on" about them like Wordsworth would be humbug.

From: *An Experiment in Criticism* (1961)

(800 words)

EXERCISE 30

Choose the best answer to each question.

1. The majority of readers, according to the writer:
    a. seldom finish a book;
    b. never read anything twice;
    c. read too slowly;
    d. read only what they like.

2. Even frequent readers, he adds:
   a. do not set much store by reading;
   b. understand little of what they read;
   c. do so with the radio on;
   d. have to skim a book before they know whether they have read it.

3. For the literary, the first reading of a literary work:
   a. can be an experience comparable with falling in love;
   b. must be repeated before it can be appreciated fully;
   c. never leaves them unchanged;
   d. will be remembered for the rest of their lives.

4. The books read by the literary minority, the writer says:
   a. are remembered but seldom talked about;
   b. provide them with quotations for all occasions;
   c. are a valued alternative to real-life experience;
   d. provide them with a means of interpreting their own experience.

5. People who love great literary works:
   a. buy them for their own bookshelves;
   b. never allow them to go out of fashion;
   c. can never find enough leisure and silence for reading;
   d. will read the same book as much as thirty times during their lives.

6. The unliterary, the writer thinks, would accuse the literary minority of:
   a. making too much fuss about books;
   b. reading the wrong books;
   c. being snobbish about their "good taste";
   d. being bookworms.

7. The majority enjoy paintings and works of music, the writer implies:
   a. for reasons that lead them to choose works in which their interest cannot long be sustained;
   b. only when they are fashionable;
   c. only occasionally, like going on holiday;
   d. only when they are in bad taste.

8. One of the objects of this passage, we may infer, is to argue that:
   a. the taste of the majority cannot be called taste at all;

b. majority tastes in literature are of much the same quality as majority taste in any other art;

c. we must give a different meaning to the word *like* when we talk about the artistic affections of the majority as compared with those of the literary few;

d. the difference between the literary and the unliterary is that the former read a few books over and over again.

9. The writer appears to be:
   a. a scholar;
   b. a snob;
   c. class conscious;
   d. a culture vulture.

10. The main idea of the passage is:
    a. Before anyone can call himself truly literary he must have read the great works many times over.
    b. There is a basic difference of attitude to the arts between the literary and the unliterary that makes the use of terms like "good taste" and "liking" books quite meaningless.
    c. When the majority are denied books, they hardly notice, but the literary few are impoverished.
    d. The difference between the literary and the unliterary is that the former prefer reading to anything else and the latter prefer anything else to reading.

SUGGESTED PRACTICE READING (PART V)

Walter Allen	*The Modern Novel in Britain and the United States*
William Empson	*Seven Types of Ambiguity*
E. M. Forster	*Aspects of the Novel*
Frank Kermode	*Puzzles and Epiphanies*
F. L. Lucas	*Literature and Psychology*
George Steiner	*The Death of Tragedy*

PART VI

LITERATURE

·16·

Difficult Books

IN A SENSE, there is no such thing as a difficult book, only difficult readers. A book may be difficult to write, but a large part of the writer's difficulty is that of making his subject easy to read. The more difficult his subject, in fact, the greater is his responsibility to *elucidate* it. And lucid writing, provided that one knows the language, is not difficult to read, whatever the subject. Of course, if the book is the *Principia Mathematica*, the score of Wagner's Ring cycle, or a little treatise on landscape gardening in Japanese, it would be difficult for most of us. But that is not the book's fault.

There are, nevertheless, all too many books that are difficult or well-nigh impossible because they are badly written. All obscure writing, in my opinion, is bad writing. So many are they, indeed, that there would be no point in making out a case for not reading them at all. Although this is what their unprofessional authors deserve, there may well be no alternative but to read them sometimes. So there is a strong case for reading them ruthlessly, employing whatever techniques eviscerate them quickly and cleanly, ensuring that we do not allow their authors' laziness or incapacity to invalidate our confidence in our own comprehension. The only people who need be harnessed to plowing laboriously through such books word by word are students ordered to do so for examinations (plow or be plowed) and others with similar limited or exclusive purposes, none of which has much to do with learning for living, or the possession of usable first-hand knowledge.

Resounding reputations for scholarship and wisdom have been

erected around amateur writers in academic or official strong-
holds on the basis of a body of published work which is virtually
unreadable, or at best lifeless and unexciting, but which no one
will admit to finding so for fear of exposing themselves to charges
of ignorance. It is a further symptom of superstition about the
printed word always to blame our own stupidity if some work
of alleged scholarship seems insufferably obscure. In *How to
Read a Page*, I. A. Richards writes that "a certain querulous
questioning tone—'What can it mean?'—is an enemy of comprehension. Read it as though it made sense," he says, "and it probably will." If it does not, one might add, it may mean that the
author does not know how to write about what he knows. It
does not follow that he should, just because he knows more about
his own subject than we do. Scholars who recommend his books
may be paying tribute to a colleague whose practical work they
rightly admire; or they may have read him from a background
of specialized knowledge, using much the same techniques that I
have described, and then evaluating the work with esoteric
criteria. Reviewers who praise bad books may be no more independent of the dogmas of academic fashion than anyone else
with a financial interest in making a safe judgment. What really
count in the last analysis are individual readers' judgments of the
work as it is personally experienced: subjective judgments, as
all judgments ultimately are, which might represent every single
shade of opinion from unreserved admiration to unqualified con-
demnation. Any possible objective elements of judgment may be
safely left to posterity. If enough honest readers of taste and
good will had the chance to voice and the courage to act upon
their disinterested judgments, we might begin to find not only
the books we read, but also every other manufactured com-
modity, evolving out of the slime of mediocrity in which nearly
all we feed upon is condemned to languish by the authority of the
average, the fashionable, the partially educated, and the pusil-
lanimous. Meanwhile, we must try to digest and transcend what
we get as easily as we can.

Perhaps there are two instances of borderline difficulty in
which the reader has a primary responsibility. One is the perverse

Difficult Books

question of style, when the reader may be so irritated by some idiosyncrasy of an otherwise competent author that he becomes unreadable. It is like finding some mannerism of someone we meet so exasperating that further acquaintance is impossible. Perhaps the way to an answer points within ourselves toward a recognition of what fault of our own creates such irrational resistance.

Another aspect of the same kind of difficulty, more susceptible to amelioration, is that order of material which can be quite simple in itself but provokes hostile reactions in the reader because of its content or implications. The reader loses all control of his speed and comprehends capriciously, if at all. The narrower his reading experience, the more often will the problem beset him. The long-term solution, of course, would be to read as widely as possible and cultivate some urbanity. The immediate one must begin with at least a frank acknowledgment by the reader of the existence of his hostility, and then continue with a courageous study of the symptoms and what provokes them. Meanwhile, the material should be read like an unpleasant job that must be well done, applying to it nothing but technique. Beyond there, the matter becomes too individualized for discussion here, for it brings us again into the hinterland between the province of the reading tutor and that of the psychologist.

The second borderline difficulty is not what I would call a difficulty at all, but rather a challenge. Chambers' Dictionary defines a difficulty as "laboriousness: obstacle: objection: that which cannot be easily understood or believed." A challenge is "a summons to a contest of any kind, but esp. a duel: a calling of anyone or anything in question." Anyone who finds a book difficult in this sense is probably not yet ready for it. The distance between reader and book is just too great and the reward, if any, would be incommensurate with the effort expended. It is best to set such a book aside after a superficial reading to assess its caliber and wait until other less difficult books have equipped one for it.

When a book is a challenge, it is because we have encountered it at a stage in our development where a change is indicated: a change that adds to our knowledge, modifies an opinion, illuminates unconsidered ground, or clarifies in some small measure our personal vision of the universe. Such a book is demanding, disturbing, infuriating, "a summons to a contest," according to how we respond within ourselves to growth and change. All worthwhile books are challenging books; one reads the other sort for relaxation or not at all.

Before deciding, by prudent skimming, whether a book is too difficult for the present or whether it is going to be a worthwhile challenge, be sure that your decision is not influenced wrongly by the apparently daunting presence of things like scientific or technical words, quotations or phrases in foreign languages, mathematical formulas, musical quotations, graphs, tables, and footnotes. Their presence should be noted during the initial skimming, but a first reading should pass through them without pausing. The reader may find that a general appreciation of the book is enough for his needs, in which case the daunting elements would not have been particularly relevant. If, after such a reading, a more detailed study is deemed necessary, a second reading will be greatly facilitated by the first; or a second skimming may be sufficient to note the details and relate them to the general context.

The importance cannot be overestimated of refusing to be browbeaten by a superficially formidable litter of scientific jargon and technical terms, unfamiliar modes of expression and explanation, and other manifestations of academic erudition, by which I mean the terminology of, say, philosophy or literary criticism as much as that of psychoanalysis, sociology, or nuclear physics. Some of it is unavoidable, because new concepts need new terms before they can be isolated and discussed. Much of it is as idle and ignorant in its own way as bureaucrats' gobbledygook. None of it need defeat the layman; and indeed none of it must. There is plenty of reason for supposing that its authors intend, unconsciously perhaps, to be obscure and intimidating, and anyone who finds them so is handing them a victory. One of the objectives of those who pursue power is to be able to wield it without having to explain themselves. We hear a lot about churches losing touch with people through a persistent use of jargon, but little about scientists, lawyers, or bureaucrats doing so for the same reason. The danger of any powerful freemasonry entrenching itself behind an entanglement of jargon and gobble-dygook, with its members unable to give a comprehensible account of themselves to any but their own initiates, is an ever-present one for all of us. If every citizen who says "I do not want to know" is forging a bar for the cage in which all our freedoms could one day be incarcerated, everyone who says "I can't be bothered with this because of its jargon" is giving fuel to the forge.

Moreover, there is an enormous personal enrichment in self-confidence and knowledge to be gained from the ability to assimilate a wide range of material without difficulty and to criticize or appraise it with the authority of an experienced lay reader.

The position of the reader grappling with jargon is not substantially different from that of anyone encountering the limits of his own vocabulary. We do not reach for a dictionary, switch off our attention, or close the book every time we meet an unfamiliar word. We may deduce its meaning from its context or ask what it means or, if that is not possible, we must wait until the word appears again. Eventually, by repetition and use, it takes its place as part of our vocabulary. We first learned to speak in much the same way as this; and so our vocabulary has grown and will continue to grow. If, however, you think that insufficient reading has left you with an immature or insecure vocabulary, it may be worth underlining unfamiliar words as you come to them for later noting and learning. Another way, especially with technical terms, is to seek them out deliberately by reading several books on the same subject, all fairly quickly and without attempting too detailed a comprehension of any of them. By the time the third or fourth book is reached, comprehension will be easier and the technical terms will be well-founded familiars.

Quotations from foreign languages ought always to be translated, either side by side or in footnotes. For ease of reading, it is preferable to have the translation as part of the main text with the original version as a footnote or, better still, reserved for an appendix where all the quotations are listed in their original languages. For the author to supply no translation at all on the assumption that anyone reading him would already be familiar with Latin and Greek, say, or French and German (and I have read such an excuse in an author's preface) is a symptom of academic cabalism displaying enough ignorance and bad manners to offset any pretensions to erudition the author might have. I would not think it unreasonable if the reader of such a book found himself provoked into questioning the significance of the author's entire thesis.

Mathematical and musical quotations are altogether another matter, because it is impossible to translate them into words. Unless the quotations are immediately recognizable by a reader familiar with their language, there is no quick way of reading them: each symbol has to be seen separately, like the letters of an unfamiliar script.[1] If the quotations or illustrations can be textually explained as well, of course it makes for easier and more meaningful reading all around.

Graphs, charts, tables, and diagrams, are all means of amplifying, and in some cases adorning, a text. Where their function is illustrative, they are usually a succinct analogue of a long and probably involved textual description. Alternatively, they may be used to summarize a mass of minor detail which would be tedious to read if it were set out in the text, in which case the text will explain the relevance of the illustration. In neither instance, therefore, is it necessary to pause over such illustrations in an initial reading. Their character and any novelty they have should be observed in the first skimming, and then they may be studied later, if desired.

Footnotes are of four kinds:

1. references to works consulted by the author or quoted in the text;

[1] I am often asked by musicians whether they can improve their reading of music by learning efficient reading techniques. I can see no way of relating their needs directly to the processes of mature silent reading because music must be either sub-vocalized (as in studying a score) or read aloud (i.e., performed). Musicians can profitably use learning techniques, however, and any confidence they gain from reading prose better ought to improve their ability in reading aloud, and vice versa, whether they read scripts or perform music. (See Chapter 6.)

2. pointers to other parts of the book to remind or compare, usually preceded by the word "see" (or its Latin equivalent, *vide*), or the abbreviation "cf." (*confer*, Latin for "compare");
3. author's afterthoughts and, in subsequent editions, amendments;
4. additional information which, if included in the text, would impede its development.

I have deliberately used all four kinds in this book and I have already suggested a way of dealing with them.[1] That was one of the second type; the footnote on the previous page is a combination of the fourth and second types. By classifying them in this way, the reader can decide, after skimming, whether or not to pause and read them as they are encountered.

Every author, in my opinion, should avoid footnotes as much as possible, and never mix the different varieties. They can be incorporated into the text or collected into an appendix. With the first type, the number of works cited must determine whether they are incorporated or appended. There is a stronger case for the second type of footnote, but a diagram at the end of the book might do the job just as well. A profusion of the third type could be evidence of an untidy mind, a lazy author, a book written in too much of a hurry, or (if it is a new edition of an older book) of a parsimonious publisher. The most justifiable type of footnote is the fourth type. They can be confined to an appendix, but much of their immediacy may be lost. The best and most prolific use of them is perhaps to be found in the earliest editions of Gibbon's *Decline and Fall of the Roman Empire*. When Thomas Bowdler got at it after scrubbing Shakespeare, it was mostly the footnotes that fell to his tumescent blue pencil.

You should have observed that during that last paragraph you kept referring back to the previous one. This is an instance where regression is right and proper and should be deliberate. And when you check your reading rate for this chapter you may also find that it is lower than of late. If it is not, ask yourself

[1] Cf. Chapter 3.

when you have done the comprehension test if you have been reading it too quickly for adequate comprehension.

The extract that follows should be read slowly enough for it to be appreciated as well as understood, but not so slowly that it is labored or disjointed. It is an extract from a book that I have heard experienced readers call difficult, a book which has been widely acclaimed as the most important book of the twentieth century, bearing something like the same relation to our time as Darwin's *Origin of Species* bore to the nineteenth century. It is *The Phenomenon of Man*, by Pierre Teilhard de Chardin (a quotation from its introduction forms the epigraph to this book) and I quote from it now not only as an example of a challenging book which is eminently readable, but also to illustrate, as best one can in a short extract, that profound ideas need not be obscure or indigestible, and to show how this author, so well served by his translator, has made them seem remarkably simple by the exquisite beauty of their development and of the language with which he adorns them.

(2,600 words)

EXERCISE 31

Choose the best answer to each question.

1. The statement "there is no such thing as a difficult book" means:
   a. with appropriate reading techniques, any book can be read easily;
   b. authors who are obscure deserve not to be read;
   c. confidence in one's comprehension makes it possible to read anything adequately for one's needs;
   d. books should be chosen and read when they are challenging, and if a book is difficult it is because the reader is not yet ready for it.
2. Obscure books, in the author's opinion, should be:
   a. read only by scholars;
   b. read ruthlessly and confidently;
   c. rewritten;
   d. avoided.

3. Critics, the author implies, are:
    a. not as disinterested as they ought to be;
    b. slaves to fashion;
    c. out of touch with the average reader;
    d. paid to make judgments which, like those of anyone, are merely articulations of subjective experience.
4. If speed and comprehension are impaired by hostile reactions, the author prescribes for the sufferer:
    a. a visit to a psychiatrist;
    b. a courageous attempt to understand them;
    c. more of the same kind of material;
    d. practice on less inflammatory material.
5. Readers who are intimidated by long words and technical terms, the author suggests, are in danger of:
    a. remaining ignorant;
    b. missing a lot of interesting knowledge;
    c. overspecializing;
    d. failing to be responsible citizens of a democracy through permitting, by neglect, the growth of potentially uncontrollable esoteric coteries.
6. The danger of gobbledygook, the author implies, is that it is:
    a. bureaucratic;
    b. anti-democratic;
    c. cabalistic;
    d. incomprehensible.
7. Scholars who use quotations from foreign literature without translating them, the author thinks, are:
    a. making a display of their erudition;
    b. out of touch with their times;
    c. bad mannered;
    d. the victims of a narrow classical education.
8. Profound ideas, the author says, can be:
    a. explained without the use of jargon;
    b. freed from obscure modes of expression;
    c. understood by any proficient reader;
    d. simply and beautifully expressed.
9. One may infer that the anti-academic observations in this chapter are made to:
    a. provoke hostile reactions by way of example;
    b. try to improve the readability of scholarly writing;

    c. encourage the self-educating reader who is daunted by "difficult" books;

    d. strike a blow at the Establishment.

10. The main idea of the chapter is:

    a. More people would be able to educate themselves if there were fewer obscure and intimidating books.

    b. There are too many amateur authors rushing into print from positions of academic importance, and they should not be encouraged, either by unwarranted praise for their writing or by readers who allow themselves to be intimidated.

    c. When we understand what elements make books seem difficult, we can eliminate those elements and read such books with ease.

    d. We must make the best we can of the books we get and refuse to be daunted by obscurities and verbiage, which is possible when we cease to regard books as Holy Writ and read them instead to take out of them whatever we need.

READING EXERCISE

The Problem of Action

BY PIERRE TEILHARD DE CHARDIN

MODERN DISQUIET

It is impossible to accede to a fundamentally new environment without experiencing the inner terrors of a metamorphosis. The child is terrified when it opens its eyes for the first time. Similarly, for our mind to adjust itself to lines and horizons enlarged beyond measure, it must renounce the comfort of familiar narrowness. It must create a new equilibrium for everything that had formerly been so neatly arranged in its small inner world. It is dazzled when it emerges from its dark prison, awed to find itself suddenly at the top of a tower, and it suffers from giddiness and disorientation. The whole psychology of modern disquiet is linked with the sudden confrontation with space-time.

It cannot be denied that, in a primordial form, human anxiety is bound up with the very advent of reflection and is thus as old as man himself. Nor do I think that anyone can seriously doubt the fact that, under the influence of reflection undergoing socialization, the men of today are particularly uneasy, more so than at any other moment of history. Conscious or not, suppressed anguish—a fundamental anguish of being—despite our smiles, strikes in the depths of all our hearts and is the undertone of all our conversations. This does not mean that its cause is clearly recognized—far from it. Something threatens us, something is more than ever lacking, but without our being able to say exactly what.

Let us try then, step by step, to localize the source of our disquiet, eliminating the illegitimate causes of disturbance till we find the exact site of the pain at which the remedy, if there is one, should be applied.

In the first and most widespread degree, the "malady of space-time" manifests itself as a rule by a feeling of futility, of being crushed by the enormities of the cosmos. The enormity of space is the most tangible and thus the most frightening aspect. Which of us has ever in his life really had the courage to look squarely at and try to "live" a universe formed of galaxies whose distance apart runs into hundreds of thousands of light-years? Which of us, having tried, has not emerged from the ordeal shaken in one or other of his beliefs? And who, even when trying to shut his eyes as best he can to what the astronomers implacably put before us, has not had a confused sensation of a gigantic shadow passing over the serenity of his joy?

Enormity of duration—sometimes having the effect of an abyss on those few who are able to see it, and at other times, more usually (on those whose sight is poor), the despairing effect of stability and monotony. Events that follow one another in a circle, vague pathways which intertwine, leading nowhere.

Corresponding enormity of number—the bewildering number of all that has been, is, and will be necessary to fill time and space. An ocean in which we seem to dissolve all the more irresistibly the more lucidly alive we are. The effort of trying conscientiously to find our proper place among a thousand million men. Or merely in a crowd.

Malady of multitude and immensity . . .

To overcome this first form of its uneasiness, I believe that the modern world has no choice but to follow its intuitive imagination unhesitatingly and right to the end.

As motionless or blind (and by that I mean so long as we think of them as motionless or blind), time and space are with good reason terrifying. Accordingly what could make our initiation into the true dimensions of the world dangerous is for it to remain incomplete, deprived of its complement and necessary corrective—the perception of an evolution animating those dimensions. On the other hand, what matters the giddy plurality of the stars and their fantastic spread, if that immensity (symmetrical with the infinitesimal) has no other function but to equilibrate the intermediary layer where, and where only in the medium range of size, life can build itself up chemically? What matter the millions of years and milliards of beings that have gone before if those countless drops form a current that carries us along? Our consciousness would evaporate, as though annihilated, in the limitless expansions of a static or endlessly moving universe. It is inwardly reinforced in a flux which, incredibly vast as it may be, is not only *becoming* but *genesis*, which is something quite different. Indeed time and space become humanized as soon as a definite movement appears which gives them a physiognomy.

"There is nothing new under the sun," say the despairing. But what about you, O thinking man? Unless you repudiate reflection, you must admit that you have climbed a step higher than the animals. "Very well, but at least nothing has changed and nothing is changing any longer since the beginning of history." In that case, O man of the twentieth century, how does it happen that you are waking up to horizons and are susceptible to fears that your forefathers never knew?

In truth, half our present uneasiness would be turned into happiness if we could once make up our minds to accept the facts and place the essence and the measure of our modern cosmogonies within a noogenesis. Along the lines of this axis no doubt is possible. The universe has always been in motion and at this moment continues to be in motion. But will it still be in motion *tomorrow*?

Here only, at this turning point where the future substitutes itself for the present and the observations of science should give way to the anticipations of a faith, do our perplexities legitimately and indeed inevitably begin. Tomorrow? But who can guarantee us a tomorrow anyway? And without the assurance that this tomorrow exists, can we really go on living, we to whom has been given—perhaps for the first time in the whole story of the universe—the terrible gift of foresight?

Sickness of the dead end—the anguish of feeling shut in . . .

This time we have at last put our finger on the tender spot.

What makes the world in which we live specifically modern is our discovery in it and around it of evolution. And I can now add that what disconcerts the modern world at its very roots is not being sure, and not seeing how it ever could be sure, that there is an outcome—*a suitable outcome*—to that evolution.

Now what should the future be like in order to give us the strength or even the joy to accept the prospect of it and bear its weight?

To come to grips with the problem and see if there is a remedy, let us examine the whole situation.

THE REQUIREMENTS OF THE FUTURE

There was a time when life held sway over none but slaves and children. To advance, all it needed was to feed obscure instincts— the bait of food, the urge of reproduction, the half-confused struggle for a place in the sun, stepping over others, trampling them down if need be. The aggregate rose automatically and docile, as the resultant of an enormous sum of egoisms given rein. There was a time too, almost within living memory, when the workers and the disinherited accepted without reflection the lot which kept them in servitude to the remainder of society.

Yet when the first spark of thought appeared upon the earth, life found it had brought into the world a power capable of criticizing it and judging it. This was a formidable risk which long lay dormant, but whose dangers burst out with our first awakening to the idea of evolution. Like sons who have grown up, like workers who have become "conscious," we are discovering that something is developing in the world by means of us, perhaps at our expense. And what is more serious still is that we have become aware that, in the great game that is being played, we are the players as well as being the cards and the stakes. Nothing can go on if we leave the table. Neither can any power force us to remain. Is the game worth the candle, or are we simply its dupes? This question has hardly been formulated as yet in man's heart, accustomed for hundreds of centuries to toe the line; it is a question, however, whose mere murmur, already audible, infallibly predicts future rumblings. The last century witnessed the first systematic strikes in industry; the next will surely not pass without the threat of strikes in the noosphere.

There is a danger that the elements of the world should refuse to serve the world—because they think; or more precisely that the world should refuse itself when perceiving itself through reflection. Under our modern disquiet, what is forming and growing is nothing less than an organic crisis in evolution.

And now, at what price and on what contractual bases will order be restored? On all the evidence, that is the nub of the problem.

In the critical disposition of mind we shall be in from now on, one thing is clear. We shall never bend our backs to the task that has been allotted us of pushing noogenesis onward except on condition that the effect demanded of us has a chance of succeeding and of taking us as far as possible. An animal may rush headlong down a blind alley or toward a precipice. Man will never take a step in a direction he knows to be blocked. There lies precisely the ill that causes our disquiet.

Having got so far, what are the minimum requirements to be fulfilled before we can say that the road ahead of us is *open*? There is only one, but it is everything. It is that we should be assured the space and the chances to fulfill ourselves, that is to say, to progress till we arrive (directly or indirectly, individually or collectively) at the utmost limits of ourselves. This is an elementary request, a basic wage, so to speak, veiling nevertheless a stupendous demand. But is not the end and aim of thought that still unimaginable farthest limit of a convergent sequence, propagating itself without end and ever higher? Does not the end or confine of thought consist precisely in not having a confine? Unique in this respect among all the energies of the universe, consciousness is a dimension to which it is inconceivable and even contradictory to ascribe a ceiling or to suppose that it can double back upon itself. There are innumerable critical points on the way, but a halt or a reversion is impossible, and for the simple reason that every increase of internal vision is essentially the germ of a further vision which includes all the others and carries still farther on.

Hence this remarkable situation—that our mind, by the very fact of being able to discern infinite horizons ahead, is only able to move by the hope of achieving, through something of itself, a supreme consummation—without which it would rightly feel itself to be stunted, frustrated and cheated. By the nature of the work, and correlatively by the requirement of the worker, a total death, an unscalable wall, on which consciousness would crash and then forever disappear, are thus "incompossible" with the mechanism of the activity of reflection (which would immediately break its mainspring).

The more man becomes man, the less will he be prepared to move except toward that which is interminably and indestructibly new. Some "absolute" is implied in the very play of his operative activity.

After that, "positive and critical" minds can go on saying as much as they like that the new generation, less ingenuous than their elders, no longer believes in a future and in a perfecting of the world. Has it even occurred to those who write and repeat these things that, if they were right, all spiritual movement on earth would be virtually brought to a stop? They seem to believe that life would continue its peaceful cycle when deprived of light, of hope, and of the attraction of an inexhaustible future. And this is a great mistake. Flowers and fruit might still go on perhaps for a few years more by habit. But from these roots the trunk would be well and truly severed. Even on stacks of material energy, even under the spur of immediate fear or desire, *without the taste for life,* mankind would soon stop inventing and constructing for a work it knew to be doomed in advance. And, stricken at the very source of the impetus which sustains it, it would disintegrate from nausea or revolt and crumble into dust.

Having once known the taste of a universal and durable progress, we can never banish it from our minds any more than our intelligence can escape from the space-time perspective it once has glimpsed.

If progress is a myth, that is to say, if faced by the work involved we can say: "What's the good of it all?" our efforts will flag. With that the whole of evolution will come to a halt—because we are evolution.

From: *The Phenomenon of Man*
Translated from the French by Bernard Wall
(2,250 words)

EXERCISE 32

Choose the best answer to each question.

1. The author argues that one of the consequences of modern man's awareness of space-time is:
   a. the advent of reflection;
   b. a fundamental anguish of being;
   c. a sense of enormity;
   d. a threat of something unknown.
2. Because of our understanding of the true dimensions of the world we are in danger of:
   a. losing our identity in the crowd;
   b. incompleteness by a failure to perceive its evolutionary nature;
   c. consciousness evaporating into limitless space;
   d. incurable despair.

3. The author's answer to those who say "There is nothing new under the sun" would be to point to:
   a. history;
   b. evolution;
   c. the noosphere;
   d. thinking man.

4. At what stage does the author of the extract suggest our perplexities should legitimately begin?
   a. Tomorrow.
   b. When we exercise our foresight.
   c. When we become aware of fears our forefathers never knew.
   d. At the point where the knowledge of science gives way to the hopes of faith.

5. By his expectation during the next century of "the threat of strikes in the noosphere," the author seems to envisage:
   a. large numbers of thoughtful people seeking a means to evade the responsibilities that their knowledge entails;
   b. an increase in the use of leucotomy, drugs, and similar forms of escape by those who cannot bear the thought of being responsible for the entire human race;
   c. widespread suicide;
   d. outbreaks of atheism.

6. The condition on which threatening strikers in the noosphere will stay at work, the author's metaphor suggests, is that:
   a. life should continue to evolve;
   b. their efforts should have a chance of succeeding;
   c. they should be assisted by more people becoming conscious of the problem;
   d. the elements of the world should not refuse to serve the world.

7. What are the minimum requirements to be fulfilled before we can say that the road ahead is open?
   a. A guarantee of no strikes in the noosphere.
   b. An assurance of the chance to fulfill ourselves.
   c. The certainty of indefinite progress.
   d. A promise of ultimate salvation.

8. What does the writer suggest are the confines of consciousness?
   a. That which the human mind can conceive.
   b. A point as far as thought can reach.

c. The fact of its being potentially unconfined.

d. The outer limits of the noosphere.

9. A good guess at the author's reply to those who say that the younger generation no longer believes in shaping a better world would be:

a. Then what's the good of it all?

b. You have no taste for life.

c. Perhaps you are right and evolution has come to a halt.

d. If you are right, there is no such thing as evolution.

10. The main idea of the extract is:

a. If, on the evidence of evolution, we can say that thinking man stands at the farthest point to which life has so far evolved, it follows that the future is in human hands and supra-mundane immensities need hold no terror for us.

b. We would all be much happier if philosophical systems explaining the nature of the universe were to be seen not as right or wrong, but as part of the process of becoming.

c. The evolution of human consciousness will eventually enable man to understand himself and dispel his fears of the unknown.

d. Scientific discoveries about the nature of the universe have more frightening implications than anything our forefathers had to face.

When you check your answers against mine, you may think that some of mine are arguable. Argue them, using the passage to support your case. The ability to do so is better evidence of efficient reading than simply a maximum score on these tests.

·17·

The Time for Slow Reading

NOWHERE IN THIS BOOK have I discussed attitudes or described techniques applicable to reading for relaxation. If you read for no other purpose than to relax, it hardly matters whether you use a technique or not. So long as the desired result is achieved, it may not even be necessary to understand or remember what you read. Most people who read for relaxation ask little more than that the material make no demands and offer no challenges. They read travelers' tales and other romances for an hour's illusion of escape from the drab lives their impoverished imaginations have created. They read detective novels for the mystery, thrillers for the suspense, horror stories for—what? The pleasure they get when they stop, perhaps. Such readers, one imagines, would reject *Hamlet* because they know how it ends, *The Possessed* because of all the unpronounceable names, and *Ulysses* because it has no story. They might try to read *Alice in Wonderland* for the sex (a pursuit which in fact demands considerable sophistication) and Dickens for the depth of his characterization, perhaps in the hope of persuading others that they are on familiar terms with the classics. But most of their reading lives will be spent awaiting the next Rex Stout or John Creasey, while they fill in with fiction forgotten on finishing.

They may admit, in that curious sniggering tone of voice with which some of the English are wont to confess an occasional taste for alcohol, to enjoying best-selling thrillers; but having been lulled by them into a stupor of fantasy addiction, they will have little chance of discovering why they enjoy them and even less of observing the formulas to which they are cut, making one barely distinguishable from the next. And the more they read, admiring, perhaps justly, the professional dexterity with which they are turned out, or their meticulous presentation of scenic detail, the less they are likely to notice that they learn nothing from them, and are no richer for having read them than if they had spent the time at a pinball machine.

My own distaste for books of which the James Bond tales are one of the latest prototypes has to do with the fact that they are psychopathic fantasies set in a partial reality (the carefully authenticated factual details) which serves only to lend substance to the sick fantasy. Their psychology is largely paranoid; their effect the artificial excitation of adrenal glands and of dream-worlds born of sex repression in which cardboard people are skillfully manipulated to make spurious responses to impossible situations and meaningless relationships. They are essentially untrue.

I do not subscribe to the contemporary superstition that fiction of this ilk, mass-communicated through various media, actually increases violence, delinquency, and irresponsibility; for I believe its popularity to be a symptom of our mores, not a cause. Its real danger, in my view, is similar to that of mnemonic memory systems: the learning process is hindered by the reduction of understanding. All living involves learning. Knowledge must be understood before it can be used. Its use should result in closer contact with reality. Hence, the reader who learns nothing usable must, in the long run, be impoverished by what he reads.

I usually discover in any group of twenty students a few who seem to think of novels as the products of authors like Agatha Christie and James Hadley Chase, and one or two among them who, presuming that all but classical or highbrow literature is frivolous or meretricious, never read novels at all. It has evidently not occurred to them that the reading of worthwhile modern novels is as serious a matter as any non-fiction they read.

For whether a book is fiction or non-fiction, it is important that it should be true, by which I mean that its underlying philosophy must be sincerely held and therefore consistently worked out: it must communicate the courage of honesty that I may test what it tells me against my own experience and thereby enlarge my experience and enrich my understanding. As Stephen Spender has it in his muddled but stimulating book, *The Struggle of the Modern:*

> The truth is that "life" without literature is unreflecting, uncritical activity, the exercise of physical reflexes, and indulgence in social prejudices. Reading does not mean leading a substitute life (though some readers might live this) but exercising judgment about experience, entering into conversation with the dead, criticizing the values of the society around one.

There is much to be learned from an honest novel that cannot be so well taught by other books. Even the least work of a minor novelist like Kingsley Amis, *I Like It Here*, will give you more useful knowledge about how a family holiday in Portugal is likely to be than all the sun-drenched travel books ever written about the country. If you want to know what it is really like to live among Greeks, read about them not as philhellenes like to dream of them, the colorful paupers of Lawrence Durrell's romanticized nostalgia in *Prospero's Cell* or *Reflections on a Marine Venus*, nor the amusing and confusedly fey gentlefolk of Dilys Powell's sentimental maunderings in *An Affair of the Heart;* but as they are at heart, the arrogant cowards and heartless fools of an impassioned novel like *Freedom and Death*, that cry of torment by one of them who survived them, Nikos Kazantzakis. *Doctor Zhivago* creates an understanding of what the daily business of living through the Russian Revolution must have been like better than a dozen history books, just as its predecessor, *War and Peace*, is a mine of social and historical information about another period. The old giant novelists were given by their publishers and readers all the freedom they liked to report on any feature of the world that for the moment absorbed them. Read Melville on whaling, Jane Austen on drawing room pastimes, Balzac on paper manufacture, Boccaccio on bubonic plague.

Modern India owes her independence as much to E. M. Forster and *A Passage to India*, published in 1924, as to the British post-

war Labor Government. If European politicians had known the
Congo as Conrad's Marlow described it at the beginning of this
century in *Heart of Darkness*, its recent history might have been
very different. The case history of the psychotic murderer
Moosbrugger presented in *The Man without Qualities* is a thirty-
year-old existential study which you will find equaled only in a
handful of recent difficult psychiatric works. No gerontologist
has described old age as unforgettably as Muriel Spark in a minor
novel called *Memento Mori*, and no approved textbook could
ever describe for young people the delight and tenderness of
sexual love as *Lady Chatterley's Lover* can.

And it is not only for what they can teach us about the world
around us that novels are worth reading. We live at a time in
human history when our survival may depend upon how well we
understand the world within. The knowledge is available to us
for developing a practical awareness of our natures with which
we shall one day view the values of even the recent past, as
embodied in literature, poetry, drama, religion, history, philosophy, and tradition, as mere curiosities, as the royal graves of Ur,
the head-shrinking Jivaro Indians, the rites of cannibals, and other
quaint practices would seem but for the contemporary recession
to them which has traumatized our future. I believe that in the
dissemination of this new quality of consciousness, self-consciousness, the novel has a part to play which will not cease when
history is seen to be empty, philosophy is played like crossword
puzzles, and religion has been transmuted into art and love.

So far, there has been precious little literature of this order.
Contemporary novelists are concerned with turning our heads
forcibly to make us acknowledge the depravity and squalor of
human life, presumably in the hope that we shall see our potential selves in the mirror and recoil, determined to make a better
world of it. Such novels have an important place, but do not deserve the entire horizon.

There have also been several great novels between *Moby Dick*
and *Lolita* in which an idea has been thoroughly worked out in
terms of action, the only realm in which any idea has value.
Animal Farm and *The Plague* are fine examples, and one could

point also to the fables of William Golding, the religious tor-
ments of Graham Greene, and some of the best science fiction.
But most of them are warnings; few are examples.

It is as examples of creative living that the novel has the most
to do and the most to teach us. Our urgent need is to know ourselves and to begin to understand one another. There are traces
of a more creative attitude to communication and personal relations in *The Alexandria Quartet* and, with less virtuosity, the
works of Agnar Mykle and Nadine Gordimer are tending in that
direction. Elizabeth Jane Howard receives less regard in this
respect than she deserves, and one day Doris Lessing may write
an exemplary novel to meet these criteria. I can think of no others
except Robert Musil. *The Man without Qualities* comes nearer
than anything I have encountered to a thorough and significant
exploration of true self-consciousness. If anyone has done more
and been published, he will be too unfashionable as yet to be
recognized. But even in the contemporary "warning" novel, there
are many redemptive moments when the author's own health
transcends his disgust and his honest observation shows us some
unfamiliar part of ourselves or gives us a new insight into someone we know.

Every statement and incident that a good novelist selects for in-
clusion in his tale should have some meaning additional to its
immediate one that gives it an inalienable place in the fabric of
the whole. It may be an elaborate metaphor or a brief anecdote
told in conversation, a single adjective about a leaf or the simple
fact of a character biting a fingernail, but it should illuminate in
one and the same moment some nook in the human heart and
something in the nature of the universe.

Consider this chatoyant extract, one of a choice of dozens in
Patrick White's *Voss*, which is about an expedition attempting
the first crossing of the Australian continent in 1845. Two of its
newly recruited members, an English ornithologist and a fresh
arrival in the country called Frank Le Mesurier, are waiting in
Sydney on the deck of the ship that will take them up the coast
to the starting point of their journey. The younger man con-
fesses to the ornithologist that he has done nothing with his life

because he has always held himself in readiness for some achievement of great beauty. He calls it his oyster delusion and adds with a laugh:

"You will think I am drunk, Mr. Palfreyman. You will not believe in my pearl."

"I will believe in it," said the quiet man, "when you bring it to me in your hand, and I can see and touch it."

Le Mesurier was not put out. The morning, shimmering and floating, was for the moment pearl enough. Listening to the humdrum grind of enterprise, of vehicles and voices in the pearly distance, he was amazed that he could have hated this genial town. But with the impact of departure it had become at last visible, as landscapes will. The past is illusion, or miasma. So the leaves of the young Moreton Bay figs were now opening their actual hand. Two aboriginal women, dressed in the poorest shifts of clothing, but the most distinguished silence, were seated on the dirt beside the wharf, broiling on a fire of coals the fish that they had caught. And a little boy, introduced especially into this regretful picture, was selling hot mutton pies that he carried in a wooden box. He was walking, and calling, and dawdling, and looking, and picking his snub nose. The little boy would not have asked to live in any other surroundings. He belonged to that place.

The nostalgia of the scene smote Frank Le Mesurier, who feared that what he was abandoning might be the actuality for which he had always craved.

An entire chapter, and perhaps a small book, could be devoted to analyzing those lines, but without saying so much so well. For their full effect they should be read in their context, but the extract may make its point here if, once you have finished this chapter, you read it again slowly, and again and again, asking of every word why the author has used it. Consider its pace, its rhythms, its mood, its temperature, its colors, the clarity of its light, then consider how much more you know at one and the same moment of the heart of Le Mesurier and the heart just beyond pioneer Sydney, in the distinguished silence of the pearly distance. Practice of this kind will in time both deepen appreciation and confirm the value of slow reading.

The Time for Slow Reading

It is because of all they have to offer in the enrichment of our understanding of ourselves and one another that I think novels that are worth reading at all are worth reading slowly. The novel offers a vicarious form of living, a prospect of sharing another's experience which, only thus, may become our own. And there is no more value in hurrying through vicarious experience than there would be in wishing our lives away. Even painful experience can teach us something. We attract to ourselves those experiences which are necessary for our growth; and perhaps that is as true for the vicarious experiences of literature as it is for the actual experiences of life.

While you are reading—and rereading—the great literature of the past and the momentous literature of the present, perhaps alternating the two kinds, do not forget the critics. And here I do not mean the weekly reviewers, but the scholars who spend their lives with books and letters and who in their articulate and scholarly appreciation are nearly as necessary to the author as he is to them. I am thinking of people like David Daiches, F. R. Leavis, C. S. Lewis, I. A. Richards and many others, English, American, and Continental, their forebears and their successors, who are for the author the articulate reader and for the reader the amplifiers of the author's impulses and intentions.

If you visited, say, the Cathedral of Chartres, with no knowledge of ecclesiastical history or Gothic architecture, you might be awed by its majesty and enchanted by its windows, but there your appreciation would end, in a kind of unspecified gasp. Similarly, there are many novels, major works of the past as well as both major and minor ones of the present, which require more than the basic ability to follow a narrative to appreciate with optimum responses and to intermingle creatively with our actual lives.

But remember that the works of literary critics are machines to think with, too. It is their stimulus that matters. It is no more necessary to agree with their opinions than mine, indulged in this chapter in the hope of awaking a new interest in literature and criticism wherever it may be needed.

As George Steiner begins *Tolstoy or Dostoevsky:*

Literary criticism should arise out of a debt of love. In a manner evident yet mysterious, the poem or the drama or the novel seizes upon our imaginings. We are not the same when we put down the work as we were when we took it up. To borrow an image from another domain: he who has truly apprehended a painting by Cézanne will thereafter see an apple or a chair as he had not seen them before. Great works of art pass through us like storm-winds, flinging open the doors of perception, pressing upon the architecture of our beliefs with their transforming powers. We seek to record their impact, to put our shaken house in its new order. Through some primary instinct of communion we seek to convey to others the quality and force of our experience. We would persuade them to lay themselves open to it. In this attempt at persuasion originate the truest insights criticism can afford.

(2,700 words)

EXERCISE 33

Answer the following questions briefly.

1. What in essence, in your own words, is the author saying?
(3 marks)
2. What reasons does the author give for his dislike of thrillers of the James Bond type? (3 marks)
3. What kind of contemporary novel does the author see as occupying the entire literary horizon today? (2 marks)
4. Why is it important, in the author's opinion, to read good literary criticism? (2 marks)

Check your answers by skimming back through the chapter.

EXERCISE 34

When you have carried out my suggestions about reading and rereading the paragraphs from Voss *quoted in the foregoing chapter, turn to the three 800-word extracts from modern literature that follow. Deal with each one separately and in the same way. Read them first at your normal speed. Then read them again more slowly, noting carefully whether they mean any more the second time. Read them aloud, again noting whether anything fresh is revealed to you. Continue reading them silently, over and over again, until you feel they have nothing more to give you, having absorbed their different styles, their moods, the way each author has used his words and the reasons for his choice of images. Then reflect on the significance of each passage, in relation to what you know of literature and of the world at large. Do the same thing from time to time with the next few novels you read until these qualities of appreciation are as natural as your ability to follow the story.*

READING EXERCISE

The River Steamer

BY JOSEPH CONRAD

We were wanderers on prehistoric earth, on an earth that wore an aspect of an unknown planet. We could have fancied ourselves the first of men taking possession of an accursed inheritance, to be subdued at the cost of profound anguish and of excessive toil. But suddenly, as we struggled round a bend, there would be a glimpse of rush walls, of peaked grass roofs, a burst of yells, a whirl of black limbs, a mass of hands clapping, of feet stamping, of bodies swaying, of eyes rolling, under the droop of heavy and motionless foliage. The steamer toiled along slowly on the edge of a black and incomprehensible frenzy. The prehistoric man was cursing us, praying to us, welcoming us—who could tell? We were cut off from the comprehension of our surroundings; we glided past like phantoms, wondering and secretly appalled, as sane men would be before an enthusiastic outbreak in a madhouse. We could not understand because we were too far and could not remember, because we were traveling in the night of first ages, of those ages that are gone, leaving hardly a sign— and no memories.

The earth seemed unearthly. We were accustomed to look upon the shackled form of a conquered monster, but there—there you could look at a thing monstrous and free. It was unearthly, and the men were— No, they were not inhuman. Well, you know, that was the worst of it—this suspicion of their not being inhuman. It would come slowly to one. They howled and leaped, and spun, and made horrid faces; but what thrilled you was just the thought of their humanity—like yours—the thought of your remote kinship with this wild and passionate uproar. Ugly. Yes, it was ugly enough; but if you were man enough you would admit to yourself that there was in you just the faintest trace of a response to the terrible frankness of that noise, a dim suspicion of there being a meaning in it which you—you so remote from the night of first ages—could comprehend. And why not? The mind of man is capable of anything—because everything is in it, all the past as well as all the future. What was there after all? Joy, fear, sorrow, devotion, valor, rage—who can tell?—but truth —truth stripped of its cloak of time. Let the fool gape and shudder —the man knows, and can look on without a wink. But he must at least be as much of a man as these on the shore. He must meet that truth with his own true stuff—with his own inborn strength. Principles won't do. Acquisitions, clothes, pretty rags— rags that would fly off at the first good shake. No; you want a deliberate belief. An appeal to me in this fiendish row—is there? Very well; I hear; I admit, but I have a voice, too, and for good or evil mine is the speech that cannot be silenced. Of course, a fool, what with sheer fright and fine sentiments, is always safe. Who's that grunting? You wonder I didn't go ashore for a howl and a dance? Well, no—I didn't. Fine sentiments, you say? Fine sentiments, be hanged! I had no time. I had to mess about with white lead and strips of woolen blanket helping to put bandages on those leaky steam pipes—I tell you. I had to watch the steering, and circumvent those snags, and get the tin-pot along by hook or by crook. There was surface truth enough in these things to save a wiser man. And between whiles I had to look after the savage who was fireman. He was an improved specimen; he could fire up a vertical boiler. He was there below me, and, upon my word, to look at him was as edifying as seeing a dog in a parody of breeches and a feather hat, walking on his hind legs. A few months of training had done for that really fine chap. He squinted at the steam gauge and at the water gauge with an evident effort of intrepidity—and he had filed teeth, too, the poor devil, and the wool of his pate shaved into queer patterns, and three ornamental scars on each of his cheeks. He ought to have been clapping his hands and stamping his feet on the bank, instead of which he was hard at work, a thrall to strange witchcraft, full of improving knowledge. He was useful because he had been instructed; and what he knew was this—that should the water in that transparent thing disappear, the evil spirit inside the boiler would get angry through the greatness of his thirst, and take a terrible vengeance. So he sweated and fired up and watched the glass fearfully (with an impromptu charm, made of rags, tied to his arm, and a piece of polished bone, as big as a watch, stuck flatways through his lower lip), while the wooded banks slipped past us slowly, the short noise was left behind, the interminable miles of silence—and we crept on, toward Kurtz. But the snags were thick, the water was treacherous and shallow, the boiler seemed indeed to have a sulky devil in it, and thus neither that fireman nor I had any time to peer into our creepy thoughts.

From: *Heart of Darkness* (1902)
(800 words)

READING EXERCISE

Silent Encounter between Two Mountain Peaks

BY ROBERT MUSIL

Neither Diotima nor Arnheim had ever loved. Of Diotima we know this already. But the great financier too possessed a—in a wider sense—chaste soul. He had always been afraid that the feelings he aroused in women might not be for himself, but for his money; and for this reason he lived only with women to whom he, for his part, gave not feelings but money. He had never had a friend, because he was afraid of being used; he only had business friends, even if sometimes the business deal was an intellectual one. So he was wily in the ways of life, yet untouched and in danger of being left on his own, when he encountered Diotima, whom destiny had ordained for him. The mysterious forces in them collided with each other. What happened can only be compared to the blowing of the trade winds, the Gulf Stream, the volcanic tremors of the earth's crust: forces vastly superior to man, related to the stars, were set in motion between the two of them, over and above the limits of the hour and the day—measureless, mighty currents.

At such moments it is quite immaterial what is said. Upward from the vertical crease of his trousers Arnheim's body seemed to stand there in the solitude of God in which the mountain giants stand. United with him by the wave of the valley, on the other side Diotima rose, luminous with solitude—her dress of the period forming little puffs on the upper arms, dissolving the bosom in an artfully draped looseness over the stomach and being caught in to the calf again just under the hollow of the knee. The strings of glass beads in the door curtains cast reflections like ponds, the javelins and arrows on the walls were tremulous with their feathered and deadly passion, and the yellow Calman-Lévy volumes on the tables were silent as lemon groves. Reverently we pass over their opening words.

Arnheim was the first to shake off the magic spell. For to linger in such a state for any length of time was, to his way of thinking, impossible; it meant either sinking into a muffled, vacant, blissfully reposeful brooding or propping up one's devotions with a solid scaffolding of thoughts and convictions, which would however no longer be of the same essential nature.

Such a means of, admittedly, killing the soul, but then as it were storing it in little tins for general use, has always been the linking of it with reason, convictions and practical action, as it has been successfully performed by all systems of morality, all philosophies and religions. God knows—as has already been said—what a soul is anyway! There can be no doubt whatsoever that the burning wish to hearken to it alone leaves one with an immeasurable field open for action, a thorough state of anarchy, and we have examples of so to speak chemically pure souls committing downright crimes. On the other hand, as soon as a soul has morality or religion, philosophy, and intensive bourgeois education and ideals in the realms of duty and of the beautiful, it is endowed with a system of regulations, conditions and directives for operation, which it has to fill out before it is entitled to think of itself as a respectable soul, and its heat, like that of a blast furnace, is conducted into beautiful squares of sand. What remains then is fundamentally only logical problems of interpretation, of the kind as to whether an action comes under this or that commandment; and the soul presents the tranquil panorama of a battlefield after the battle, where the dead lie quiet and one can at once observe where a scrap of life yet stirs or groans. And so man makes this transition as fast as he can. If he is tormented by religious doubts, as occasionally happens in youth, he goes straight over to the persecution of unbelievers; if love deranges him, he turns it into marriage; and if any other enthusiasm overwhelms him, he disentangles himself from the impossibility of living perpetually in the fire of it by beginning to live for that fire. That is, instead of filling the many moments of his day, each of which needs a content and an impetus, with his ideal state, he fills them with the activity for the sake of his ideal state, in other words, with the many means to the end, the hindrances and incidents that are a sure guarantee that he need never reach it. For only fools, the mentally deranged, and people with *idées fixes*, can endure unceasingly in the fire of the soul's rapture. A sane man must content himself with declaring that life would not seem worth living without a flake of that mysterious fire.

From: *The Man without Qualities* (1930)
translated by Eithne Wilkins and Ernst Kaiser
(800 words)

READING EXERCISE

Molloy

BY SAMUEL BECKETT

Coming up to four or five of course there is the night shift, the watchmen, beginning to bestir themselves. But already the day is over, the shadows lengthen, the walls multiply, you hug the walls, bowed down like a good boy, oozing with obsequiousness, having nothing to hide, hiding from mere terror, looking neither right nor left, hiding but not provocatively, ready to come out, to smile, to listen, to crawl, nauseating but not pestilent, less rat than toad. Then the true night, perilous too but sweet to him who knows it, who can open to it like the flower to the sun, who himself is night, day and night. No there is not much to be said for the night either, but compared to the day there is much to be said for it, and notably compared to the morning there is everything to be said for it. For the night purge is in the hands of technicians, for the most part. They do nothing else, the bulk of the population have no part in it, preferring their warm beds, all things considered. Day is the time for lynching, for sleep is sacred, and especially the morning, between breakfast and lunch. My first care then, after a few miles in the desert dawn, was to look for a place to sleep, for sleep too is a kind of protection, strange as it may seem. For sleep, if it excites the lust to capture, seems to appease the lust to kill, there and then and bloodily, any hunter will tell you that. For the monster on the move, or on the watch, lurking in his lair, there is no mercy, whereas he taken unawares, in his sleep, may sometimes get the benefit of milder feelings, which deflect the barrel, sheathe the kris. For the hunter is weak at heart and sentimental, overflowing with repressed treasures of gentleness and compassion. And it is thanks to this sweet sleep of terror or exhaustion that many a foul beast, and worthy of extermination, can live on till he dies in the peace and quiet of our zoological gardens, broken only by the innocent laughter, the knowing laughter, of children and their elders, on Sundays and Bank Holidays. And I for my part have always preferred slavery to death, I mean being put to death. For death is a condition I have never been able to conceive to my satisfaction and which therefore cannot go down in the ledger of weal and woe. Whereas my notions on being put to death inspired me with confidence, rightly or wrongly, and I felt I was entitled to act on them, in certain emergencies. Oh, they weren't notions like yours, they were notions like mine, all spasm, sweat and trembling, without an atom of common sense or lucidity. But they were the best I had. Yes, the confusion of my ideas on the subject of death was such that I sometimes wondered, believe me or not, if it wasn't a state of being even worse than life. So I found it natural not to rush into it and, when I forgot myself to the point of trying, to stop in time. It's my only excuse. So I crawled into some hole somewhere I suppose and waited, half sleeping, half sighing, groaning and laughing, or feeling my body, to see if anything had changed, for the morning frenzy to abate. Then I resumed my spirals. And as to saying what became of me, and where I went, in the months and perhaps the years that followed, no. For I weary of these inventions and others beckon to me. But in order to blacken a few more pages may I say I spent some time at the seaside, without incident. There are people the sea doesn't suit, who prefer the mountains or the plain. Personally I feel no worse there than anywhere else. Much of my life has ebbed away before this shivering expanse, to the sound of the waves in storm and calm, and the claws of the surf. Before, no, more than before, one with, spread on the sand, or in a cave. In the sand I was in my element, letting it trickle between my fingers, scooping holes that I filled in a moment later or that filled themselves in, flinging it in the air by handfuls, rolling in it. And in the cave, lit by the beacons at night, I knew what to do in order to be no worse off than elsewhere. And that my land went no further, in one direction at least, did not displease me. And to feel there was one direction at least in which I could go no further, without first getting wet, then drowned, was a blessing. For I have always said, First learn to walk, then you can take swimming lessons. But don't imagine my region ended at the coast, that would be a grave mistake. For it was this sea too, its reefs and distant islands, and its hidden depths. And I too once went forth on it, in a sort of oarless skiff, but I paddled with an old bit of driftwood. And I sometimes wonder if I ever came back, from that voyage. For if I see myself putting to sea, and the long hours without landfall, I do not see the return, the tossing of the breakers, and I do not hear the frail keel grating on the shore. . . .

From: *Molloy*
(800 words)

·18·

On Becoming a Mature Reader

HE KNOWS NOT and knows that he knows not: he is honest, emulate him. He may also be a well-read man, for the well-read man is a self-confident man who knows that he knows enough to be able to admit without shame to his ignorance. He has read enough and lived enough to have preserved a restless child-like curiosity that drives him to ask questions, the commonest of which is: Why? He knows that all his knowledge has been gleaned during a long and complex series of experiences which are nothing if not accidental; and that everyone else's knowledge is equally the consequence of accident. Hence he will never feel disdain for another man's ignorance, unless it is the ignorance that arrogantly says: But *surely* you know that! His profoundest contempt, or perhaps pity, is reserved for him who does not want to know.

The well-read man is urbane except toward manifestations of inurbanity; he is tolerant of all but intolerance. He reads in such a way that, to quote Barzun again:[1]

> He comes to see that in the realm of mind as represented by great men, there is no such thing as separate, isolated "subjects." In Shakespeare's English are tags of Latin, allusions to medicine, elements of psychology, facts from history—and so on ad infinitum. Nor is this true of fiction alone. The great philosophers and scientists are—or were until recently—universal minds, not in the sense that they knew everything, but in the sense that they sought to unite all they knew into a mental vision of the universe.

[1] Op. cit.

And in his own personal vision of the universe, the well-read man may see individual intolerance growing from something as unconsidered as the opening of a single-sex comprehensive school, or universal inurbanity fermenting in the microcosm of an ordinary home.

The well-read man need not have read many books, but he will have dipped into a wide variety of subjects. He need not have read very systematically, preferring to follow his whims or intuitions, but he will never be at a loss about what to read next and whatever he reads he will assimilate without distortion into a personal body of knowledge, rejecting the waste. No new knowledge, whatever its implications, will frighten him into preferring ignorance. He will continually broaden his horizons, discovering as he does so the truth of Ian M. L. Hunter's observation in his comprehensive little book, *Memory: Facts and Fallacies*, that:

> the wider our range of past experience and the greater the variety of our already completed learning, the easier it becomes for us to learn yet more and more new material because of the richness of the "cabinet" into which it may be "filed."

The well-read man may not be a mature reader, but the mature reader will be, among other things, a well-read man. There is probably no such thing as a fully mature reader, any more than there is a fully mature person. But if a good working definition of a realistically mature person, of which one may occasionally meet a walking example, is an individual who behaves at a standard appropriate to his age and experience and yet is capable of being, at will, the person he has been at any period in his past life, then perhaps the mature reader may be usefully defined as he who reads efficiently whatever is appropriate to his age and knowledge and yet is equally capable of using any of the reading methods appropriate to his past reading life.

He will certainly not be too proud to read and learn from children's books, nor too arrogant to presume that he knows a book from having read it once. He will often choose to read a book a second or third time, confident in the knowledge that, in a sense, you cannot read a book twice because, as Plato observed all those years ago, neither you nor it is the same.

The mature reader will be able to read proofs accurately, word by word, if he has to do so; and he will never read documents like legal contracts so carelessly that he fails to notice a deliberate ambiguity or a condition hiding in small print. Neither will he be taken in by the cheap deceptions of advertisers: he will not read, say, an advertisement for a cruise as costing two hundred dollars when it says "From $200"; and he may even know enough to suspect with justification that two hundred dollars buys a berth in one of two six-berth cabins on E deck, and that the next price up the scale for all other accommodation is three hundred dollars. He will also read $2.95 as three dollars and not two, and $695 as seven and not six hundred. And if he reads, as I have, the publisher's blurb to a book on rapid reading that begins: "If you do not read at 1,000 words a minute, this book will help you," he will toss it aside with contempt, noting that it is aimed at everyone and therefore no one, and that whatever it might help you to do it will not, presumably, help you to see the deception in a statement like that.

If you have read this far, you may well have some of the qualities of the mature reader yourself. Tenacity and fortitude are (perhaps) necessary to have done so, but if not, at least you have not closed the book forever in anger at the provocative statements I have permitted myself in order to enliven what some people make a very dull subject, and also, I confess, in order to challenge your ability to read thoughtful and provocative material and to touch upon a few of the wider ramifications of an innocent-seeming subject like developmental reading.

You may have found it difficult not to be confronted by the underlying philosophy of this book. The mature reader will discover a philosophy underlying everything he reads. There is one to be found even in workaday subjects like upholstery. (The condition matters not of what is hidden from the eye; appearance is all.)

The mature reader will never need to pretend to have read what he has not, for the confidence of knowing what he has will be impressive enough. He may keep a simple diary of the author, title, publisher, and date of publication, of every book he reads, a practice which, if it is not slavish, is to be more warmly recommended than Lionel McColvin implied in the reading extract that followed Chapter Nine. The mature reader remembers what he reads, but not in the unrealistic way that the immature reader usually expects. He will remember the things he learns and wants to remember, and the facts he constantly uses, but mostly he will merely know where information is to be found. He will not expect to have all the facts that he ever needs continually at his fingertips, but he may be able to marshal any number of them to his fingertips quite quickly by drawing on a reference library or his own bookshelves.

The mature reader is quite likely to deny that he is a mature reader; but this is not to say, of course, that everyone who makes such a denial is really a mature reader. I am not a mature reader; neither am I a well-read man. But one day I hope to become both. I will admit to being a self-educated man, but that much must be obvious from the anti-academic flavor of many of my remarks in this book. For many years I was limited by average reading ability. Then I took an evening course in efficient reading and saw its possibilities. Today I am a more powerful reader than I was, and that power is increasing my power to educate myself. I have tried to articulate as much as I can remember of the processes by which I became the kind of reader I am, in such a way that I hope others can make use of them, too. I have tried to point out a few of the ways along which further progress might be directed. Now we are each of us alone. But if you have accompanied me this far, you have the ability to develop further. Go in peace. Keep your curiosity alive. And develop your personality with diligence.

(1,400 words)

EXERCISE 35

Make a list of ten qualities that the author attributes to the mature reader (one mark for each), defining each one in your own words. Then rearrange them in your own order of priority. Do not refer back to the foregoing chapter until you check your list.

EXERCISE 36

After a suitable interval for the most intensive reading you can manage, read this book again.

The list of suggested practice reading that follows is a random sample of challenging or demanding books that may exemplify some of my observations in Chapter Sixteen.

SUGGESTED PRACTICE READING (PART VI)

Norman O. Brown	*Life against Death*
Norman Cohn	*The Pursuit of the Millennium*
G. Rachel Levy	*The Gate of Horn*
Michael Polanyi,	*Personal Knowledge*
Wayland Young	*Eros Denied*
R. C. Zaehner	*Mysticism Sacred and Profane*

APPENDIXES

Answers

Answers to multiple-choice recognition tests

Question No.	1	2	3	4	5	6	7	8	9	10
Exercise 1	d	b	c	a	c	a	c	b	b	d
Exercise 2	c	a	c	b	b	d	d	b	c	c
Exercise 3	d	b	a	b	c	c	d	a	a	c
Exercise 4	b	b	a	a	a	c	d	d	c	d
Exercise 5	c	d	c	c	b	c	a	a	b	b
Exercise 8	d	b	b	b	a	d	b	d	b	a
Exercise 9	d	c	a	c	d	a	b	a	c	c
Exercise 18	a	b	c	d	a	a	d	c	a	a
Exercise 20	b	b	c	b	c	d	c	d	a	d
Exercise 21	b	a	a	a	a	c	d	d	d	b
Exercise 25	c	b	a	c	b	c	a	b	c	a
Exercise 26A	c	c	b	a	d	a	c	b	b	b
Exercise 26B	a	a	c	c	b	c	a	a	b	d
Exercise 26C	c	c	b	a	d	c	a	b	b	b
Exercise 30	b	a	a	d	d	a	a	c	a	b
Exercise 31	d	b	d	b	d	b	c	b	c	d
Exercise 32	b	b	d	d	a	b	b	c	d	a

EXERCISE 10A

Migration Gave Australia 58 Per Cent of Postwar Population Increase

Australia's population reached 11 million last Saturday, on official estimates prepared by the Commonwealth Statistician. Speaking in Adelaide, the Minister of Immigration, Mr. Downer, said that about 58 per cent of the net postwar population increase could be attributed to immigration.

Although it took 80 years for Australia's population to rise to one million, it is only four years and eight months since the 10 million mark was passed, said Mr. Downer. The number of people in Australia has been increasing steadily since 1949 at about 213,000 a year.

Mr. Downer said that since World War II, and allowing for departures, 1,460,000 people from Britain and Europe had settled in Australia. This was 39 per cent of the postwar net gain of population.

To this must be added 720,000 children born in Australia to families where one or both the parents were migrants. These comprised 19 per cent of the 3.7 million births reported in Australia since 1945.

Immigration had thus contributed about 58 per cent of Australia's total postwar population increase. Without immigration Australia's population would not have reached 11 million until 1975.

The Minister was speaking at a special church service held on the banks of the Port Adelaide River to mark the 125th anniversary of the first landing in Australia of members of the Lutheran Church. The service was at the spot where, in 1838, about 200 Lutherans went ashore after a sea voyage of 19 weeks from Hamburg, Germany.

Mr. Downer said that of nearly 1.5 million people from Europe and Britain who had settled in Australia since World War II, about 95,000 were Germans, many of them Lutherans.

Australian News
November 21, 1963

EXERCISE 10B

Odd Ways at Westminster

The oddest thing about the House of Commons is the meeting-place in which its sessions were held for more than 100 years. This unique chamber was gutted during the German air raids in the Second World War, but was restored in its original rectangular shape. Legislative halls in other countries are so planned that every member can have a seat and can sit with his face to the presiding officer. But in the House of Commons there have never been benches for more than two-thirds of the members. And those who occupy them do not face the Speaker of the House; they face their opponents. New members sometimes do not always realize that no individual seats are assigned and there are current stories of freshman commoners making early application to the clerk in the hope of getting well placed. A first glance around the old chamber gave the impression of a chapel or huge choir stall. The subdued light which fell from overhead threw a mellowness over the place. There was an air of dignity, leisure, and comfort intermingled with venerableness—all in sharp contrast with the bustling auditorium in which the American House of Representatives semicircles around its Speaker.

It is not astonishing that time had rendered the old House of Commons too small to seat all the members. It is understandable, too, that its peculiar plan of antiphonal banks of seats derived from the historical accident of its original meeting-place in a choir-chapel. Some there were who wanted a new and completely up-to-date design. But the characteristically English decision was to reconstruct the bombed-out chamber just as it was in its two essentials: the banks of benches for "government" and "opposition" facing each other, and seats for about two-thirds of the members. Winston Churchill spoke eloquently in favor of retaining the old arrangements. The oblong shape, he said, favors the two-party rather than the group type of political affiliation. To slip a bit to left or right is easy; to "cross the floor" is a decisive act "which requires serious consideration." A small chamber facilitates the easy, conversational style of speaking, traditional in the Commons, rather than "harangues from a rostrum." It also prevents the feeling of being lost in a vast hall when the business is not such as to call for a full House. Furthermore, "there should be on great occasions a sense of crowd and urgency," with all seats full and members jammed at the back and in the gangways.

From: *The Governments of Europe*
by William Bennett Munro and Morley Ayearst (1952)

EXERCISE 10C
What Do We Mean by "Thinking"?

Aristotle selected rationality, the capacity to think, as the defining attribute of Man. Descartes sought to distinguish mind from matter by characterizing the former as "that which thinks." It is not surprising that these two philosophers should seize upon one of the most distinctive human capacities in their definitions. It is true that many of the activities involved in human thinking are present lower down the evolutionary scale, particularly among vertebrate animals; but the human animal has developed these activities to such an extent that there is a huge gap between man and the next most intelligent living creature. Thought is not necessarily the most significant psychological function, but no understanding of human behavior can be complete without some study of the fact that human beings have the capacity to think in ways which no other animal is able to achieve. No psychology can be complete without some attempt to describe and explain what a man does when he is described as "thinking"—however much certain psychologists emphasize the irrational and unconscious factors in human make-up.

But what is thinking? This might seem a pointless question, since everyone knows by acquaintance what thinking is from his own first-hand experience of doing it. We all think from time to time. Even if we are not philosophers or scientists we have at least followed an argument put to us by a schoolteacher or preacher. We have sometimes been bright enough to spot a flaw in such an argument and have managed to formulate a cogent objection against it. We have been defeated by chess or bridge problems or have battled with such teasers until we have succeeded in reaching a solution. We know very well how some thinking sticks to the point and moves steadily toward its conclusion while other thinking runs around in circles or drifts off into blind alleys or gets bogged down! Some answers to problems come to us in a flash, while at other times we are confused and befuddled in spite of hard efforts. In brief, we know quite a lot about thinking from our own practical experience of thinking.

From: *The Psychology of Thinking*
by Robert Thomson (1959)

EXERCISE 22

The World of Books

This article is an adaptation brought up to date of an earlier one which contained, if anything, even less factual information. It was published in a highly respectable British weekly journal and has been used in its present disguise to warn the reader that increased efficiency in reading must include a sharper critical acumen in order to resist the caprices of the brainwashed.

The table from which the figures were culled is followed by two-thirds of a page of explanatory footnotes in English and French. The books were classified in accordance with the Universal Decimal Classification and each title was counted as one unit. "They are understood, unless otherwise stated, to cover all non-periodical publications, including pamphlets, first editions of originals and (new) translations, re-editions, and more important government reports." The following statements otherwise, associated as footnotes with the U.K., U.S.A. and U.S.S.R. respectively, are therefore especially worthy of notice.

U.K. Including books published in Ireland. Books and pamphlets priced at less than sixpence omitted.

U.S.A. Books only, excluding pamphlets which are defined as works of less than 49 pages; the statistics refer only to the production of the book trade (namely, the industry engaged in the publishing of books for sale to the general public) and omit a large part of total book production (publications of the federal state, and local governments, universities, churches and other organizations, most reports and accounts of proceedings, dissertations, laboratory manuals, wordbooks).

U.S.S.R. 43,822 titles of books placed on market, of which 38,453 first editions; the rest are distributed free.

Bibliography

A. Short list of background reading in subjects covered by this book
B. Sources of reading extracts
C. Sources of quotations in the text
D. Alphabetical list of suggested practice reading

For the sake of consistency, and to avoid presenting readers with irrelevant difficulties at the early stages of instruction, the reading extracts from British sources have been Americanized in spelling and punctuation. The sole exception, the extract from the *Report of the Committee on Weights and Measures Legislation,* is presented in its original form for the reasons given on page 231. The texts of the reading extracts have been taken from the British editions in all cases. The publisher and date of the first American edition is also noted where a work has been published in both countries, and a comparison with the American source might therefore reveal some minor differences.

Throughout the following lists, with one exception, each author is represented by only one work. Other works by the same authors may also be consulted. Titles mentioned in the text in passing are not included here; paperback editions, where they exist, are listed here only. The two unsigned articles are my own.

O.W.

A. SHORT LIST OF BACKGROUND READING IN SUBJECTS COVERED BY THIS BOOK

Manuals

Spache, George D., and Berg, Paul C. *The Art of Efficient Reading.* New York, Macmillan, 1955.
Waldman, John. *Rapid Reading Made Simple.* New York, Doubleday, 1958.

Wilking, S. V., and Webster, R. G. *A College Developmental Reading Manual.* Boston, Houghton Mifflin, 1943.

Research

Carmichael, Leonard, and Dearborn, W. F. *Reading and Visual Fatigue.* Boston, Houghton Mifflin, 1947; London, Harrap, 1948.

Vernon, M. D. *The Psychology of Perception.* Baltimore, Penguin, 1962.

Welford, A. T. *Ageing and Human Skill.* London, Oxford University University Press, 1932.

Learning

Bartlett, Frederic C. *Remembering.* Cambridge (Eng.), Cambridge University Press, 1932.

Meredith, Patrick. *Learning, Remembering and Knowing.* London, English Universities Press, 1961.

Weinland, James D. *How to Improve Your Memory.* New York, Barnes and Noble, 1957.

Studying

Mace, Cecil A. *The Psychology of Study.* London, Methuen, 1932; Baltimore, Penguin, 1962.

Maddox, Harry. *How to Study.* New York, Fawcett, 1964. London, Pan Books, 1963.

Wertheimer, Max. *Productive Thinking.* New York, Harper, 1945.

(Other titles have been mentioned in the text in passing.)

B. SOURCES OF READING EXTRACTS

Chapter

1. Richards, I. A. *How to Read a Page.* New York, Norton, 1942; London, Routledge & Kegan Paul, 1943; New York, Beacon.
2. Young, Wayland. "Pot," *Guardian.* Manchester, October 23, 1963.
3. Thouless, Robert. *Straight and Crooked Thinking.* London, English Universities Press, 1936; Pan Books, 1953.
4. Chaytor, Henry J. *From Script to Print.* Cambridge (Eng.), Cambridge University Press, 1945.
5. Munro, William Bennett, and Ayearst, Morley. *The Governments of Europe.* New York and London, Macmillan, 1954.

Thomson, Robert. *The Psychology of Thinking*. London and Baltimore, Penguin, 1959.

6. Chase, Stuart. *The Tyranny of Words*. New York, Harcourt, 1938; London, Methuen, 1938.

7. Huxley, Aldous. *The Art of Seeing*. New York, Harper, 1942; London, Chatto, 1943.

8. Newsam, Sir Frank. *The Home Office*. London, G. Allen, 1954.

9. McColvin, Lionel. *How to Use Books*. Cambridge (Eng.), Cambridge University Press, 1933, 1948.

10. Barlow, Fred. *Mental Prodigies*. New York, Philosophical Library, 1952.

13. Mares, Colin. "Reading at the Double," *Sunday Telegraph*. London, May 30, 1962.
Winnicott, D. W. "Strength out of Misery," *Observer*. London, May 31, 1964.

14. *Report of the Committee on Weights and Measures Legislation*, London, H.M.S.O., Cmd. 8219, May, 1951.

15. Lewis, C. S. *An Experiment in Criticism*. Cambridge (Eng.), Cambridge University Press, 1961.

16. Teilhard de Chardin, Pierre. *The Phenomenon of Man*. New York, Harper, 1959.

17. Conrad, Joseph. *Heart of Darkness*. New York, Doubleday, 1902.
Musil, Robert. *The Man Without Qualities*. London, Secker and Warburg, 1953–1960.
Beckett, Samuel. *Molloy*. New York, Grove Press, 1955.

C. SOURCES OF QUOTATIONS IN THE TEXT

1. Buswell, Guy. *How Adults Read*. Chicago, University of Chicago Press, 1937.

2. Durrell, Lawrence. *Key to Modern Poetry*. London, Peter Nevill, 1952.

3. & 4. Perry, William G., Jr., and Whitlock, Charles P. *Instructor's Manual*, Harvard University Reading Course. Cambridge (Mass.), Harvard University Press, 1949.

4. & 81. Barzun, Jacques. *Teacher in America*. Boston, Little-Atlantic, 1945.

6. Burt, Cyril. *A Psychological Study of Typography*. Cambridge (Eng.), Cambridge University Press, 1959.

Chapter

13. Miller, Henry. *The Colossus of Maroussi.* New York, New Directions, 1941.
17. Spender, Stephen. *The Struggle of the Modern.* London, H. Hamilton, 1963.
    Steiner, George. *Tolstoy or Dostoevsky.* London, Faber, 1960.
    White, Patrick. *Voss.* New York, Viking, 1957.
18. Hunter, Ian M. L. *Memory: Facts and Fallacies.* Baltimore, Penguin, 1957.

D. ALPHABETICAL LIST OF SUGGESTED PRACTICE READING

Adler, Mortimer J. *How to Read a Book.* New York, Simon and Schuster, 1940, 1956.

Allen, Walter. *The Modern Novel in Britain and the United States.* New York, Dutton, 1964.

Arendt, Hannah. *The Human Condition.* Chicago, University of Chicago Press, 1958.

Bronowski, Jacob, and Mazlish, Bruce. *The Western Intellectual Tradition.* New York, Harper.

Brown, Norman O. *Life Against Death.* Middletown (Conn.), Wesleyan University Press, 1959; Vintage.

Cohn, Norman. *The Pursuit of the Millennium.* New York, Oxford University Press, 1957.

Empson, William. *Seven Types of Ambiguity.* New York, New Directions, 1930; Meridian.

Forster, E. M. *Aspects of the Novel.* London, E. Arnold, 1927; New York, Harcourt, 1956.

Fromm, Erich. *The Art of Loving.* New York, Harper, 1956; Bantam.

Gabor, Dennis. *Inventing the Future.* New York, Knopf, 1964.

Gaddis, Thomas E. *Birdman of Alcatraz.* New York, Random House, 1955; Signet.

Hecht, Selig. *Explaining the Atom.* New York, Viking, 1960.

Heyerdahl, Thor. *Kon-Tiki.* New York, Rand McNally, 1950; Pocket Books.

Hoggart, Richard. *The Uses of Literacy.* London, Chatto and Windus, 1957; Boston, Beacon, 1961.

Kermode, Frank. *Puzzles and Epiphanies.* New York, Chilmark, 1962.

Koestler, Arthur. *The Lotus and the Robot.* New York, Macmillan, 1960.

Levy, G. Rachel. *The Gate of Horn.* London, Faber, 1948; New York, Harper Torchbooks.

Lin Yutang. *The Importance of Living.* New York, John Day, 1937.

Lucas, F. L. *Literature and Psychology.* London, Cassell, 1951; Ann Arbor, University of Michigan Press, 1957.

MacMurray, John. *Reason and Emotion.* New York, Barnes and Noble, 1962.

Maxwell, Gavin. *Ring of Bright Water.* New York, Dutton, 1961; Fawcett.

Moorehead, Alan. *Cooper's Creek.* New York, Harper, 1964; Dell.

Mumford, Lewis. *The Culture of Cities.* New York, Harcourt, 1938.

Polanyi, Michael. *Personal Knowledge.* New York, Harper.

Rawicz, Slavomir. *The Long Walk.* New York, Harper, 1956; Ace Books.

Russell, W. M. S. and Claire. *Human Behaviour.* London, A. Deutsch, 1961; Boston, Little, Brown, 1961.

Steiner, George. *The Death of Tragedy.* New York, Knopf, 1961; Hill and Wang, 1963.

Storr, Anthony. *The Integrity of the Personality.* New York, Atheneum, 1960; Penguin.

Symons, A. J. A. *The Quest for Corvo.* London, Cassell, 1934.

Thoreau, Henry David. *Walden.*

Wells, H. G. *The Outline of History.* New York, Macmillan, 1921; Washington Square Press, 1960.

Williams, Raymond. *The Long Revolution.* New York, Columbia University Press, 1961.

Young, Wayland. *Eros Denied.* New York, Grove Press, 1964.

Zaehner, R. C. *Mysticism Sacred and Profane.* New York, Oxford Galaxy Books, 1957.

Zinsser, Hans. *Rats, Lice and History.* Boston, Atlantic Monthly Press, 1935; Bantam, 1960.

Conversion Table to Determine Reading Rate

To use the following table, you will need to know the number of words in a passage and the number of seconds you took to read it.

1—In the top row find the figure corresponding to the number of words.

2—Round off your reading-time seconds to the nearest zero (as 148 to 150 or 252 to 250) and locate this figure in the column headed "seconds."

The point at which these two lines cross gives you your reading rate in *words a minute* to the nearest five.

NUMBER OF WORDS IN PASSAGE

seconds	560	800	850	900	1000	1200	1400	1450	1600	1700	2100	2200	2250	2350	2400	2600	2700	3000	3650	4000	4250	seconds
70	495	685	730	770	860																	70
80	420	600	640	680	750																	80
90	375	535	570	600	670	800																90
100	336	480	510	540	600	720	840	870	960													100
110	305	435	460	490	550	650	760	790	870	930												110
120	280	400	425	450	500	600	700	730	800	850												120
130	260	370	390	415	460	550	650	670	740	780												130
140	245	345	365	385	430	510	600	620	690	730												140
150	225	320	340	360	400	480	560	580	640	680	840	880	900	940	960							150
160	210	300	320	340	375	450	530	540	600	640	790	830	840	880	900							160
170	195	280	300	320	355	425	495	510	560	600	740	780	790	830	850							170
180	185	270	285	300	335	400	465	485	530	570	700	730	750	780	800							180
190	175	250	270	285	315	380	440	460	510	540	660	690	710	740	760							190
200	170	240	255	270	300	360	420	435	480	510	630	660	680	710	720							200
210	160	230	245	255	285	345	400	415	455	485	600	630	650	670	690							210
220	150	215	230	245	275	325	380	395	435	465	570	600	610	640	650	710	740	820				220
230		210	220	235	260	315	365	380	415	450	550	575	590	610	630	680	700	780				230
240		200	210	225	250	300	350	365	400	425	530	550	560	590	600	650	675	750				240
250		190	205	215	240	290	335	350	385	410	510	530	540	560	580	620	650	720				250
260		185	195	210	230	275	325	335	370	390	485	510	520	540	560	600	630	690	840			260
270		180	190	200	220	265	310	320	355	380	465	490	500	520	540	580	600	670	810			270
280		170	180	195	215	255	300	310	345	365	450	465	480	495	520	560	580	640	780			280
290		165	175	185	205	250	290	300	330	350	435	450	465	485	495	540	560	620	760	830		290
300		160	170	180	200	240	280	290	320	340	420	440	450	470	480	520	540	600	730	800	850	300

READING TIME IN SECONDS

314

	310	320	330	340	350	360
310	820	770	710	580	520	500
320	795	750	680	560	510	490
330	770	730	660	550	490	475
340	750	710	640	530	475	460
350	730	690	630	510	465	445
360	710	670	610	500	450	435
370	690	650	590	485	440	420
380	670	630	580	475	425	410
390	650	620	560	460	415	400
400	640	600	550	450	405	390
410	620	590	530	440	395	380
420	600	570	520	430	385	370
430	590	560	510	420	375	365
440	580	550	500	410	370	355
450	565	530	485	400	360	345
460	555	520	475	390	350	340
470	540	510	465	385	345	330
480	530	500	455	375	340	325
490	520	490	445	365	330	320
500	510	480	440	360	325	310
510	500	470	430	355	320	305
520	490	460	420	345	310	300
530	480	455	415	340	305	295
540	470	445	405	330	300	290
550	460	435	400	325	295	285
560	455	430	390	320	290	280
570	450	420	385	315	285	275
580	440	415	380	310	280	270
590	430	405	370	305	275	265
600	425	400	365	300	270	260
610	420	395	360	295	265	255
620	410	385	355	290	260	250
630	405	380	350	285	255	250
640	395	375	340	280	255	245
650	390	370	335	275	250	240
660	385	365	330	275	245	235
670	380	360	325	270	240	235

310 320 330 340 350 360 370 380 390 400 410 420 430 440 450 460 470 480 490 500 510 520 530 540 550 560 570 580 590 600 610 620 630 640 650 660 670

READING TIME IN SECONDS.

315

NUMBER OF WORDS IN PASSAGE

seconds 60	560	800	850	900	1000	1200	1400	1450	1600	1700	2100	2200	2250	2330	2400	2600	2700	3000	3650	4000	4250	seconds 60
680										150	185	195	200	205	210	230	240	265	320	355	375	680
690											185	190	195	205	210	225	235	260	315	350	370	690
700											180	190	195	200	205	225	230	255	315	345	365	700
710											175	185	190	195	205	220	230	250	310	340	360	710
720											175	185	190	195	200	215	225	245	305	335	355	720
730											175	180	185	190	195	215	220	245	300	330	350	730
740											170	180	180	190	195	210	220	240	295	325	345	740
750											170	175	180	185	190	210	215	235	290	320	340	750
760											165	175	180	185	190	205	215	235	290	315	335	760
770											165	170	175	180	185	205	210	230	285	310	330	770
780											160	170	175	180	185	200	210	230	280	305	325	780
790											160	165	170	180	180	195	205	225	275	305	320	790
800											160	165	170	175	180	195	205	220	275	300	320	800
810											155	165	165	175	180	195	200	220	270	295	315	810
820											155	160	165	170	175	190	200	215	265	295	310	820
830											150	160	165	170	175	190	195	215	265	290	305	830
840											150	155	160	165	170	185	195	215	260	285	305	840
850											150	155	160	165	170	185	190	210	260	280	300	850
860												155	155	165	165	180	190	210	255	280	295	860
870												150	155	160	165	180	185	205	250	275	295	870
880												150	155	160	165	175	185	205	250	275	290	880
890													150	155	160	175	180	200	245	270	285	890
900													150	155	160	175	180	200	245	265	285	900
910														155	160	170	180	200	240	265	280	910
920														150	155	170	175	195	240	260	275	920
930														150	155	170	175	195	235	260	275	930
940															155	165	170	190	235	255	270	940
950															150	165	170	190	230	255	270	950
960															150	165	170	190	230	250	265	960
970																160	165	185	225	245	265	970
980																160	165	185	225	245	260	980
990																160	165	180	220	240	260	990
1000																155	160	180	220	240	255	1000

READING TIME IN SECONDS

316

ABOUT THE AUTHOR

OWEN WEBSTER *was born in London, England. Until he emigrated recently to Melbourne, Australia, he worked in London in various journalistic capacities—as a reporter, feature writer and critic of the arts—at the same time lecturing on the subject that has become his principal interest: efficient reading. Mr. Webster has helped academic, industrial and professional groups (representing more than 60 professions and occupations) to improve their reading efficiency, memory and comprehension. The broad appeal of his new approach to reading skills is based on common sense and the author's sympathetic understanding of human nature.*